CROSSING OPINION

The Step into Fact-Based Faith

Dustin T. Holcombe

Copyright © 2019 by Dustin T. Holcombe

All rights reserved. This book is protected by the copyright laws of the United States of America. This book may not be copied or reprinted for commercial gain or profit. However, the use of short quotations or occasional copying of pages for personal or group study is permitted and encouraged. Permission will be granted upon request.

Published in the United States   First edition, June 2019
ISBN: 978-0-578-50727-9

Author: Dustin T. Holcombe
Cover: Virtually Possible Designs
Interior Layout: Olivier Darbonville

Publisher: H Publishers

crossingopinion.com

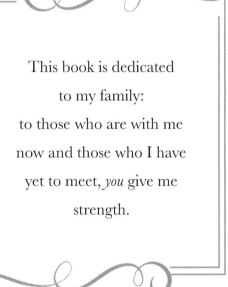

This book is dedicated
to my family:
to those who are with me
now and those who I have
yet to meet, *you* give me
strength.

CONTENTS

1. Why We Believe What We Believe • 7
Does Truth Matter When It Comes to Our Religious Beliefs?

2. An Eternal or Finite Universe? • 31
Was the Universe Created or Has It Always Been Here?

3. A Precise Universe? • 63
Does the Universe Show Signs of Design?

4. Is Mankind Just a Cosmic Accident? (Part 1) • 105
Intelligent Design vs. Evolution

5. Is Mankind Just a Cosmic Accident? (Part 2) • 137
What the Unique Code in Our DNA Tells Us

6. Morality and Consciousness (Part 1) • 177
How Exactly Do We All Know Right From Wrong?

7. Morality and Consciousness (Part 2) • 211
What Free Will Tells Us About the Spiritual Realm

8. A Historical Investigation of the Resurrection (Part 1) • 251
Did Jesus Even Exist?

9. A Historical Investigation of the Resurrection (Part 2) • 291
Are There Theories About Why Jesus' Tomb Was Found Empty?

10. Salvation • 323
What Can We Know About Life's Biggest Mystery?

Bibliography • 351

WHY WE BELIEVE WHAT WE BELIEVE

Detective Sherlock Holmes and his friend Dr. Watson were out on a camping trip. A few hours had gone by after finishing their campfire dinner and falling asleep. Holmes awoke and nudged Watson awake:

"'Watson," he said, "look up at the sky and tell me what you see."

"I see millions and millions of stars," Watson replied.

"What does that tell you?" Holmes questioned.

Watson pondered the question and then said, "Astronomically, it tells me that there are millions of galaxies and potentially billions of planets. Astrologically, I observe that Saturn is in Leo. Horologically, I deduce that the time is approximately a quarter past three. Theologically, I can see that God is all-powerful and that we are small and insignificant. Meteorologically, I suspect that we will have a beautiful day tomorrow. What does it tell you?" Holmes was silent for a minute before speaking. "Watson, you idiot!" he said with a measure of restraint. "Someone has stolen our tent!"[1]

Infamously referred to as "Donna the Deer Lady," Donna once called in to a North Dakota-based radio program to express her major concern: the local deer crossing signs needed to be relocated in order to persuade the deer to walk across certain roads in areas that had less traffic.² Never mind that the call was very likely a prank, what would you say was the main problem with her concern? That it would be difficult getting enough signatures on a petition to relocate the signs? Persuading a county board to hire a crew to do the work? Or possibly the fact that *deer cannot read road signs*?

The Invisible Gorilla Test was a study conducted in 1999 at Harvard University to demonstrate what psychologists had recently coined "inattentional blindness." In the study, one is to watch a video of six people – three dressed in white T-shirts and three dressed in black T-shirts – randomly moving around a room and passing basketballs back and forth as you keep close count of the exact number of passes made by those specifically in the white T-shirts. Half-way through the video, a person dressed in a gorilla costume casually walks into the middle of this crowd, pounds their chest, and walks away. Oddly enough, even after being on-screen for a total of ten whole seconds, roughly half of the viewers will entirely miss seeing the gorilla! This is because of the way our brains process visual information and create perceptual blind spots to things not primarily focused on.

These three stories illustrate one less very well: we can focus so much of our attention on things that comparatively do not matter in the grand scheme of things that we entirely miss the big picture of what is in front of us. For the topic at-hand, far too many today are not at all focused on something which should be crucially important to each and every one of us: *truth*.

DO NOT TAKE ANY WOODEN NICKELS

Every person struggles with life's most essential questions: where did we come from, why are we here, how should we live, and what happens to us after we die? When pondering our purpose in life, for instance, what are some examples that we tend to come up with? Well, we can earn and store up our money, try and become famous, protect the environment, settle down and have children, and be happy over all. But are any such answers anything more than our opinions? Of course not. Yet, even though we are intimately aware that such answers to these questions are lackluster as far as being true for everyone, such as a comb having the primary purpose of combing hair and not cooking eggs, many of us go about each day as if personal opinions are the only "answers" we can find.

If not the route of personal opinion, then, what about the mysterious route of religion? Is picking and choosing in the buffet line of religious beliefs for what suits our style of life the best any different? With religions and denominations within each religion bickering over so many differing beliefs, what we are missing is the obvious point that even the most well-intentioned sermons and traditional doctrines, like personal opinions, are a mere waste of attention if we are not seeking out whether or not they are actually *true*.

When we are asked by someone why we hold our particular religious beliefs, by far the most common answer that is given is simply, "Because I was raised to have these beliefs." If you attend church, look around; nearly every person is there because of that very reason. It is a clear fact that, say, if you are born in the United States, the chances are considerably high that you will become a Christian; or, if you are born in the Middle East, probability greatly favors the odds that you will become a Muslim. You can sit around all day and say, "I am so happy that the religion I was raised in just so happens to be the truth," but the reality is that, if you were born in a different region of the world, you would most likely be a follower of a different religion entirely and would still apply *that very same quote*!

Now, of course, this does not take away the fact that a religion you were culturally brought up in could just so happen to be true; thus, this is not at all a genetic fallacy stating something on the lines of, "If someone who is a Buddhist now had been born in Pakistan, they would likely be a Muslim instead. Therefore, a belief in Buddhism is unjustified." After all, if you had been born in, say, ancient Greece, it is likely that you would have believed the Sun orbits the Earth. But does that imply if you were born at that time and in a location which (correctly) believed the Earth orbits the Sun then that belief was unjustified? Obviously not.

Maybe, though, you are a slight exception and do not fall into the traditional category. Perhaps you hold specific beliefs because of an invitation you received to a religious event you subsequently attended, or perhaps you started going to a particular church after seeing an eye-catching flyer on a bulletin board at the grocery store. Whatever the case may be, can you *honestly* say that any answers similar to those are sufficient reasons for you or any other person to follow a religious belief system? Think about it: what if you had been invited to an event by your Buddhist friend instead of your Christian friend; would you be a Buddhist now? Or what if you saw a flyer on that bulletin board for another religion?

Or, let us continue with this line of thought: what would *you* tell someone if they asked you why you hold to your religious beliefs? That a specific friend invited you to their church, you started meeting up to chat and have white chocolate mochas at the church's coffee shop, you joined a mid-week study group, and then you were converted? What does that sound like to the person asking you that question? If the answer to the question of why you started holding to your religious beliefs is *how* and not *why* you do, that sounds exactly like you started hanging around a group of people and they brainwashed you! The person asking you that question knows that your beliefs are all by chance; again, you could have been invited by your Buddhist friend instead of your Christian friend, and started having mochas somewhere else, and so on.

With that said, it is of the utmost importance that we move from these all-too-common, woefully inarticulate answers. And, because of our immense past and present inability in doing that, there are many, almost irreparable repercussions that all religious backgrounds must own up to and face. Take, for instance, the rate at which Christian youth in the U.S. are leaving their faith behind entirely. Are you pretty confident that percentage is quite low? Is it five percent? It might be a stretch, but could it even be as high as 15%? It is much worse:

> "A significant majority of our church's youth are leaving the foundations of their faith when they transition from high school," said Paul Fleischmann, president of the National Network of Youth Ministries. Researchers found between 69-94% of Christian youths forsake their faith after leaving high school. The Barna Group reported 64% loss after college graduation. The Assemblies of God conducted a 10-year study and found 75% loss of their students within one year of high school graduation, while the Southern Baptists found that number to be even higher at 88% loss. And Josh McDowell Ministries reports 94% fallout within two years of high school graduation.[3]

Some youth will simply put their traditionally held faith on a hiatus after high school to simply negotiate it on their own terms, but many (especially from mainline churches) will have a very difficult time ever coming back to it even once they have settled down with a spouse and have children. Religion, then, is like being on a really bad date you know is going nowhere; you want to smile and be polite until you are in the clear, and then you do not want to hear from them ever again to avoid a waste of time and effort. So what is the main culprit causing this exodus of youth from not only Christianity but *all* religions? With aid from the rise of the Internet and its exposure to other people and ideas, "According to The National Study of Youth and Religion," says author, professor, and national youth speaker Dr. Sean McDowell, "the most common answer . . . teens offered for why they left their faith was intellectual skepticism."[4]

In other words, they have been taught by older generations *what* to believe but very rarely have they been taught, engaged, or encouraged to critically think on their own as to *why* to believe it. They are not encouraged to ask questions, as older generations often resort to taking out of context the teaching behind Jesus' words to have the faith of a child (do they not realize how many questions children ask?). All too often, sermons are aimed at going through the motions, going on and on about what we should not be doing, tugging at your heartstrings, and everything else under the Sun besides stimulating minds to ask questions. The youth of today have seen this played out far too many times and are concluding that all religions have zero real substance. To them, being told to "just have faith" is interpreted as merely a polite way of saying "take a blind leap into the dark," to "leave your brain at the door before you take a seat," and that "faith is the belief in what you know probably does not exist." And what do you call people who believe in things that do not exist: delusional. How political commentator and television host Bill Maher has put it would sum up their frustrations well: "Faith means making a virtue out of not thinking. It's nothing to brag about. And those who preach faith, and enable and elevate it are intellectual slaveholders, keeping mankind in a bondage to fantasy and nonsense."[5]

Being convinced there are many counterfeit religions out there, the youth of today know to be careful not to take any wooden nickels. As any holy book could be, the world's smallest Bible is engraved on an ultra-flat silicon chip roughly the size of a grain of salt.[6] And, ironically, it is becoming believed more-so than ever that one can take any form of scriptures with a grain of salt. Youth can see right through what they conclude to be a shallow faith that is based on nothing more than feelings alone. For those who attend college, it is even more difficult to be convinced that their particular faith is of any real substance, because their peers, professors, and society as a whole will mock faith (mostly Christianity) as a mere fairytale and make believers out to be behind-the-times Neanderthals who cannot defend their positions in any way. The university, then, has become viewed as "Thinking 101" whereas faith is simply "Feelings 101."

SUBJECTIVE VS. OBJECTIVE

We hear the quote "That is true for you but not true for me" more often than pharmaceutical lawsuit commercials. But let us delve into that quote to see why it is entirely foolish. When children at a birthday party play the game of guessing how many pieces of candy are in a filled jar, are all of their "answers" correct? Similarly, because there are lots of differing "answers" given, does that negate the fact there *really is one true answer?* Of course not. Further, pretend you go to a bank and ask to have ten million dollars withdrawn.[7] Would your request actually correspond with reality in regards to the balance of your bank account? Or if you were to say you have a wine red 1968 Camaro, does that description of a car actually correspond with reality in regards to what is sitting in your garage? No matter how much wishful thinking you have, nor how many times you say "That is true for you but not for me," reality will smack you when your bank teller thinks you are a comedian (or calls the police!) and your wife tells you to stop daydreaming and to go find the chicken nuggets the kids dropped between the seats a week ago in your beige minivan! Whatever the balance of your bank account may be, or whatever vehicle you have parked in the garage at a given time, it is true no matter who says otherwise.

So does it really matter what a person believes as long as they are sincere and their beliefs help them become better people? Yes, it matters a great deal, because belief and sincerity of belief do not create truth. While we are all entirely entitled to our own *beliefs*, we are not at all entitled to our own *facts*. Contrary to what you may think, truth is *not* what you make it. As the fictional character sheriff Walt Longmire states, "People can play games with it if they want, but the truth is the truth."⁸ And as syndicated columnist and New York Times bestseller Ben Shapiro writes, "Facts don't care about your feelings" and, "We can't have conversations with each other if all we do is say the facts don't matter."⁹ ¹⁰

The distinction between belief and fact is misunderstood is because there are two types of truth: subjective and objective. Author and speaker Greg Koukl gives an obvious example of each type:

> Think about the difference between ice cream and medicine.... Do you spend time trying to convince others they are wrong if they prefer chocolate over vanilla? Of course not. Our choice of ice cream flavors is a matter of personal preference. It is *subjective*. My favorite flavor of ice cream is true for me but you might have a different favorite flavor. No problem. But do we take this same approach when it comes to medical choices? If doctors were to discover you had Type 1 (or Insulin-dependent) diabetes would you ask for a treatment you like or prefer? Of course not. You want... what is *objectively* true. The cure is in no way dependent on your preference or belief. You might *believe* ice cream can control diabetes but . . . in the case of Type 1 diabetes you *need* insulin, not ice cream [emphasis added].¹¹

With such examples in mind, the distinction between the two types of truth is clear. *Subjective* truths, such as choosing your favorite ice cream flavors or making a list of your favorite movies, are internal truths which are no more valid than the preferences of another person and, therefore, do not apply to other people. On the other hand, *objective* truths, like the statements "insulin controls diabetes," or "George Washington was the first President to serve under the U.S. Constitution" are external truths which are independent of what anyone thinks or how anyone feels about them and, therefore, are true for all people.

Basing objective truth on opinion is like a hundred people closing their eyes, each pointing in the direction they think is south, opening their eyes to see hands pointed in a hundred different directions, and claiming all of them are objectively true! It is *subjective* truth that is based on opinion, whereas objective truth is based on facts (like a working compass). No matter if ninety-nine out of one-hundred people agree on something, opinion never creates objective facts. Take, for instance, an illustration from an elementary school show-and-tell:

> This young girl brought in a puppy for the class to enjoy. The classmates began to wonder about the gender of the puppy, but none of them knew how to ascertain it. The young girl raised her hand, 'I know how we can tell,' she explained. 'We can vote.' While we may snicker at her childish response, she illustrated the most common view of truth in our culture – majority rules. . . . Obviously we cannot merely decide on truth, because truth is indifferent to what we think and believe. . . . Hopefully our beliefs will match up with reality, but we have no power to create truth any more than we can decide the gender of a puppy by voting on it.[12]

It is sad, really, that we even have to discuss this topic, let alone discuss it in such basic terms. But, it is entirely necessary seeing as how the word *truth* is used so loosely that we are on the verge of losing its very definition altogether. In fact, 81% of youth in the U.S. believe that *all* truth is subjective.[13] As philosopher Allan Bloom observed, "There is one thing a professor can be absolutely certain of: almost every student entering the university believes, or says he believes, that truth is [subjective]. . . . The students, of course, cannot defend their opinion. It is something with which they have been indoctrinated."[14]

Take, for instance, a college professor who once tried to make the point that all truth is subjective: "Some people to this day still believe the Earth is flat. Therefore, the Earth being round is true for some but not true for others. See, truth cannot exist for everyone." No hands in the class were raised to present an objection to the contrary, but there was one student who could not let that remark go: "Everyone, this man before you claims to be your teacher. But since truth, of course, is created by subjective opinions, it is true for me that *I* am your teacher. *I* also say there will be no more homework, no more tests, and no more class for the rest of the semester. How about we all get out of here and enjoy the rest of the day?" Of course, no one got up and left, and that spoke volumes; their common sense told them there was only one professor in that classroom. The student, changing their sarcastic tone, continued: "Just because someone thinks that the Earth is flat does nothing to change the fact that the Earth is and has always been round. You claim that nothing can be true for everyone and, therefore, that all truth is subjective; but, in stating that nothing can be true for everyone, you are saying *that very statement* is true . . . for *everyone*! In other words, you are saying it is *objectively* true that *objective* truth *does not exist*; it is a self-defeating statement." The professor just grinned and, in fact, would go on to defend objective truth when the topic came up again later in the semester. (Oh, and as for that one student, you are reading his book right now).

For those who believe all truth is subjective, none of them truly live that way. After all, none of us want a pilot of an aircraft who states, "Well, my instruments say that if we keep steady at this altitude, we will soon crash into the side of a mountain. But, because that is not *my* opinion, I am going to flip the autopilot on and take a quick nap." And none of us want a boss who states, "Well, the computer says you worked forty hours this week. But *my* opinion is that you worked and should only be paid for fifteen hours." In light of real-world application, it is clear that the statement "That is true for you but not for me" is utter nonsense. Yet, when the topic switches gears to religion, pluralistic cultures have diligently tried to ingrain into each and every one of us that we must put aside our common sense and, without our slightest thought to the contrary, automatically compartmentalize even our own most sacred religious beliefs into the opinionated realm of subjective opinion instead of objective fact.

THE GOSPEL OF OPRAH

You hear statements like, "Christianity is true for you, but Islam is true for me." That is *exactly* like saying, "Coke is your choice, but I prefer Pepsi." Most people who are dedicated to their religious beliefs feel their beliefs are equally true when compared with different beliefs from around the world and, thus, that all roads lead to the same God. According to a recent U.S. Religious Landscape Survey by the Pew Research Center, 65% of those who are affiliated with a religion (not including atheism) believe that "many religions" are equally true.[15] It is not surprising, then, that such statistics are in harmony with statements commonly made by influential celebrities.

Look no farther than media giant Oprah Winfrey when she stated, "I am a Christian who believes that there are certainly many more paths to God other than Christianity. I'm a free-thinking Christian who believes that, who believes in my way, but I don't believe that it is the only way, with six billion people here on the planet."¹⁶ In another instance, while disagreeing with an audience member, she exclaimed, "There could not possibly be just one way!"¹⁷ Or take musician Willie Nelson, when he said in an interview: "'I realized there's a higher power. There's somebody smarter than I am out there, and I'm not picky about who it is. It's like Kinky [Friedman] says: "May the God of your choice bless you." If you've got one, you're all right.'"¹⁸ And then there is filmmaker George Lucas, when he stated in Times Magazine: "I remember when I was 10 years old, I asked my mother, "If there's only one God, why are there so many religions?" I've been pondering that question ever since, and the conclusion I've come to is that all religions are true.'"¹⁹

Most people are happy to agree that God exists, but it has become politically incorrect to claim that God can be found only through one particular religion. Even the word *tolerance* has slowly but surely developed into having a newfound meaning; whereas it has always prominently been defined as, "respecting the different views of others," it has now taken form as, "believing every view is equally true." The fact of the matter, though, is that this way of viewing world religions reveals a number of critical misunderstandings – the first being that *no religion teaches that all religions are true!*

Now, while you may think exclusivity is an arrogant and narrow-minded claim to insist, let us view the picture from another perspective. In regards to those who believe all religions are equally true, theologian and author Timothy Keller rightly observes,

> Ironically, the insistence that doctrines do not matter is really a doctrine itself. It . . . is touted as superior and more enlightened than the beliefs of most major religions. So the proponents of this view do the very thing they forbid in others. . . . Therefore, their view is also an "exclusive" claim about the nature of spiritual reality. If it is

not narrow to hold this view, then there is nothing inherently narrow about holding to traditional religious beliefs. . . . It is no more narrow to claim that one religion is right than to claim that one way to think about all religions (namely that all are equal) is right. We are all exclusive in our beliefs about religion, but in different ways.[20]

To those who say a religion cannot claim exclusivity to truth because that is close-minded, ironically, they *themselves* would meet their supposed criteria for being close-minded. In other words, to say that *only* their belief is true (i.e., that all religions are true) *is also an exclusive belief* and, thus (like the college professor), due to the use of that self-defeating statement, pulls the rug from beneath their own feet! And it should also be pointed out that one would not even hold to the belief in the first place that all religions are equally true unless they grew up in a culture that encouraged such thoughts of religious pluralism; if again, they had been born in, say, Pakistan, they very likely would not hold to such a thought process and, instead, would believe their particular monotheistic religion (Islam) was true!

The faulty logic of saying all religious beliefs are equally true and that all religions lead to the same God is, of course, due to the faulty assumption that all religions teach the same thing. While the mantra may sound nice, this prevalent belief is simply a myth that is entirely untrue. *All* religions disagree and contradict one another on virtually every single major issue in life, and by no means do they share the same concept of God. While it is true that many religions do share some basic, common sense teachings (e.g., do good unto others), they are polar opposites when it comes to their core teachings. While we could go into many of those differences, it is sufficient to focus on just a small handful of them in regards to the religions referred to (in descending order of adherents) as the world's greatest and most well-known by which all minor religions derive: Christianity, Islam, Hinduism, Buddhism, and Judaism.

THE IDENTITY OF GOD

Christianity   God the Father (Yahweh), the Son (Jesus), and the Holy Spirit are one entity
Islam   Allah
Hinduism   Brahman (manifested through 330 million gods and goddesses)
Buddhism   None (atheistic)
Judaism   YHWH (Yahweh)

THE IDENTITY OF JESUS

Christianity   The Son of God (crucified and resurrected as the Savior of the world)
Islam   A prophet of Allah (not crucified nor resurrected)
Hinduism   Non-historical figure but example of how to live (not crucified nor resurrected)
Buddhism   Historical figure and example of how to live (not crucified nor resurrected)
Judaism   Blasphemous rabbi (crucified as a criminal and not resurrected)

SALVATION

Christianity   God seeks a personal relationship with us, and we are given this free gift by trusting Jesus as our Savior. It is a guarantee which lasts forever
Islam   Must be earned by works in the hope that your good deeds outweigh your bad deeds. Since it must be earned, obtaining it is not guaranteed
Hinduism   Must be earned by escaping the endless cycle of death and

	reincarnation by the realization that our lives are just an illusion and that we are one with the universe. Since it must be earned, obtaining it is not guaranteed
Buddhism	Must be earned by eliminating all desires and escaping the endless cycle of death and reincarnation by following the Eightfold Path: Right understanding, right thought, right speech, right action, right livelihood, right effort, right mindfulness, and right concentration. Since it must be earned, obtaining it is not guaranteed
Judaism	Must be earned by keeping laws specific to Judaism. Since it must be earned, obtaining it is not guaranteed

THE AFTERLIFE

Christianity	The eternal soul continues to exist in another world (Heaven or Hell)
Islam	The eternal soul continues to exist in another world (Heaven or Hell)
Hinduism	Through the process of reincarnation, the eternal soul reinhabits a new form of life by means of a possibly infinite cycle of death and rebirth based on karma in of reaching Moksha (merger into a oneness; the individual is liberated and ceases to exist)
Buddhism	No soul exists. No afterlife exists, as the world is eternal. Through the process of Samsara, energy reinhabits a new form of life by means of a possibly infinite cycle of death and rebirth based on karma) in hopes of reaching nirvana (a state of non-existence, "extinction")
Judaism	The eternal soul continues to exist in another world (Heaven or Hell)

Clearly it is a blindly held position to believe that all religions are one and the same. Thus, even if they are all false, religions cannot be categorized alongside subjective preferences. A perfect example of this fact is Jesus' physical appearance: if Jesus really did live on Earth, then He definitely was not pale-skinned with blue eyes and flowing locks of golden blonde hair, nor was He African American or Asian. No matter what cultures commonly believe or what personal opinions we might hold, they do not change the fact that within the given location that Jesus would have lived, he had the physical features of a Jewish male. With that said, the main point is that all religions can be *false*, but they cannot all be *true*.

Due to their contradictory teachings, the idea that all religions teach the same thing would be a violation of a fundamental law of logic called the law of noncontradiction: two opposing statements cannot both be true at the same time and in the same context. For example, either you do or do not have that sweet Camaro. The first statement ("I have a Camaro") excludes the possibility of the second statement ("I do not have a Camaro") as being true. Therefore, to say both statements can be true at the same time and in the same context is to use faulty logic. Likewise, for example, either the identity of Jesus according to Christianity is true or is not true; we cannot have it both ways. Core religious teachings either do or do not correspond with reality; they cannot be true for one person and not true for the next person. Thus, the list of world religions can quickly be narrowed-down based on what teachings *actually match reality*.

Before we continue on with that line of thought, if you are an atheist reading this you may think you are off the hook for the rest of this book (that was a nice rhyme, eh?). But as we will see when we get to subsequent chapters, that is not at all the case. Those who believe in a deity may think the burden of proof is only on themselves when, in fact, every worldview makes their own truth claims and, therefore, must be justified by means of intellectual scrutiny. After all, atheism is also a religion. Keller explains:

> Let's begin by asking what religion is. Some say it is a form of belief in God. But that would not fit Zen Buddhism, which does not really believe in God at all. Some say it is belief in the supernatural. But that does not fit Hinduism, which does not believe in a supernatural realm. . . . What is religion then? It is a set of beliefs that explain what life is all about, who we are, and the most important things that human beings should spend their time doing. For example, some think that this material world is all there is, that we are here by accident and when we die we just rot, and therefore the important thing is to choose to do what makes you happy and not let others impose their beliefs on you. Notice that though this is not an explicit, "organized" religion, it contains a master narrative, an account about the meaning of life along with a recommendation for how to live based on that account of things. . . . It is an implicit religion.[21]

Atheism is not merely a lack of belief in a deity, but is a religion in and of itself that may even take *far more* faith to follow its theological beliefs than any other religion. Thus, we must add atheism to our list as we look to see if any religions match reality.

CROSSING OPINION

At this point you may be thinking, "Fine, I concede that world religions are not one and the same. We still cannot put them into test tubes, though." But this way of thinking adheres to the assumption that it is an either-or situation; that one must choose between either faith or reason (the mindset, for instance, of 65% of evangelical youth).²² So, adding to the myth that all religions teach the same thing, the claim that we cannot test the truth of religious teachings is also a myth.

With Islam, for instance, its supposed justification for being the truth is a mere circular argument: one should believe Muhammad is the chief prophet of Allah because the Qur'an says so, and we should believe that the Qur'an is the word of Allah because Muhammad says so. A Muslim's upbringing to never doubt a single word of the Qur'an is evident with such a circular argument. Furthermore, Islam says that Jesus was never placed on a cross nor killed (let alone resurrected from the grave as the Savior of the world). But because followers of Islam are not supposed to question the Qur'an, they are never once led to study for themselves and verify that claim or other claims.²³ Or take a religion that we have yet to discuss – Mormonism – and you will see that their argument for why they believe the Book of Mormon is true is because of a burning sensation within their bosom.²⁴ So we are supposed to commit our lives to Islam because some guy went into a cave alone and was supposedly presented with divine revelation?²⁵ And we are supposed to commit our lives to Mormonism based on a feeling that could easily be mistaken as heartburn from eating too many tacos? If all religions are not to be questioned and are feelings-based alone, no wonder so many people are giving up on their traditional belief systems!

Fortunately, there is *one* exception: Christianity invites you – even *dares* you – to test its claims. For instance, in 1 Corinthians 15:14, the apostle Paul states very confidently and bluntly that, "If Christ has not been raised, your faith is worthless." In other words, getting straight to the heart of the matter, Christianity *either stands or falls* on whether or not Jesus Christ was resurrected from the grave. This event, then, unlike private revelation in a cave or an internal burning in the bosom, is *public evidence* that we can investigate to see whether or not this event – the very cause of the birth of Christianity –

actually occurred. Whereas verifiability is discouraged at all costs with any other religion, Christianity wants you to test its public claims. The Bible is clear when it says we should be careful about letting feelings influence us: "The heart is more deceitful than anything else."[26] Thus, Christianity is unique in that it was never meant to be a blind leap into the dark, as it embraces that faith and reason are to hold hands.

Paul is confident that the Bible's claims hold up to historical inquiry, and all we have to do is observe the historical record for ourselves. Because we can all test this event to see if it matches with reality, one does not have to be a follower of any particular belief system in order to perform this investigation. Just like with the Camaro parked in your garage, or with the ten million dollars sitting in your bank account, the claim within this verse is not something that can just be "true for you but not true for me." Either Jesus was or was not resurrected from the grave; there is not an in-between position that anyone can take. This is a journey by which we must be willing to follow the evidence wherever it leads. As historian Philip Schaff states well, "It is not the business of the historian to construct a history from preconceived notions and to adjust it to his own liking, but to reproduce it from the best evidence and to let it speak for itself."[27] If the historical record goes against these words from Paul, Christianity would lose every bit of credibility and another religion possibly could hold the truth. But if it matches Paul's words, the contradictory core teachings from all other religions would lose all credibility and we would be justified in trusting that what is stated in the Bible is objectively true. Thus, we can place everyone's belief in *any* religion (including atheism) to the test on this one verse.

Before we get into specifically this historical investigation, there is a roadmap to a much larger investigation we must explore first. Since truth should be taken with the most absolute, utmost attention, one must not only look at the historical evidence but at *multiple* avenues of evidence in order to make a well-reasoned, objective, overarching conclusion. And the very best way for us to discuss these other avenues in our subsequent chapters just so happens to be by seeking the answers to life's most essential questions that we introduced earlier (i.e., where did we come from, why are we here, how should we live, and what happens to us after we die?).

Once we address those questions in that order and find out how Christianity and the other major world religions holds up to significant scrutiny, we either will or will not have good reason to believe a supernatural being like Jesus could even exist. If we find there is good evidence that the God of the Bible exists, then it is reasonable to believe that a miraculous event like the resurrection could be possible. Such an investigation is necessary; after all, someone miraculously rising from the grave does not happen every day! It is only then that we can build a bridge over the bottomless chasm of subjective opinions on which religion, if any, is true. With that said, the beginning of our overall investigation deals with an even greater miracle that, if found to be true, would make the miracle of a resurrection out to be like child's play for the God of the Bible to accomplish.

BELIEFS CAN HAVE ETERNAL CONSEQUENCES

The stats are out: ten out of ten people are going to die (roughly 156,000 people dying each day and 57 million each year).[28] What we choose to believe not only has temporary consequences for ourselves and others in the here and now, but it has eternal consequences as well. If one wholeheartedly thinks, say, that rat poison cures a common cold, such an incorrect belief will obviously have undesired consequences. Likewise, as we must base our religious beliefs on well-reasoned knowledge instead of opinions alone, to put one's trust in or to not put one's trust in Jesus will most definitely have eternal consequences. *Every* religion says something drastically different about the characteristics of God, about creation, purpose in life, sin, salvation, and the afterlife. These differences are why it is so crucially important to genuinely do a comprehensive investigation into which religion – if any – is true.

Even though it is not politically correct to state only one religion can be true, would it be loving to state otherwise? While we should respect the choices that others make, would it be loving to play along when "modernized" cultures say, "What is true for you may not be true for me"? Of course not. Writes author and educator Alex McFarland, "If there's one thing that Americans don't want to hear, it's that their neighbor Joe, a super nice guy who serves at a soup kitchen every holiday and who dabbles in Buddhism every once in a while, might be going to hell. We don't like to offend people, especially when it comes to matters of faith."[29] If Christianity really is true, the only loving thing to do would be kindly telling others about the coming consequences of not putting their trust in Christ. As C.S. Lewis rightly said, "Christianity, if false, is of no importance, and, if true, of infinite importance. The one thing that it cannot be is moderately important."[30] After all, the Bible says in the book of John that Jesus is *the* way, *the* truth, *the* life, and that no one comes to God the Father except through Him.[31] If that is all true, to not tell someone about it would be like shrugging your shoulders as they are about to take that rat poison for their cold. Atheist and half of the famous magic and comedy team, Penn & Teller, Penn Jillette adds to this line of thought:

> If you believe that there's a Heaven and Hell and people could be going to Hell or not getting eternal life, and you think that it's not really worth telling them this because it would make it socially awkward – and atheists who think people shouldn't proselytize and who say just leave me alone and keep your religion – how much do you have to hate somebody . . . to believe everlasting life is possible

and not tell them that? I mean, if I believed beyond the shadow of a doubt that a truck was coming at you, and you did not believe that truck was bearing down on you, there is a certain point where I tackle you. And this is more important than that.[32]

We put helmets on before riding bicycles and seatbelts on in cars; how much more important is it to protect our souls? Is it smart to risk meeting death's door with a faith system that is likely an invention of man and completely discourages verification altogether? Given the stakes at hand, we should be significantly more careful in the decisions about our faith and let the evidence speak for itself. According to a 2017 survey from the Innovation Center for U.S. Dairy, seven percent of American adults believe that chocolate milk comes from brown cows.[33] That math works out to be 17.8 million people (nearly the entire population of New York state!). So, yes, it is quite clear that human opinion could be mistaken when it comes to things much more important! Depending on feelings alone is dangerous. Truth matters. And the unexamined faith is not worth betting your soul on.

Like the financially poor mother who would give her child the good meat while she ate the fat and lied saying she liked it better, or the father who would wear old, uncomfortable shoes that do not fit while his kids had the latest and greatest, we need more people who make the selfless sacrifices for our youngest generations. We must wake up to reality, do the work, and find this stuff out for them. So regardless of where you are starting from, before you decide whether to continue, if not for yourself, at least join the rest of us on this journey for your family and other loved ones.

The reality of the seriousness of our mortality should not only hit us in those intimately helpless times, such as riding out a severe storm without electricity, our homes and belongings being destroyed by the elements, or when a loved one is deathly sick in the hospital. To simply brush off the truth as not being worth your time is a very dangerous thing to do. It cannot be stressed enough this is a journey that has never been more important to trek than now. Depending on the final conclusions, no matter what religion (including atheism) you may adhere to, we will all have an important decision to make. So, whether you are a firm believer in a particular religion (including atheism), or are a seeker who is somewhere in between belief and unbelief, let us discover the truth together.

AN ETERNAL UNIVERSE OR A FINITE UNIVERSE?

"Who am I? Why am I here?" asked Admiral James Stockdale in the 1992 vice presidential debate. Now, while this *probably* was not the best setting to bring up such questions, they happen to be in-line with two of the four very questions we seek to answer: "Where did we come from?" and "Why are we here?" As humans from all cultures and all times in history have pondered their existence, these two questions about our origin and our meaning and purpose in life especially have left us all many times anxiously wrestling with them wide awake at the foot of our beds. Take, for instance, Leo Tolstoy, who is regarded as one of the greatest authors of all time:

> My question – that which at the age of fifty brought me to the verge of suicide – was the simplest of questions, lying in the soul of every man . . . a question without an answer to which one cannot live. It was: "What will come of what I am doing today or tomorrow?

What will come of my whole life? Why should I live, why wish for anything, or do anything?" It can also be expressed thus: Is there any meaning in my life that the inevitable death awaiting me does not destroy?[1]

With our rapidly growing modern-day advances in every field of science, and with so many different approaches from all the religions of the world, are there any solidly confirmed facts where science and religion both agree? With that challenge, conducting a reasonable investigation into the truth of these two questions will require discussing multiple fields of science within our next handful of chapters.

With that said, it is only natural to start at square one by going all the way back to see whether or not the universe itself had a beginning. This, then, would have us enter into a discussion on cosmology (the study of the origin, development, and structure of the universe), which leads us to what is referred to as the *Kalam Cosmological Argument*:

1. Whatever begins to exist has a cause.
2. The universe began to exist.
3. Therefore, the universe has a cause.

This argument will aid us in an organized fashion with investigating how – and potentially why – the universe came about in the first place. Of course, given the rules of how a valid argument logically works, if we find solid evidence that the first and second premises are both true, the third premise (the conclusion) necessarily follows. Therefore, if the argument as a whole is found true, this would give us great insight and work as a launching point for digging even deeper into more points in our continued investigation. Thus, let us begin by looking for such evidence for premise one.

PREMISE 1:
WHATEVER BEGINS TO EXIST HAS A CAUSE

No matter what it is, there is absolutely, positively *nothing* that begins to exist that does not have a cause. Suppose one finds a small box of marbles at the top of a mountain. Would it be at all reasonable for you to simply conclude there is no explanation for the box of marbles being there; that it just popped into existence by itself? No. You would know, for sure, that someone either purposefully placed or accidentally dropped it there. Now, what if that box were the size of a vehicle, a football field, a moon, and so on? No matter how much you decrease the size or increase the size of any entity, the same conclusion would ultimately be reached: it did not just pop into existence by itself and, therefore, it needs an explanation for its cause. In the exact same way, you cannot say everything that has a beginning has a cause and then somehow exempt the universe; it is no different than anything else, and doing so would be a direct violation of *the* fundamental principle in all of science – the Law of Cause and Effect (i.e., for every *effect* there is a definite *cause*, and for every *cause* there is a definite *effect*) – thus rendering science impossible.

For another illustration, author Mark Mittelberg writes, "'If you loan someone your car, and he brings it back with a fresh dent in the bumper, you don't want to enter into a philosophical discussion about whether or not "dents that begin to exist need a cause"; you just want to know what your friend ran into – and how he's going to pay for the repairs.'"[2] William Lane Craig observes: "The idea that things can come into being uncaused out of nothing is worse than magic. At least when a magician pulls a rabbit out of a hat, there's the magician and the hat! . . . Nobody worries that while he's away at work, say, a horse might pop into being, uncaused, out of nothing, in his living room, and be there defiling the carpet."[3]

The philosopher David Hume, who was an atheist in all but name, regarded this position as ridiculous and never denied causation. In the late eighteenth century he wrote that he "never asserted so absurd a proposition as that anything might arise without a cause."[4] But it is the position of fringe atheists since the mid-1900s to somehow actually believe the exact opposite; that everything *but* the universe itself needs a cause because it somehow popped into existence out of nothing all on its own. For instance, philosopher, essayist, and mathematician, Bertrand Russell held that very position in the famous BBC Radio debate against Frederick Copleston.[5] This kind of thinking becomes even nuttier once you grasp what *absolute nothingness* is; scientist and philosopher Aristotle had a perfect definition: "Nothing is what rocks dream about."

So beyond philosophical and common sense facts which all clearly show that our first premise is undeniably true, are there scientific facts that back them up which unquestionably refute the fringe atheistic position and show that the universe did, in fact, begin to exist in the finite past and, therefore, requires a cause? This leads us to our second premise.

PREMISE 2:
THE UNIVERSE BEGAN TO EXIST

Yes, fringe atheists hold to the belief that the universe just popped into existence on its own and needed no cause. Nevertheless, they still know it had an ultimate beginning.

That the universe had a beginning is now an indisputable scientific fact from multiple avenues of observation. Surprising, seeing as how much it gets wrong, this is even evident in forms of entertainment. For instance, the feature story on the cover of a 2001 issue of *Time* magazine was entitled, "How the Universe Will End."[6] Of course, if the universe will have a definite end, it had a definite beginning. Even the narration in the latest installment of the kid's movie, *Ice Age: Collision Course*, states this without a second thought: "The universe, a vast expanse of space and matter. It includes all that we see and all that we know. Since the beginning of time, we have wondered how it came to be."[7] But the factual understanding that the universe had a beginning a finite time ago was not always the case.

Just as it was long assumed the Earth was the center of the entire universe, until we later figured out we are not even in the center of our own galaxy nor our own solar system, at least as far back as the ancient Greek philosophers, nearly everyone but those from certain religious backgrounds assumed that the universe was eternal – having always existed with no beginning. It was not until the early 1900s that this understanding changed. So what was it that dramatically swayed nearly everyone's minds to the exact opposite conclusion? While there were good arguments based on logic alone to be made for a finite universe, there was not any confirmed way to scientifically determine which of the two views was correct. But this all began to change with two laws of thermodynamics that, though, of course, they have been laws of the universe since its creation, were empirically developed in the nineteenth century.

FIRST AND SECOND LAWS OF THERMODYNAMICS

Thermodynamics is the branch of physical science that studies relationships between all forms of energy. And according to the First Law, a closed, isolated system like the universe (meaning no energy is coming into existence or out of existence) will have a finite amount of energy that remains constant. In other words, energy cannot be made nor destroyed—there will never be an increase or decrease in the amount of energy – but, instead, is merely converted into another form of energy. States mechanical engineer Jeff Miller, "This can be demonstrated by the burning of a piece of wood. When the wood is burned, it is transformed into a different state. The original amount of energy present before the burning is still present. However, much of that energy was transformed into a different state, namely, heat. No energy disappeared from the Universe, and no energy was brought into the Universe."[8] The only question, then (that we will discuss in depth in premise 3), is if energy can neither be created nor destroyed, where did all of the energy in the universe come from in the first place?

Further, according to the Second Law, the universe is not constantly being depleted of energy but depleted of *usable* energy. Miller continues: "Extending our wood burning illustration above, after the wood is burned, the total amount of energy is still the same, but transformed into other energy states. Those energy states (e.g., ash and dissipated heat to the environment) are less retrievable and less accessible." This is where engineers come in to address ways of minimizing energy loss and maximizing useful energy before it is wasted.

With these laws in mind, nature goes from order to disorder. This principle, which can be slowed down but not stopped, is called entropy. For instance, a freshly painted house will eventually chip, peel, and quickly become dilapidated if not being lived in and being kept, an automobile will rust, living things will die and then decompose, etc. Isaac Asimov, author and Professor of biochemistry at Boston University, explained,

> The universe is constantly getting more disorderly! Viewed that way we can see the Second Law all about us. We have to work hard to straighten a room, but left to itself it becomes a mess again very quickly and very easily. Even if we never enter it, it becomes dusty and musty. How difficult to maintain houses, and machinery, and

AN ETERNAL UNIVERSE OR A FINITE UNIVERSE?

our own bodies in perfect working order: how easy to let them deteriorate. In fact, all we have to do is nothing, and everything deteriorates, collapses, breaks down, wears out, all by itself – and that is what the Second Law is all about.⁹

So what does this have to do with our understanding of the universe having a beginning? Well, eternal things do not "run down." It makes zero sense that the universe has always existed, because all of its usable energy would have been used up infinitely long ago. Think of this like you would an automobile or a flashlight, writes Geisler and Turek:

> If your car has only a finite amount of gas . . . and whenever it is running it continually consumes gas . . . would your car be running right now if you had started it up an infinitely long time ago? No, of course not. It would be out of gas by now. In the same way, the universe would be out of energy by now if it had been running from all eternity. . . . If you leave a flashlight on overnight, what's the intensity of the light in the morning? It is dim, because the batteries have used up most of their energy. Well, the universe is like a dying flashlight. It has only so much energy left to consume. But since the universe still has some battery life left . . . it cannot be eternal – it must have had a   beginning.¹⁰

As the Galaxy And Mass Assembly (GAMA) team leader and Senior Principal Research Fellow for the International Centre for Radio Astronomy Research (ICRAR) at the University of Western Australia, professor Simon Driver states, "The Universe will decline from here on in, sliding gently into old age. The Universe has basically sat down on the sofa, pulled up a blanket and is about to nod off."¹¹

According to these well-established scientific laws, just as the fuel will eventually burn up as the engine of an automobile is running, or a flashlight will run out of battery power if left on overnight, the universe will eventually run out of its finite amount of usable energy. But unlike an automobile or a flashlight, cosmologists know that the universe will die in thermodynamic equilibrium (heat death) when it runs out of this energy. If the universe were eternal, our Sun would have exhausted its fuel reserves, the cycle of death and rebirth of stars would have stopped, and we would have reached this point of equilibrium an infinite time ago. Yet, our Sun burns bright, an estimated 400 million stars are born every day, and we are still here, all because the universe is not eternal with an infinite amount of usable energy.[12] With these two laws in mind, it is unavoidable both with common sense and scientific fact that, as astronomer Robert Jastrow states, "The laws of thermodynamics . . . [point] to one conclusion . . . that the Universe had a beginning."[13]

EXPANSION OF THE UNIVERSE

Further evidence to scientifically determine whether or not the universe had a beginning a finite time ago came to us when an unknown clerk, Albert Einstein, working in the Swiss patent office developed equations for ten long years and published in November of 1915 his General Theory of Relativity.[14] With his equations, Einstein completely changed the way we look at the universe. For instance, he showed that our assumptions about the universe being spatially three-dimensional was wrong; there are at least four bound-together spatial dimensions – up and down, left and right, forward and backward, and time itself. To the surprise of everyone that the three are not distinct from the one, there is actually a direct link between space and time – the time-space continuum. This, then, led to yet another assumption held by

AN ETERNAL UNIVERSE OR A FINITE UNIVERSE?

everyone which was shown to be wrong: our thoughts on gravity.

When Sir Isaac Newton first theorized in 1665 that objects stay on and fall to Earth's surface due to how, for instance, the moon stays in orbit around the Earth, he was right and all. But the glaring problem with his theory, even though he accurately described its strength, was that he actually did not know how, what he called "the force of gravity," actually works. It would then take 250 years for the facts to be understood, when Einstein would revolutionize our understanding of the universe, showing how matter such as stars and planets can warp space and change time and light (time actually runs differently at, say, the bottom and top of a skyscraper, or even from the distance between two shelves), and that this phenomenon causes what he and everyone referred to as the force of gravity.

Imagine gridlines running across the entire universe, and that this interwoven fabric of flexible space-time can be curved by mass (greater the mass equals greater the curve). It is like the fabric of a trampoline with a bowling ball in the middle: once you roll a marble at an angle, it will begin to orbit around the bowling ball until it loses energy (something that a celestial body does not have to worry about in this sense). So, with what we perceive as a force, gravity is the effect of the curvature of space-time; the Sun, for instance, does not have a gravitational pull that forces the Earth to orbit around it, but instead the effect of space-time caused by the Sun's enormous mass has stretched and curved the area well beyond that of Earth and is actually pushing Earth in a very nearly circular orbit around it at a speed of 67,000 miles per hour.

Despite all of the ways Einstein revolutionized our scientific understanding of the universe, though, there was one significant aspect that perplexed him. Going beyond explaining the motion of planets and other celestial bodies, Einstein believed that the attractive nature of all the objects within the universe should have caused the entire universe to collapse on itself. When Russian physicist and mathematician Alexander Friedmann and Belgian astronomer and professor of physics Georges Lemaître applied Einstein's equations to the universe as a whole, they found that, because the amount of matter within the universe sculpts its curvature, and because of the vast amount of energy it contains, the equations strongly indicated the exact opposite: the universe must be *expanding* with time.

This was perplexing to Einstein only because, just like the assumptions from most ancient Greek philosophers up to the assumptions from most scientists of his time, he had always simply followed the consensus view that the universe is eternal, static, and unchanging (things within the universe were changing, but the universe itself was at rest). Regardless of whether it was contracting back upon itself or expanding, he now knew that the indications from his equations meant the universe was finite, dynamic, and changing. There was no way around what was directly in front of him: the universe had a beginning.

The story goes on that, as astrophysicist Neil deGrasse Tyson states, "With a non-static universe staring him in the face, Einstein botched the opportunity to predict it and, out of aesthetic preference, instead favored the static model."[15] Personally not liking the thought of a beginning, Einstein then dismissed the information, referred to it in a letter to mathematician, physicist, and astronomer Willem de Sitter as "irritating," and continued with his personally preferred belief that the universe was eternal. Of course, this was only until empirically decisive proof came along showing that his equations, as described by Friedmann and Lemaître, had been right all along; the first piece of scientific confirmation of the universe having a beginning coming in the 1920s in the form of proof that the universe is, in fact, expanding.

Up until this time, most scientists believed that the universe consisted only of our Milky Way galaxy in the vastness of space. But with the world's largest telescope having been completed and at the disposal of American astronomer Edwin Hubble at the Mount Wilson Observatory in Los Angeles County, California, we came to learn that there are far, far more galaxies (then referred to as *extragalactic-nebulae*) beyond our own. Continuing his research and using previous research from astronomers Henrietta Swan Leavitt and Vesto Melvin Slipher who were hot on the trail but did not have a way to expand on and confirm their research, Hubble, who did have the required equipment, then began to measure the distances between galaxies.

In doing so, Hubble was able to confirm that all galaxies and objects in space are moving away from one another, causing a Doppler effect. A Doppler effect is, for example, what you experience when a vehicle with its siren or horn blowing approaches and goes passed you; when the vehicle moves toward you, the sound of the siren or horn has a higher and higher pitch (higher frequency), and once it passes you it has a lower and lower pitch (lower frequency). The same effect is true for stars and galaxies as a whole, whereas, instead of sound waves, we can use special equipment to accurately measure the frequencies of light waves to conclude whether they are moving closer or farther away. If, say, a galaxy is moving closer to the observer, the light waves are more compressed, representing a higher frequency and the light will move to the blue side of the light spectrum. On the other hand, if a galaxy is moving farther from the observer, the light waves are more spread out, representing a lower frequency and the light will move to the red side of the light spectrum. This movement to the red side of the light spectrum is what astronomers refer to as *red shift*, and is crucially important to the discussion at hand.

By observing shifts in spectral color, Hubble was able to conclude that all galaxies were rushing away from one another at enormous velocities. Furthermore, once he developed a graph with plot points for the amount of red shift in relation to their distances, called the *Hubble plot*, he was also able to conclude that galaxies are incrementally receding more rapidly as t distance incrementally increases. This observation, then, that every galaxy is receding with a speed which is in direct proportion to its distance, became known as *Hubble's Law*.

The reason that the universe had not collapsed, as both Newton and Einstein thought was inevitable, is that it had been expanding all along. Einstein himself went to the Mount Wilson Observatory to take a look at the red-shifting galaxies and ultimately concluded this made for the first concrete evidence that the universe has definitively been expanding and growing in size just as was previously predicted by the Friedmann-Lemaître model. He stated, "The red shift of distant nebulae has smashed my old construction like a hammer blow."[16]

Of course, it is not the actual *galaxies* that are expanding but *space* itself that is expanding. Take a balloon with stickers on it as an example. If you were to blow air into this balloon what would happen to the stickers? They would move farther and farther away from one another as the balloon grew bigger and bigger. But it is not the stickers themselves that are moving; it is the air (space) that is expanding and making the distance between them grow. Imagine, then, what would happen if all the air from the balloon was released. Yes, a funny, suggestive sound, but also the stickers would move closer to one another. Similarly, if we were to "let the air out" of the entire universe and rewind it we would see everything contract back unto itself. But unlike the balloon, the universe would keep contracting until the distance between objects becomes zero at a point of absolute nothingness. This cosmological fact that the universe came onto the scene out of nothingness and rapidly expanded to what we know today is what would later become known as *the*

mes to this term – the big bang – there are some commonly s. We will discuss one of two significant misconceptions ter, but the other is the fact it is sometimes believed that, before the big bang occurred, there was just a dull, object-less void of space and that the big bang would eventually come along and suddenly fill it with expanding galaxies. But it would be entirely false and not at all in line with what the model states to believe the universe itself is eternal while its contents began to exist a finite time ago.

As Janna Levin, Professor of physics and astronomy at Columbia University, for instance, succinctly states, "The universe had a beginning. There was once nothing and now there is something."[17] What *nothingness* means is just that: absolutely *nothing*; as Aristotle said, "What rocks dream about." So to ask the question "What was the universe like before the big bang?" is nonsense; there was *nothing* before the big bang because a state of existence *before* the big bang is not even a possibility. As Arizona State University physicist, cosmologist, and astrobiologist Paul Davies states, "The big bang represents the creation event; the creation not only of all matter and energy in the universe, but also of spacetime itself."[18]

As the late Stephen Hawking (world-renowned theoretical astrophysicist, cosmologist, and former Director of Research at the Centre for Theoretical Cosmology at Cambridge), and mathematical physicist Roger Penrose stated, "The universe, and time itself, had a beginning at the Big Bang."[19] And astronomer, planetary physicist, Director of *Mount Wilson* Observatory, and founder and director of NASA's Goddard Institute for Space Studies Robert Jastrow states, "Now both theory and observation [point] to an expanding universe and a beginning in time."[20]

We know that what has been coined "the big bang" was an explosive event of creation where everything – matter, energy, space, time, and even the scientific laws – began to exist at the exact same moment in the finite past. The debate on whether or not the universe had a beginning has long been over and, now, scientists are simply conducting experiments to see how fast the universe's expansion, which is due to this explosion, has been accelerating.

LIGHT ELEMENTS

The event at which matter, energy, space and time all came into existence, as with the subsequent expansion of the universe, had all gone beyond mere theory to being empirically observed, indisputable, cosmological facts. And, since this discovery was made, we have found even further confirmation through experimental observations; one, for instance, having to do with the origin and abundance of light elements, such as hydrogen and helium, throughout the universe.

Hydrogen is by far the lightest (14 times lighter than air) and most abundant (nearly 92% in number and 74-75% in mass) element in the universe. Helium is a distant second in weight (nearly 4 times lighter than air) and abundance (nearly 8% in number and 24-25% in mass). But while it is an interesting tidbit that the universe consists of comparatively insignificant amounts of all the other elements, it is the origin of these two and other light elements that are most relative to our discussion at hand.

It had long been the prevailing theory (Burbidge, Burbidge, Fowler, Hoyle; "BBFH" Theory) that all elements were produced within the outer envelopes and interior of stars (stellar nucleosynthesis) and released when they exploded (a supernova). But come to find out, that is not the case. While it is true that heavy elements are formed and dispersed in this fashion, it is not true concerning light elements because, if this were their only source of production, either they (like the element deuterium) would be destroyed or there would only be trace amounts throughout the universe. In fact, the BBFH Theory estimated that only trace amounts of helium should exist in the universe today because of this very fact. Of course, with helium taking up 25% of the universe's mass, it was clearly flat-out wrong. So, if light elements cannot form efficiently whatsoever through stellar nucleosynthesis like heavy elements can, how is it the case that the universe is composed almost entirely

AN ETERNAL UNIVERSE OR A FINITE UNIVERSE?

of hydrogen and helium with only small concentrations of heavy elements?

In studying what the conditions of the universe were like as it exploded into existence in the big bang, long before the first stars were ever formed, we know that the creation event was, to say the least, very hot. While it was much, *much* hotter just prior at an estimated temperature of over 10^{34} degrees Fahrenheit (that is a 1 with 34 zeros, compared to the temperature of the Sun at slightly under 10,000 degrees Fahrenheit!), after roughly three minutes had elapsed and the universe cooled considerably to just under two billion degrees Fahrenheit, the production of light elements (big bang nucleosynthesis) could take place to initially form a great abundance of hydrogen and helium (and also much smaller amounts of lithium and beryllium).[21]

The formation of light elements depended very strongly on this event's incredible heat, and also the high density of the newly created, incredibly small universe. The chance of light elements forming in even the hottest and most luminous supernova is very rare, as they can barely form even trace amounts. The big bang, though, allowed for an environment in which the building blocks of all matter was greatly condensed, which allowed for protons, neutrons, and electrons to collide and combine with one another in multiple fashions extremely rapidly to start the process of forming stable light elements on a grand scale. And in regards to why big bang nucleosynthesis created so much hydrogen and helium and only small amounts of other light elements, we find our answer in the period between when the universe was merely a fraction of a second old to the point that it cooled off considerably after a few minute's time.

At just a fraction of a second old, though there were not many protons and neutrons at this time compared to electrons and neutrinos which outnumbered them by roughly a billion to one, the universe contained roughly an equal 50/50 split amount of protons and neutrons. But after the universe had a few minutes to cool down, it became much more difficult to find proton-electron pairs with the energy needed to create neutrons compared with neutron-neutrino pairs creating proton-electron pairs, thus changing this 50/50 ratio to roughly 88/12 in favor of protons. At this point in which we can build our way up the periodic table, nearly every neutron combines with another neutron and two protons to form helium-4 atoms, therefore using up an equal amount of protons (12%) in this process. This, then, left protons and electrons to combine into hydrogen atoms, thus causing the universe to have a mass ratio of roughly 74-75% hydrogen and roughly 24-25% helium along with much smaller amounts of lithium and beryllium.

Heavy elements, on the other hand, such as carbon and oxygen, could not have formed in the big bang. Once the first stars formed long after the event took place, heavy elements have always relied on being synthesized in stars and dispersed through supernova explosions (an event that is incredibly rare in and of itself, as it is estimated that supernovae occur, on average, about once per century in the entire galaxy).[22] As you can see, then, the universe did not start off with heavy elements.

Unlike the BBFH Theory, the measurements of the big bang model predict all of this. These measurements not only tell us when light and heavy elements formed for the first time but also tell us the percentages at which each element should account for the entire universe today (such as the abundance of hydrogen and helium being the same ratio ever since mere minutes after the big bang). One way that we can be sure of this is by comparing the predicted percentages with actually observed percentages.

Because the farther away an object is, the longer it has taken for its light to travel to our eyes, when we look out into the distant universe, we are looking back into its distant past closer and closer to the big bang event itself. Thus, a telescope is similar to a time machine. So, just like it takes the Sun's light roughly eight minutes and thirty seconds to travel to Earth (we would not know for 8.3 light-minutes if the Sun exploded), and light from Proxima

AN ETERNAL UNIVERSE OR A FINITE UNIVERSE?

Centauri, the star closest to our solar system, takes over four light-years to reach Earth, we can look deep into the past and observe the ancient light from the oldest stars; the equivalent of looking at their baby pictures. And when we do so we find that, similar to the gas giants Jupiter and Saturn (or planet Bespin, home to Cloud City in the movie The Empire Strikes Back), but unlike Earth because it is not massive enough to gravitationally hold on to helium well, the first stars to ever form contained 75% hydrogen, 25% helium, and trace amounts of newly formed heavy elements.[23] Thus the predictions are observed to be spot-on accurate, and NASA states that this accuracy "is in very good agreement with observations and is another major triumph for the Big Bang."[24]

COSMIC MICROWAVE BACKGROUND RADIATION

Another prediction from the big bang model has to do with the temperature of what is called the cosmic microwave background radiation (CMBR). Let us look at a couple of illustrations to get better acquainted with this term.

If you have ever watched a tube TV in a dark room, you have experienced a noticeable faint glow of light around the screen that lasts for a few seconds after the set has been turned off. This afterglow, called phosphorescence, is the remnant heat coming off the screen. Or, as J. Warner Wallace writes,

> I served for three years on our SWAT unit, and during that time, we were repeatedly asked to flush out barricaded suspects. We employed a "flash-bang" grenade in nearly all these SWAT entries. The grenades are designed, of course, to "flash" and "bang"; they make a lot of noise, light, and heat. We typically threw a grenade in the room where the suspect was barricaded. When the grenade hit

the ground, it exploded violently, lighting the room, deafening the suspect, and filling the space with debris and heat. In that instant, as the suspect was distracted, our team came in from the opposite corner. Flashbangs are excellent distraction device because they leave a lingering impact in the space where they are deployed.[25]

Similarly, the CMBR is the detectable remnant light and heat coming off the universe which has been left over from the incredibly powerful event of creation; the smoking gun if you will. In fact, speaking of TV sets, we now know that a sizeable amount of the static, or "snow" shown on improperly tuned analog channels is actually due to this remnant radiation. And the same is true for the "white noise" you hear on FM radios when tuned to a frequency that is in-between stations.

The CMBR was first predicted in connection with work on big bang nucleosynthesis from George Gamow, Ralph Alpherin, and Robert Herman in 1948. They argued that, because the light and heat from the big bang would not dissipate as it would from, say, an explosion from a bomb, and because the big bang explosion occurred everywhere at the same time, its remnant light and heat must be equally spread throughout the entire universe. Further, it was predicted that, because the incredibly hot, dense, early universe began to expand and the ultra-hot gas within it started to cool as time went on long before the formation of the very first stars and galaxies, the CMBR, which should have been emitted shortly after the universe cooled to the point that stable atoms of hydrogen began to form, should now be diluted and cooled to the point that it is now slightly hotter than absolute zero (a temperature of −459.67 degrees Fahrenheit, the coldest and impossible-to-reach temperature because it is then when atoms would stop moving). Thus, the remnant light and heat from this time has been traveling through space ever since, should be isotropic (coming equally from all directions of the sky) and, thus, able to be detected all around us.

Sure enough, at a time when specialized instruments able to potentially detect such radiation invisible to the naked eye in specific regions of the electromagnetic spectrum was newly developed, and when teams were already underway devising experiments specifically to find the CMBR, it was found accidentally and confirmed in 1964 by physicists and radio astronomers Arno Penzias and Robert Wilson as background noise from electromagnetic waves (strongest in the microwave region because they have red shifted from high frequencies and short wavelengths to much lower frequencies and longer wavelengths) coming from every direction and having a temperature of approximately -454 degrees Fahrenheit. In fact, if the naked eye could see microwaves, the entire sky would be bathed in a glow from this remnant radiation. The discovery of the CMBR, which was made using the Holmdel Horn Antenna at New Jersey's Bell Labs, would go on to earn both Penzias and Wilson the 1978 Nobel Prize in Physics.

At this point, there was no way to deny that the big bang creation event happened. As Jastrow stated, "The clincher, which has convinced almost the last Doubting Thomas, is that the radiation discovered by Penzias and Wilson has exactly the pattern of wavelengths expected for the light and heat produced in a great explosion."[26] But convincing these very few skeptics got even better. While this discovery was entirely incredible, confirming the presence and even the temperature of the CMBR is not where the most excitement eventually arose.

In 1989, NASA launched the Cosmic Background Explorer (COBE) space satellite to observe this radiation much more closely. Of course, it takes a long time to do these experiments because of dust in the galaxy and the radiation coming off the Sun and distant stars. But because all of these sources come in different wavelengths than the CMBR (which itself is in the microwave region of the electromagnetic spectrum because the wavelengths have stretched to be that length as time has gone by), we are able to subtract them to collect accurate data of strictly those wavelengths. And in 1992 its results showed that, while almost entirely smooth, the CMBR actually has very slight density fluctuations (ripples), termed anisotropies, within its temperature – roughly one part in 100,000 (the equivalent of the tallest mountain on Earth being 300 feet instead of 30,000 feet).[27]

Hawking would praise the discovery of these ripples as "the most important discovery of the century, if not all of time."[28] So why was this particular discovery so exciting and deserving of so much praise?

Keep in mind that the remnant light and heat COBE observed is from the very distant past. Therefore the results of the project, which is literally a map of the initial conditions of the early universe when light was first made, show us how these density variations, which led to slight variations in the temperature of the CMBR, precisely allowed matter to congregate as "seeds" that would grow over time into the stars, planets, galaxies, and superclusters of galaxies.[29] In other words, it is absolutely vital that these ripples were exactly how they were because, if the universe were perfectly smooth or if there were any slight variations of these initial conditions, no cosmic structures (and eventually mankind) would be here. So not only was it the discovery of these ripples that amazed scientists, but their *perfect precision* to allow for everything that exists to date. This also goes to show that the big bang was not just a chaotic mess but instead was an incredibly intricate creation event.

Astrophysicist, cosmologist, and leader of the COBE project who announced its findings, George Smoot, along with fellow astrophysicist and cosmologist, John Mather, would go on to earn the 2006 Nobel Prize in Physics for their work with the project. Then in 2001, NASA launched a second, significantly more technically sophisticated space satellite to measure the CMBR. This satellite, called the Wilkinson Microwave Anisotropy Probe (WMAP), was designed to make much more precise measurements of these ripples (anisotropies) compared to COBE. Further, in 2009, the European Space Agency launched the third space satellite, Planck, for measurements of the CMBR at even higher resolution than obtained by WMAP. Being successful in their results, both satellites confirmed the findings from COBE with increasing accuracy, as well as providing an increasingly more detailed picture for how the universe looked soon after creation. As WMAP principal investigator Charles L. Bennett stated, "It amazes me that we can say anything about what transpired within the first trillionth of a second of the universe, but we can."[30]

PREMISE 3:
THEREFORE, THE UNIVERSE HAS A CAUSE

Just like many were mistaken for so long about the Earth being flat, many were mistaken about the universe having always existed. It is clear the universe had a beginning in the finite past and, for those uncomfortable with that idea, there is no getting around it being a solid fact. Einstein, being "irritated" by the expanding universe, was one of those people. Astronomer, physicist, and mathematician Sir Arthur Eddington shared Einstein's displeasure with what the facts showed about the universe having a beginning, stating, "Philosophically, the notion of a beginning . . . is repugnant to me. . . . I should like to find a genuine loophole."[31]

Speaking towards scientists like Einstein and Eddington, the director of the Institute of Cosmology at Tufts University, Alexander Vilenkin, once said, "It is said that an argument is what convinces reasonable men and a proof is what it takes to convince even an unreasonable man. With the proof now in place, cosmologists can no longer hide behind the possibility of a past-eternal universe. There is no escape, they have to face the problem of a cosmic beginning."³² Vilenkin is absolutely correct. But why exactly would the beginning of the universe make some people so uncomfortable; why is this fact so irritating, repugnant, and such a problem?

THEOLOGICAL IMPLICATIONS

Let us go down the line to list what we know about the premises of the Kalam Cosmological Argument. Premise one stated that whatever begins to exist has a cause. That premise is obviously true. Second, we also know from the five examples of scientific proof we have discussed that the universe began to exist. This, then, means that the second premise is also true. Thus, given the rules of logic, the two premises necessarily lead to the inevitable conclusion – being premise three – that, therefore, the universe has a cause. It is impossible for something to begin to exist without a cause, and we know for certain that the universe is not exempt from this fact. So the question, anymore, is not whether or not the universe began to exist; it is what *caused* it to begin to exist.

Of course, we will populate the list more and more as we go on with subsequent chapters. But, in regards to what we have discussed in this chapter alone, what can we know already about this cause?

Well, since space, time, and matter began to exist all at once in the creation event, and since something cannot just come out of nothing, the cause must be without space (spaceless), outside of time (timeless), and not be made of physical matter (immaterial). In other words, nothing in the universe could create the universe; because the universe had a beginning, it must be caused by something outside itself. A created thing cannot be the cause that brought itself into creation. And to even suggest, as philosopher Daniel Dennett has, that the universe created itself is to present a brutally obvious, laughable, self-contradictory position.³³ In order for something to be self-caused, it would have to exist, before it existed, to cause its own existence! This is impossible

52

on all levels. For someone to say they are searching for a natural cause of the universe's beginning would be the equivalent of them saying, "Give me more time and I'll discover that I gave birth to my own mother!"[34]

Additionally, having created time and not being bound to it, and since change is a product of time, the cause must, therefore, be changeless. The cause must also be uncaused because there is no such thing as infinity and an infinite regress of causes; powerful to have created the universe out of nothing; intelligent to have created the universe with such precision out of nothing; and, because impersonal forces like gravity cannot choose to do anything and purpose directly implies plan and intention, the cause must also be personal (not in the sense of having personal closeness with humans, but in the sense of having the human characteristics of rationality, being conscious of their own existence, having an intellect, free will, emotion, etc.) to have decided to even create the universe. As Alex McFarland writes, "We know that an uncaused effect is impossible; it does not exist – clocks do not wind themselves, baseballs do not throw themselves. So the universe was *intentionally* caused" [emphasis added].[35] Thus, a personal cause could exist without creation and then choose to bring creation into existence by an act of will. William Lane Craig adds to this line of thought:

> Causal explanations can be either of two types: it can be a scientific explanation in terms of laws and initial conditions, or it can be a personal explanation in terms of an agent and his volitions. So, for example, if I walk into the kitchen and see a kettle boiling and I say to [my wife], "Why is the kettle boiling?" she could say to me, "Because the heat of the flame is being conducted by the copper bottom of the kettle to the water causing the molecules to vibrate more violently until they're thrown off in the form of steam." Or she could say to me, "I put it on to make a cup of tea. Would you

like one?" One is a scientific explanation, and the other is a personal explanation. Both of them are equally legitimate forms of causal explanation. . . . Now, when it comes to a first physical state of the universe, there cannot be a scientific explanation of that in terms of initial conditions and natural laws because it *is* the first physical state; there is nothing prior to it from which you could deduce it by natural laws based on prior conditions. So the only kind of causal explanation that's available will be an explanation in terms of an agent and his volitions. And that gives you a personal Creator.

It's the only way in which you can explain how to get an effect with a beginning from an eternal Cause. If the Cause is sufficient to produce its effect, then if the Cause is always there and is permanent, then the effect should be always there as well. For example, if the cause of waters freezing is the temperature being below zero degrees Celsius, then if the temperature were below zero degrees from eternity past, it would be impossible for the water just to begin to freeze a finite time ago; any water that was around would be frozen from eternity. If the cause is there, its effect must be there as well. So how do you get a cause which is permanent and eternal and an effect like the universe which only began to exist [a finite time] ago? The only answer to this conundrum, I think, is if the Cause is a personal agent, endowed with freedom of the will, who can therefore create a new effect spontaneously without any antecedent determining conditions; for example, a man sitting from eternity could freely will to stand up, and thus you would have an effect with a beginning arise from an eternal and permanent cause.[36]

Since a cause cannot come after its effect, and since the universe (nature)

AN ETERNAL UNIVERSE OR A FINITE UNIVERSE?

did not even exist prior to the big bang, it cannot be its own cause. Thus, the cause must be outside of nature, being "supernatural." It is entirely reasonable, then, to move from the idea that an impersonal *something* created the universe to the fact that a personal, supernatural *Someone* is the only possible explanation for its creation. Therefore, since the universe had a *creation*, this obviously implies that the universe did not just have a cause, but, to be specific, a *Creator*.

This sounds entirely like a god. To sum up, then, the relation between a god and the big bang, the big bang did not just happen on its own; it had a *Big Banger*.

Yes, this sounds entirely like a god, yet notice that we did not have to use *any* scriptures to conclude what characteristics the Creator must have. Even scientists of agnostic and atheistic leanings from all different fields of science who constantly study this information know that nature cannot be its own cause and that, therefore, the Creator must be outside of nature.

For instance, Hawking wrote that, "It would be very difficult to explain why the universe should have begun in just this way, except as the act of a God who intended to create beings like us."[37] Further, stating to a reporter: "The odds against a universe like ours emerging out of something like the big bang are enormous.... I think clearly there are religious implications whenever you start to discuss the origins of the universe. There must be religious overtones. But I think most scientists prefer to shy away from the religious side of it."[38] Davies wrote that, "One might consider some supernatural force, some agency beyond space and time as being responsible."[39] Eddington (who found the beginning of the universe repugnant), ultimately concluded, "The beginning seems to present insuperable difficulties unless we agree to look on it as frankly supernatural."[40] Einstein, says Jastrow, was irritated with a beginning of the universe "because of its theological implications."[41] And Jastrow himself stated,

Astronomers now find they have painted themselves into a corner because they have proven, by their own methods, that the world began abruptly in an act of creation to which you can trace the seeds of every star, every planet, every living thing in this cosmos and on the earth. And they have found that all this happened as a product of forces they cannot hope to discover. . . . That there are what I or anyone would call supernatural forces at work is now, I think, a scientifically proven fact.[42]

Beyond the theory that Dennett proposed of the universe having created itself, other agnostic and atheistic scientists have tried and tried positing more theories to try and bypass a Creator. For instance, Hawking similarly theorized what is scientifically impossible – that the universe can be the cause and effect – writing in his book *The Grand Design*, "Because there is a law like gravity, the universe can and will create itself from nothing."[43] Well, first of all, the laws of the universe do not have causal powers to create and, therefore, could not be responsible for the creation of anything. Second, he believes the universe just popped into existence all by itself out of "nothing" due to the law of gravity. But, obviously, it is not difficult to see that the law of gravity is not "nothing." This is a reminder of a recent Craftsman tools commercial: "We were born to make something out of nothing."[44] Common sense says that these tools are *something* and what they are to be used on is *something*; therefore there is no making something from "nothing" at all. The law of gravity was not here before the universe existed, because there was truly, absolutely, positively, *nothing*.

Similarly, theoretical physicist Lawrence Krauss wrote in his book, *A Universe From Nothing: Why There Is Something Rather Than Nothing*, that perhaps a quantum vacuum can explain how the universe came into being from "nothing."[45] Again, the problem rests on the pesky little word "nothing." If you press Krauss, he admits that his use of the word "nothing" is not *really* talking about "nothing" but, instead, is speaking of an entirely theoretical microscopic sea of fluctuating energy.[46] But all he has done is renamed *something* (the quantum vacuum) "nothing," when clearly it is something!

Further, chemist and professor of chemistry at Oxford University, Peter Atkins, believed the universe could have' been created due to swirling mathematical points. And professor of biochemistry at Boston University, Isaac Asimov, believed it could be due to positive and negative energy.[47] Each of the theories, in trying to bypass a Creator, are trying to say things that came *after* the creation event caused the creation event; all that these theories do is discuss what the early stages of the universe were like *after* the universe was *already* created and do not at all touch on the moment of *creation itself* – which is *the whole point*! Even further, they have not even attempted to deal with the fact that one must explain where space, time, matter, energy, and the physical laws came from in the first place. So, as the most dreaded question of a parent is about where babies come from, theirs is, "Where do(es) space, time, matter, energy, and the physical laws come from?" As Oxford mathematician and philosopher John Lennox concludes, "Nonsense remains nonsense, even when talked by world-famous scientists."[48]

A cosmic beginning due to a Creator outside of nature is inescapable. Speaking of them, Hawking noted, "Together with Roger Penrose . . . [we] showed that . . . any reasonable model of the universe must start with a [beginning]. This would mean that science could predict that the universe must have had a beginning, but that it could not predict how the universe should begin: for that one would have to appeal to God."[49] Hawking similarly concluded: "One would have to appeal to God.'"[50]

Knowing that a cosmic beginning leads to a Creator is exactly what is so bothersome to those who call themselves agnostics or atheists and who know this is the inevitable conclusion. This is the implication of the beginning of the universe, putting the self-described agnostic or atheist in a real philosophical pickle. But if they know the truth, why do they not just follow the evidence wherever it leads and do away with developing ridiculous theories trying to avoid it? After all, for centuries they believed in an eternal universe, so why do they suddenly have an issue believing in an eternal Creator? Jastrow, an agnostic himself, gives insight to this:

> Theologians generally are delighted with the *proof* that the Universe had a beginning, but astronomers are curiously upset. Their reactions provide an interesting demonstration of the response of the scientific mind – supposedly a very objective mind – when evidence uncovered by science itself leads to a conflict with *the articles of faith* in our profession. It turns out that the scientist behaves the way the rest of us do when our beliefs are in conflict with the evidence. We become irritated.[51]

It has nothing whatsoever to do with science. Instead, it is their *faith* that a Creator does not exist which keeps them from following the evidence wherever it leads.

CROSSING OPINION

At the beginning of our investigation into finding the one true God, we listed four essential questions in life in which every single person seeks answers. With the area of cosmology covered, we cannot reach a conclusive answer yet as to a *specific* God, but we do know that it must be *some* God having the characteristics which include being spaceless, timeless, immaterial, changeless, uncaused, powerful, intelligent, purposeful, and personal.

AN ETERNAL UNIVERSE OR A FINITE UNIVERSE?

The religion of atheism, which states the universe is eternal and no gods exist, obviously does not have the right answers and is eliminated as being the truth (nevertheless, we will continue discussing its viewpoints on all of the topics in our subsequent chapters). When it comes to other religions, again, we have not looked into any scriptures whatsoever in order to make decisive conclusions about both the beginning of the universe and its Creator. But what happens when we *do* look into them? Are there any religions that hold beliefs which match the facts described by the cosmological evidence?

Because it is an atheistic religion, and because it holds to the belief that the universe has simply existed eternally, Buddhism does not teach of a beginning or a Creator. Because it is taught that the universe is eternal, and because Brahman is simply an impersonal ultimate reality, Hinduism also does not teach of a beginning or a Creator. Further, Hinduism teaches that the universe goes through an endless cycle of collapse and reemergence. This is done through a process involving a lotus flower emerging from the belly button of Vishnu (the maintainer and preserver), who has four faces, and who is sleeping on a giant snake which has a thousand heads in a vast ocean. Thus, both Buddhism and Hinduism do not have the right answers and are also eliminated as being the truth (though, again, we will continue discussing their viewpoints in subsequent chapters). Islam, though it does believe in the creation of the universe, is not so straightforward. This is because Muslims are oftentimes split on whether the Qur'an is allegorical or not when stating Allah has a solid, material body (therefore, being bound by space, bound by time, bound by matter, and not being changeless). Though Islam may potentially not be a strong contender at this point, we will discuss its viewpoints in subsequent chapters.

Christianity and Judaism, on the other hand, teach that their specific deities created the universe and have the characteristics of being spaceless, timeless, immaterial, changeless, uncaused, powerful, intelligent, purposeful, and personal. The cosmological evidence, then, lends credence for the existence of a supernatural being (God), that an event like a resurrection could be possible, and that, since the first verse of the Bible – "In the beginning God created the heavens..." – seems to be true, every verse after it is also possibly true.[52]

While the cosmological evidence does not get us to one specific God, it does get us all the way to proving the existence of *some* God that is entirely consistent with the Christian God. Many scientists have also connected these dots. For instance, Jastrow writes, "Science, unlike the Bible, has no explanation for the occurrence of that extraordinary event."[53] Further, he adds, "Now we see how the astronomical evidence leads to a biblical view of the origin of the world. . . . The essential elements in the astronomical and biblical accounts of Genesis are the same: the chain of events leading to man commenced suddenly and sharply at a definite moment in time, in a flash of light and energy."[54] Smoot famously observed that the ripples in the CMBR are the "fingerprints from the maker" and that, "If you're religious, it's like seeing God."[55][56] Further, he adds: "There is no doubt that a parallel exists between the big bang as an event and the Christian notion of creation from nothing."[57] And Penzias stated to the *New York Times*, "The best data we have are exactly what I would have predicted had I nothing to go on but the . . . Bible as a whole."[58]

The Bible's prophets and apostles stated explicitly and repeatedly the two most fundamental properties of the big bang: a cosmic beginning a finite time ago, and a universe undergoing continual expansion. The characteristic of the universe stated more frequently than any other in the Bible is its expansion; being "stretched out."[59] Regardless if Christianity is found to be true in subsequent chapters, with the cosmological facts stated here, it is unavoidable that science simply needed to catch up (with the first verses being recorded over thirty-five hundred years ago!) to see this view has always

AN ETERNAL UNIVERSE OR A FINITE UNIVERSE?

matched reality in regards to the creation of the universe at a point in the finite past and also its expansion. Craig adds to this line of thought:

> What's important to understand . . . is how reversed the situation is from, say, a hundred years ago. Back then, Christians had to maintain by faith in the Bible that . . . the universe was not eternal but was created out of nothing a finite time ago. Now, the situation is exactly the opposite. It is the atheist who has to maintain, by faith, despite all of the evidence to the contrary, that the universe did not have a beginning a finite time ago. . . . So the shoe is on the other foot. The Christian can stand confidently within biblical truth, knowing it is in line with mainstream astrophysics and cosmology. It is the atheist who feels very uncomfortable and marginalized today.[60]

Atheism is clearly more than mere nonbelief in God; it has its own worldview, and atheists must give solid reasons why that worldview is true. And as you can begin to see, with cosmology being merely the tip of the iceberg at this point, it takes much more faith to believe in atheism than it does to believe in Christianity (or any of the religions that believe in a creator with those characteristics). The conventional belief espoused by the New Atheists is that you must rely on blind faith in order to believe in God. But as we have seen already just within this chapter alone, it takes blind faith to *not* believe in God. Now, while still in the realm science, let us continue our overall investigation and expand (no pun intended) on what we have covered in this chapter to see whether or not the universe itself, from the moment of creation all the way down to the conditions on Earth today, shows signs of intricate design.

DOES THE UNIVERSE SHOW SIGNS OF DESIGN?

In William S. Paley's book, *Natural Theology*, he popularizes the argument that if we were to find a watch in a field, and yet lacked the knowledge of how it got there, we would logically conclude, due to its exquisite complexity and design having the purpose to tell time, that it was the product of purpose by a designer rather than having been randomly formed. Paley writes:

> In crossing a heath, suppose I pitched my foot against a stone, and were asked how the stone came to be there; I might possibly answer, that, for any thing I knew to the contrary, it had lain there forever; nor would it perhaps be very easy to show the absurdity of this answer. But suppose I had found a watch upon the ground, and it should be inquired how the watch happened to be in that place; I should hardly think of the answer which I had before given, that, for any thing I knew, the watch might have always been there. Yet why should not this answer serve for the watch as well as for the stone? Why is it not as admissible in the second case, as in the first? For this

reason, and for no other, namely, that, when we come to inspect the watch, we perceive (what we could not discover in the stone) that its several parts are framed and put together for a purpose, e. g. that they are so formed and adjusted as to produce motion, and that motion so regulated as to point out the hour of the day; that, if the different parts had been differently shaped from what they are, of a different size from what they are, or placed after any other manner, or in any other order, than that in which they are placed, either no motion at all would have been carried on in the machine, or none which would have answered the use that is now served by it.

To reckon up a few of the plainest of these parts, and of their offices, all tending to one result: We see a cylindrical box containing a coiled elastic spring, which, by its endeavor to relax itself, turns round the box. We next observe a flexible chain (artificially wrought for the sake of flexure), communicating the action of the spring from the box to the fusee. We then find a series of wheels, the teeth of which catch in, and apply to, each other, conducting the motion from the fusee to the balance, and from the balance to the pointer; and at the same time, by the size and shape of those wheels, so regulating that motion, as to terminate in causing an index, by an equable and measured progression, to pass over a given space in a given time. We take notice that the wheels are made of brass in order to keep them from rust; the springs of steel, no other metal being so elastic; that over the face of the watch there is placed a glass, a material employed in no other part of the work, but in the room of which, if there had been any other than a transparent substance, the hour could not be seen without opening the case. This mechanism being observed . . . the inference, we think, is inevitable, that the watch must have had a maker; that there must have existed, at some time, and at some place or other, an artificer or artificers who formed it for the purpose which we find it actually to answer; who comprehended its construction, and designed its use.[1]

In other words, Paley's saying that nothing could convince you otherwise; the watch was not merely a fluke of nature that spontaneously appeared out of nothing by itself. Obviously, a watch requires a *watchmaker*. The same goes for anything else that shows complex design. When you ponder Mount Rushmore, for instance, do you automatically assume those faces formed by a combination of wind and rain-induced erosion? This reasoning by Paley is not from analogy but, instead, is from an inference to the best explanation. Whenever something shows evidence of having been made for a purpose it points us back to a purposeful *designer*.

Does this common sense hold when it comes to the universe – from the moment of creation all the way down to the conditions on Earth today? Is the universe merely a chaotic mess that shows no signs of design whatsoever, or is it another example – the grandest example – of something that requires a purposeful designer?

This is the first premise of our next argument: the *Teleological Argument*, which derives its name from the Greek word *telos*, meaning "purpose" or "goal." In this chapter, in which we will move from a discussion in cosmology and enter a discussion into astronomy (the study of stars, planets, and space), we will fill in the blanks below with the topic at hand – the Heavens and the Earth:

1. Where there is design, there must be a designer.
2. [   ] have/has design.
3. Therefore, [   ] have/has a designer.

PREMISE 2:
[THE HEAVENS AND THE EARTH] HAVE/HAS DESIGN

Thanks to developments in cosmology and physics from around the time the cosmic microwave background radiation (CMBR) was found and confirmed in 1964, scientists have continually discovered solid evidence that confirms the fact that the universe has been breathtakingly ordered from its outset. As Paul Davies has since written, we now know that science would be impossible if the universe was not "ordered in a rational and intelligible way. You could not be a scientist if you thought the universe was a . . . jumble of odds and ends haphazardly juxtaposed."[2]

COSMOLOGY, PHYSICS . . . AND GOLDILOCKS?

Starting our discussion with the universe itself and making our way down to the Earth, the initial conditions of the universe at creation, as well as the number of parameters that literally hold the universe together (e.g., the fundamental laws of nature and constants of physics) had to be incomprehensibly precise at the very onset not only for the formation and sustainment of galaxies, stars, planets, or even chemistry itself, but for the formation of *life* to be remotely possible. In fact, because it is now understood for one to say that the possibility for life is balanced on a razor's edge is a complete understatement, scientists cannot help but conclude that the universe ultimately had life in mind from the very beginning. In other words, as theoretical physicist and mathematician Freeman Dyson says, "The universe in some sense must have known we were coming."[3] Sean McDowell gives an analogy of this observation:

> I want you to imagine that you are hiking through the mountains

and you come across what appears to be an abandoned cabin. But, as you walk up, you notice something very strange. You smell the scent of your favorite meal. In fact, in the background, you hear your favorite song playing. You walk through the door and you see the fireplace already lit. You see the books you like to read on the table [and] the DVD's you watch on the TV. As you walk over to the bathroom you notice the toiletries that you normally use. Now, what would you think? Obviously, you would suspect that somebody knew you were coming. In the past few decades, scientists have learned that, in many ways, the universe is just like this cabin: that the many conditions that allow humans to live here are set precisely for human life.[4]

This display of discoveries, while formally named the *Anthropic Principle*, has become coined as the *Goldilocks Enigma*; the universe is "just right" for life in the same fashion that the porridge, chair, and bed were "just right" in the story of Goldilocks and the Three Bears. According to theoretical physicist, professor, and author Michio Kaku, "It is shocking to find how many of the . . . constants of the universe lie within a very narrow band that makes life possible. If a single one of these . . . were altered, stars would never form, the universe would fly apart . . . and so on."[5] Lee Strobel adds:

> Martin Rees, who became . . . professor of astronomy at Cambridge . . . and was named Astronomer Royal by Queen Elizabeth in 1995, could not ignore how the cosmic parameters are so incredibly choreographed to create a life-friendly universe. If the . . . numbers that underlie the fundamental physical properties of the universe were altered "even to the tiniest degree," he said, "there would be no stars, no complex elements, no life."[6]

As Davies puts it, "The cliché that 'life is balanced on a knife-edge' is a staggering understatement in this case: no knife in the universe could have an edge *that* fine."[7] And as Stephen Hawking wrote, "The remarkable fact is that the values of these numbers seem to have been very finely adjusted to make possible the development of life."[8] Further, he writes, "The emergence of the complex structures capable of supporting intelligent observers seems to be very fragile. The laws of nature form a system that is extremely fine-tuned, and very little in physical law can be altered without destroying the possibility of the development of life as we know it."[9]

This is a reminder of the scene from the 1984 movie called *This Is Spinal Tap*, when the character Nigel Tufnel explains the unique setup of his Marshall electric guitar amplifiers. Pointing to the knobs that control the volume, treble, and so on (which always have the highest setting of ten), Tufnel proudly explains, "These go to eleven." As unique as his amps were, eleven pales in comparison to the possible settings for each of the parameters of the universe. Instead, picture the universe having dozens and dozens of knobs, each having trillions upon trillions of possible settings which must be precisely set in an exceedingly narrow range for life and all that makes up the universe to even be possible let alone be sustained to this day.

This precise calibration has been coined the "fine-tuning" of the universe. And in the simplest terms possible, let us go over some quick examples to demonstrate just how narrow the life-permitting ranges are for each of these interdependent parameters. Starting with the ratio between the number of electrons to the number of protons in the universe, astrophysicist Hugh Ross writes,

> Unless the number of electrons is equivalent to the number of protons to an accuracy of one part in 10^{37} or better, electromagnetic forces in the universe would have so overcome gravitational forces

that galaxies, stars, and planets never would have formed. One part in 10^{37} is such an incredibly sensitive balance that it is hard to visualize. The following analogy might help: Cover the entire North American continent in dimes all the way up to the moon, a height of about 239,000 miles. . . . Next, pile dimes from here to the moon on a billion other continents the same size as North America. Paint one dime red and mix it into the billions of piles of dimes. Blindfold a friend and ask him to pick out one dime. The odds that he will pick the red dime are one in 10^{37}.[10]

Put another way, that is one in .0000000000000000000000000000000 000001 or better! Another example is gravity. This universal attraction has a force throughout the entire universe which is determined by the value of the gravitational constant. William Lane Craig writes, if the gravitational constant varied "by just one in 10^60 parts, none of us would exist. . . . If the gravitational constant had been out of tune by just one of these infinitesimally small increments, the universe would either have expanded and thinned out so rapidly that no stars could form and life could not exist, or it would have collapsed back on itself with the same result: no stars, no planets, and no life."[11] Of course, that is .0000000000000000000000000000000000000000 00000000000000000001 percent or better. This would be the same probability as "a blindfolded man finding one marked grain of sand somewhere in the vastness of the Sahara Desert – and doing it . . . three different times."[12]

Speaking of expansion, the next example is what drives the expansion speed of the universe: the energy density of space referred to as the cosmological constant. This constant acts as a repulsive force counter to the law of gravity, and an alteration in any way of "1 in 10^120," writes Jay W. Richards, co-author of *The Privileged Planet: How Our Place in the Cosmos Is Designed for Discovery*, would cause the universe to expand too rapidly and fly apart, or expand too slowly and collapse on itself.[13]

As amazingly small as these calibrations have been so far, our final example of the initial distribution of mass energy at the time of the creation event is even more impressive. Cambridge University mathematical physicist Roger Penrose was the first to calculate that if this highly ordered distribution were not calibrated to one part in ten billion multiplied to itself one hundred and twenty-three times – 1 in $10^{10^{(123)}}$ – the orderly universe we know today would instead be immensely chaotic and hostile to the possibility of life. Penrose would go on to state that it would be impossible to actually write such a number down in full, as it would require more zeros than the number of all elementary particles in the universe.[14]

These are just four quick examples, and we can go a step further. The dozens and dozens of parameters that we could list not only have to be precisely calibrated in and of themselves, but also in *their ratios relative to one another*. Yes, the initial conditions are independent of the physical constants and so on, but all parameters are also an *interdependent team*; meaning, if even one of the "knobs" were turned in any way whatsoever, all of the other knobs would be affected resulting in a lethal universe. For instance, an alteration in any way of one part in 10^{40} between the ratio of the electromagnetic force constant and the gravitational force constant would be catastrophic. If increased slightly, all stars would burn up too quickly to support life. If decreased slightly, all stars would not be able to produce heavy elements. Of course, we could go on and on with such examples, but as you can see, all of the parameters multiply and multiply with one another until the statistics in precision are absolutely mind-boggling.

And that is just the beginning. We can now multiply all of those parameters with the "local" parameters found on the steady journey down to Earth.

LOCAL PARAMETERS

In regards to recent images from NASA's Dawn Spacecraft of what appeared to be one bright light and one dim light on the dwarf planet Ceres, Fox News host Neil Cavuto asked Apollo 17 Commander (and the last man to walk on the moon) Captain Eugene Cernan, "Wouldn't that be a kick if that is some sort of life there? What do you think?" Cernan replied: "Well, you know, I get that question all the time Neil. People want to know if I've seen . . . other life in outer space. And the answer is no, I've not. And I've gone out there . . . three times. So, you know, I had my chances. But that doesn't mean it is not out there. You know, mathematically, statistically, there is other life in space of some kind."[15]

As with Cernan's "old school" attitude, it would have been understandable back in the 1960s and early 1970s to think that life is likely to be plentiful in space. After all, this seemingly reasonable line of thinking, made popular during that time by the late astronomer Carl Sagan, is derived from the observation that, since there are so many galaxies full of numerous planets and stars in the incredibly vast universe, chance alone must account for it being absolutely teeming with advanced life in every direction. As Ross writes, "In the early 1960s astronomers could identify just a few solar system characteristics that required fine-tuning for human life to be possible. . . . The odds that any given planet in the universe would possess the necessary conditions to support intelligent physical life were shown to be less than one in ten thousand."[16]

Up until the sixteenth century, man believed that Earth was the center of the galaxy. Of course, we did not scientifically know much about the size of the universe – or really anything about the universe – at that time. Nevertheless, the observation made by Copernicus that the Earth is not actually at the center of the universe but, instead, orbits around the Sun, made us think twice about Earth's significance and led scientists to ponder whether the Earth could simply be an average planet.

It is with confidence to assume that the vast majority of viewers definitely took Cernan's words as a hard fact. But, today, with our great advancements in scientific understanding of the cosmos, are those words at all sound? To answer that question we must start by discussing the characteristics of the vast number of galaxies.

THE GOOD, THE BAD, AND THE UGLY (WHICH ARE ALSO BAD)

Up until the 1920's, the prevailing view of astronomers was that the entire universe was comprised simply by what we now know as our Milky Way *galaxy*. Soon thereafter, what we knew the size of the universe to be was about to get significantly bigger, as the newly hired Edwin Hubble began his research at the Mount Wilson Observatory. As it was a pressing question, Hubble's interest focused primarily on what was thought to be clouds of gas and dust presiding in the Milky Way. Eventually, he would discover that much of what was being observed was not clouds of gas and dust at all but were entire galaxies – dozens of which he would go on to identify. Of course, upon further research of these distant bodies, he would also go on to make the breakthrough discovery that the universe not only is much bigger than we previously knew but that it is expanding from the point of creation.

With the vastly more advanced equipment of today, we know that the universe does not house just dozens of galaxies but is estimated to have *hundreds of billions* of galaxies. So, with this much larger number of known galaxies out there, this surely gives us a good idea there are other civilizations out there, right?

Upon the discovery of multiple galaxies, it was noted that they each took the form from one of three unique categories. First, like our Milky Way, is the spiral galaxy which, due to the symmetrical spiral "arms" that circle the center, is shaped similarly to that of a pinwheel or a nautilus shell. Second is the elliptical galaxy, which lacks these arms and instead ranges from a circular shape to an elongated shape like an egg. Third is the irregular galaxy, which lacks arms and lacks really any particular shape. These categories are very important when determining whether or not life has the possibility to be within a given galaxy.

For starters, even though they remind you of a piece of exercise equipment that makes it sound quite fit for life, elliptical galaxies are actually anything but habitable. One major problem is that they lack the heavy elements required to form Earth-like planets, defined as "terrestrial planets," which potentially may have similar composition – silicate rocks or metals – as well as potentially similar environmental conditions and liquid water as found on Earth. As astrophysicist and author Guillermo Gonzalez states, "The bigger the galaxy, the more heavy elements it can have, because its stronger gravity can attract more hydrogen and helium and cycle them to build heavy elements. In the low-mass galaxies, which make up the vast majority, you can have whole galaxies without a single Earth-like planet."[17] A second major problem is the fact that, even if an Earth-like planet ever formed, the planet would still not be habitable due to the stars that planets must orbit. As Gonzalez states, the stars in elliptical galaxies have "very random orbits, like bees swarming a beehive. . . . The stars visit every region, which means they'll occasionally visit the dangerous, dense inner regions."

So what about irregular galaxies? Are they at least more habitable to life than elliptical galaxies? "Like the elliptical, they also don't provide a safe harbor. In fact, they're worse" continues Gonzales. "They're distorted and ripped apart, with supernovae going off throughout their volume. There are no safe places where there are fewer supernovae exploding."[18] (Supernovae, being star explosions which can release built-up matter with velocities up to 25,000 miles per *second*).

Thus, these two categories, which make up approximately 85% or more of the total number of galaxies in the entire universe, are out of the running as possible homes for life. Therefore, we have now boiled down the number to no more than 15% of all galaxies that have the *most basic* required characteristic for the habitability of life: being in the right (spiral) type of galaxy.

It should also be noted that, of the remaining 15%, we must also take into account the number of spiral galaxies that do not meet the required size, leaving us with less than 15% of all galaxies that pass the test at this point. An abundance of heavy elements (e.g., iron, oxygen, silicon, magnesium, sulfur, nickel, calcium, aluminum) – are needed to form Earth-like planets. If a spiral galaxy is not large enough, for instance, it simply will not have the sufficient strength of gravity needed to attract the building blocks for these elements. Our galaxy just so happens to be at the very top of the class when it comes to being the most massive and also the most luminous.

But even from these remaining galaxies which have these two basic requirements of the right shape and the right size, they are still home to many hazards that prohibit life. This leads us to our next requirement: being in the right location.

Even if Earth-like planets were to form in these remaining spiral galaxies, they most likely could never be sustained – one reason being because of those pesky heavy elements. The outskirts of the galaxy, for instance, when compared to other regions, will not have enough building material to make planets. Close to the center, yes, there is an ample amount of heavy elements, but it is a very dangerous region that, as Ross puts it, is "too congested with billions of stars in a relatively small volume" and the "gravitational tug-o-war [makes] the survival of life-supportable planets impossible."[19] It is also home to a supermassive black hole (which can be millions and even billions of times more massive than our Sun) that will rip to shreds everything that comes near its path. There is also a large abundance of deadly radiation, which Ross says is "far too intense for life."

In the region between the outskirts and the center, though it has the amount of elements needed and is far enough away from the dangers of the center, a planet's habitability is still is not out of harm's way. Located primarily in the spiral arms, there are vast regions which are very active in the formation of stars. That process does not sound too bad, until you realize these regions, along with other hazards, account for a high rate of supernovae. With that said, Earth just so happens to be located exactly within the only safe area – the "Galactic Habitable Zone" – required for life to flourish, *between* the Perseus and Sagittarius spiral arms. As Gonzalez says about this location, we are in "the best possible place."[20] Richards agrees:

> The propaganda of the Copernican Principle has been that the long march of science has shown how common and ordinary our situation is. But the trend is in the opposite direction. The more you pile on the threats we're discovering in most places in the universe, and you contrast that with the many ways we're in a cocoon of safety, the more our situation appears special. . . . Very often the Copernican Principle describes properties that do not matter. Who really cares whether we're in the physical center of the galaxy? It is irrelevant! What really matters is being in the place that's most conductive to life. And that's exactly where Earth finds itself.[21]

As the common expression in real estate goes: "location, location, location." Thus, to answer the present question of whether or not there are "local" parameters which must be finely tuned for life, we know that Earth is located not only in the right type of galaxy, or in the right type of galaxy having the right size, but in the right area in the right zone in the right type of galaxy having the right size!

These are merely a small handful of parameters that must be met for galaxies. So as we move from the category of galaxies to the categories of solar systems within galaxies, we then ask, are there even further parameters which are required for a planet even possibly to be habitable to life?

GUARDIANS OF THE SOLAR SYSTEM

While some of us enjoyed the Marvel comic series long before it was cool amongst the masses, the movie "Guardians of the Galaxy" took the box office by storm in the summer of 2014. Now, while many are familiar with that particular pictured team of characters (Star-Lord, Drax the Destroyer, Gamora, Groot, and Rocket Raccoon), Earth, for instance, has its own guardians in the form of our large, outer planets Jupiter, Saturn, Uranus, and Neptune.

Jupiter, being the largest planet in our solar system (able to fit roughly 1,312 Earth's inside!), is especially crucial to our continued existence. Its gravitational force is so strong that it acts as both a shield and a magnet, either deflecting most of the dangerous comets and other space debris away or attracting them into its depths to take the hit. One such example – the very first eyewitnessed observation of two solar system bodies colliding in space – was the 1994 comet named Shoemaker-Levy 9 (SL9). Prior to impact, Jupiter's tidal gravitational force ripped SL9 apart into 21 separate fragments. Between July 16 and July 22, the world watched as each fragment – lined up similarly to a string of pearls stretching hundreds of thousands of miles – took its turn at Jupiter. Though each had impressive statistics, the most damaging fragment would come to be fragment G. Clocking in at 133,000 miles per hour, this fragment alone struck Jupiter with the energy equivalence of *six trillion tons* of TNT (roughly 400 million times stronger than the atomic bomb dropped on Hiroshima, Japan in World War II). It sent fireballs into space over 10,000 miles high (half the distance around the entire Earth!), and left a visible, dark scar in Jupiter's atmosphere twice the diameter of Earth! This one example of the many, many hits that Jupiter takes for us makes it easy to say that Earth would be void of life and likely would not exist at all were it not for Jupiter, its neighboring outer planets, and even our local planets and our moon at their given locations in our solar system.

Another reason why primarily these four planets play an important role in our sustainment is due to their nearly circular orbits around the Sun. If their orbits were more elongated (elliptical) their gravitational force would pull on and destabilize Earth's circular orbit in the same fashion. This would cause the Earth to be much too close to the Sun at times and much too far during others, therefore being subjected to lethal temperature variations. To avoid the drastic, uninhabitable effects that would come, Earth is required to maintain a stable, almost perfectly circular orbit around the Sun. In the rare instances that we have found planets orbiting host stars, says Gonzalez, "Most of their orbits are highly elliptical; very few are circular. These strongly non-circular orbits utterly surprised astronomers. Because they strongly subscribed to the Copernican Principle, they had expected that other planetary systems would be just like ours. And that expectation was basically dashed."[22]

THE UNIQUE SUN

Einstein once said, "The most beautiful thing we can experience is the mysterious. It is the source of all true art and science. He to whom the emotion is a stranger, who can no longer pause to wonder and stand wrapped in awe, is as good as dead; his eyes are closed."[23] For those who can experience it, gazing up at a night's sky filled with stars is a universal way in which awe can cause instant relaxation and for our priorities to be straightened. In such moments, life is at its most mysterious and yet makes the most sense when we are able to sit still and take in everything.

And when you do look up, to the naked eye you would have a difficult time keeping track of the number of stars you see. You probably have the idea that, if given enough time, you could eventually count them all. In reality, though, the number that can be seen (roughly 2,500) absolutely pales in comparison to what is truly out there (an estimate of at least 70 billion trillion stars in the universe, with our galaxy alone having between 100 and 400 billion stars). You probably also have the idea that each star is just a hop, skip, and a jump from Earth, when in reality the average distance between each star in the Milky Way is roughly 30 trillion miles. Not just a short car ride after all. In fact, if you were to drive to the nearest star (Alpha Centauri) from ours (the Sun) at a speed of 55 miles per hour, it would take you roughly 60 *million* years to get there!

These figures, by the way, are very important parameters for a galaxy themselves. If the amount of stars are too big or too little in a safe area of a spiral galaxy, and therefore the distance between them altered to be closer together or farther away, solar systems could not be life-permitting nor could they even exist in the first place. If the amount was too big, and the distance between each star was closer, planetary orbits would be too erratic and would cause extreme temperature variations. If the amount was too little, and the distance between each star was farther, the density of heavy elements would be too scattered to form adequate sized planets.

With just the few examples we have discussed, we have already greatly boiled down the locations in which an Earth-like planet could be. The fact is, though there are a large number of stars in spiral galaxies, the vast majority of those stars have nowhere near the characteristics required for an Earth-like planet to possibly be habitable for life. So, what is special about our Sun in particular? Having just spoken about distances, the parameter of the distance between a host star and an Earth-like planet is a great place to start.

The Sun is roughly 300,000 times closer to Earth than Alpha Centauri. Driving at a speed of 55 miles per hour would still take you nearly 200 years to reach it. If it were a mere one percent closer to Earth, our water would vaporize. A mere two percent farther from Earth and our water would freeze. Either way, life would not exist. This distance also goes hand-in-hand with its mass.

While the Sun is among the top 10% most massive among all stars, there are some that are much too massive to support life. Take, for instance, the most statistically impressive star in this category – referred to as R136a1 – which those behind the find of this star believe once had 320 times the mass of the Sun. One crucial reason why an Earth-like planet's host star cannot be too massive is that such monstrous stars live a considerably shorter life cycle. Further, higher mass comes with higher luminosity. You would assume that such a star would live longer due to the obviously increased amount of fuel that it can burn, but that assumption would be wrong. Producing significantly more light – with R136a1, for example, burning at roughly *8,700,000* times as bright as the Sun – comes from a significantly faster rate of nuclear fusion within its much larger core, causing it to rapidly deplete its fuel supply and to have very unstable ranges of luminosity.

We say that R136a1 *once* had 320 times the mass of our sun. This is because its fast, exciting lifestyle has used up a big chunk of its hydrogen. As astrophysicist Paul Crowther, who led the team that discovered this star and its similarly massive neighbors, states, "Unlike humans, these stars are born heavy and lose weight as they age. . . . R136a1 is already 'middle-aged' and has undergone an intense weight loss program, shedding [more than] a fifth of its initial mass."[24] Even after having slimmed down, it still holds the record for mass at 265 times that of the Sun. Like other massive stars, it will soon run out of fuel and end its life cycle as a violent supernova.

On the other side of the scale, around nine out of every ten stars have significantly less mass – as low as 10% when compared to the Sun. Similar to the more massive stars, they also cannot support life. One crucial reason why the mass of an Earth-like planet's host star cannot be too low is that with lower mass comes lower luminosity – as low as 0.01% when compared to the Sun. If the luminosity of a host star is too low, a planet's home would have to be in a location much closer to such a star to have the right amount of heat needed for liquid water and a habitable environment for life overall. When located so close, this causes a planet to stop spinning – its rotation being synchronized with its orbital motion – and, instead, to be "tidally-locked" into a permanent position. Having then only one of its sides facing its host star at all times (just as the moon is locked to the Earth, hence why we only see one side of the moon at all times), this would lead to an uninhabitable rise in radiation and temperature levels on the sunlit side of the planet whereas the dark side of the planet would remain frozen and also uninhabitable.

While this one parameter of an Earth-like planet's host star being the right mass has eliminated from contention more than 90% of all the stars that are in the rare, safe areas of a spiral galaxy, there are even more parameters that can boil down the remaining number even further. For example, also determined by its mass, luminosity, and age, a star must emit the right colors of light in the electromagnetic spectrum. Emitting the wrong colors – such as more massive stars having too much blue light, and those with a lower mass having too much red light – leads to insufficient energy for the life-essential process of photosynthesis which then leads to an insufficient production and buildup of oxygen in the atmosphere. Another example is that a star must have the right metal-rich composition (metallicity), having a high abundance of elements that are heavier than helium. If this amount is too high, radioactivity would make life impossible; too low and there would be an insufficient amount for life chemistry. Also, just as planets are required to have a nearly perfect, circular orbit around a host star, a host star itself must not only also have the same type of orbit around a given spiral galaxy but exactly the right rate at which it orbits the galaxy. This ensures that the Sun is not swept from its safe area, staying in the "co-rotation radius," thus ensuring the protection of entire solar systems from a galaxy's lethal outskirts, lethal spiral arms, and lethal center.[25]

As a final example, there is the brutally obvious parameter: that a planet *even has* a host star! Called "rogue" or "lonely" planets, these are planets that do not orbit a host star. In fact, many stars do not have planets at all. Even if the remaining stars that are closely matched to the characteristics of the Sun have planets, that number is usually limited to just one planet. Of course, in having only one planet, the orbit would be much too close and there would be no other planets to protect it. Further, there are some planets that orbit two stars (like Luke Skywalker's home planet, Tatooine, in *Star Wars*) and even three stars, which introduce even further lethal problems: lethal gravitational forces, tide cycles, highly elliptical orbits, extreme temperatures, ultraviolet radiation, solar flares, and so on!

The Sun uniquely passes the test on all of these required parameters and many more. As the list of parameters which it passes could go on and on, such as how it is considerably stable in comparison to other stars, these examples alone are sufficient for us to quickly see that, the more we learn about the Sun, the more we learn it is anything but an average star.

THE UNIQUE MOON

Our moon also plays a significant role in our habitability. This is obviously because we mine and bring back on spaceships its yummy cheese. Well, not exactly. But there are many reasons. Similar to those of the Sun, there is an ever-growing list of parameters that lead scientists to come to this conclusion. Let us start with why having a moon is important.

At one-fourth the diameter of Earth (nearly the size of the continental United States) and at 240,000 miles away (receding two inches per year), these statistics make the moon's gravitational pull exactly the strength that it needs to be so that the angle of Earth's axial tilt (obliquity) is stabilized at a constant 23.5 degrees in relation to the Sun. This precise tilt allows for the Earth's Northern and Southern hemispheres to point either towards or away from the Sun at just the right amount to ensure mild seasonal changes year-round, giving Earth the only life-friendly climate in the solar system. If the axial tilt were greater or less, this would account for extreme, uninhabitable surface temperatures.

Another example for why these statistics of comparable size and distance are so important is because, as Johannes Kepler correctly predicted, Earth's tides are caused by the oceans being attracted by the *moon's* gravitational pull. The distance of the moon from the Earth and its mass are just right to account for the mild ebb and flow of the rising and falling of sea levels. While the gravitational pull of the Sun accounts for slightly more than 40% of the strength of the ocean tides, the moon picks up the majority of the work and accounts for slightly less than 60% of the strength. For instance, if the moon was closer or was more massive, and therefore its gravitational pull and orbiting speed around the Earth was greater, ocean tides would be so drastic that immense global flooding, tidal waves, earthquakes, and volcanism would occur. Needless to say, it would be much too extreme for life. As bad as that would be for Earth, if the moon were to get close enough, it would reach what is called Roche limit – the point at which a celestial body would be torn apart by the Earth's gravity – and leave behind merely a ring of debris from its destruction.

Even further, the moon's gravitational pull keeps Earth's rotation at a twenty-four-hour rate. If the moon was closer or more massive it would slow the Earth's rotation considerably more, causing extreme temperature swings. If it took Earth more than twenty-four hours to make a full rotation, this would account for uninhabitable temperature swings between daytime and nighttime. On the other hand, if it took Earth less than twenty-four hours to make a full rotation, this would account for an uninhabitable increase in atmospheric wind speeds.

The moon's role in sustaining life on Earth is also displayed by its ability to be a punching bag for meteorite impacts. Looking at zoomed-in pictures of our moon's surface, or simply by looking up at the night's sky, you can see evidence of a good track record in the form of numerous craters. While the outer planets divert or take hits from the vast majority of impacts, our moon is the very last line of defense against space debris.

It is safe to say that if our moon was slightly more massive, less massive, closer, or farther away, we would not be here to observe its uninhabitable effects. While there are 168 confirmed moons orbiting planets in our solar system (with the number steadily growing as our technology for better detection becomes more advanced), Earth is the only planet that has just one moon. While there are problems that come with a planet having a moon with the wrong attributes, and problems with planets that have more than one moon, there are also many planets – such as Mercury and Venus – that do not have a moon at all. With that said, these parameters (and all other parameters that can be discussed) show that, just like the Sun, our moon is uniquely anything but average. Therefore, we can continue to narrow down the remaining potential Earth-like planets that could potentially be habitable for life to an even further incomprehensibly small number.

THE EARTH

From discussing galaxies, solar systems, host stars, and moons, we have moved down the line from the most distant categories of the universe to our closest. With those behind us, we have finally made our way home. With all of this talk about how numerous parameters within these categories are required to interconnect for life to be sustained on potential Earth-like planets, the obvious question that we must now address is what exactly makes *Earth* so "Earth-like."

For starters, there are basically two different types of planets throughout the universe. Like the outer planets in our solar system, there are the gas giants. Then, like Earth and its inner neighbors (Mercury, Venus, and Mars), there are what are known as the terrestrial planets. While there are many differing characteristics between these two types, the most significant difference comes down to either having or lacking solid surfaces. Gas giants, much like stars, are predominantly made-up of hydrogen and helium. This means that, if you were to (hypothetically) jump out of an orbiting spaceship in hopes of landing on such a planet, you would never actually land *on* it. On the other hand, terrestrial planets all have solid exterior surfaces due to a substantially different interior structure compared to that of gas giants. For instance, Earth is composed of a roughly 11,000 degree Fahrenheit solid iron inner core, a liquid iron-nickel alloy outer core, a mantle layer of mostly silicate rock that is rich in iron and magnesium, and a crust layer made of iron, oxygen, silicon, and magnesium.

While gas giants could never be habitable to life, terrestrial planets are very unlikely candidates themselves. In fact, of the terrestrial planets in our solar system, Earth is the only one that is even remotely close to having the parameters required for sustaining life. To delve further into the topic and give examples for why this is the case, we are led to our first parameter that is required of a terrestrial planet: having an atmosphere that is precisely just right for life.

When we left off discussing the mass of potential host stars, we were discussing how a star with too low of mass requires a planet to be located incredibly close to obtain sufficient heat. Of course, we know that such an area is completely lethal to life. But avoiding lethal areas in a solar system is not bound to only avoiding a close proximity to a host star. In fact, while a terrestrial planet is partly defined as being found within close proximity to a host star, its location can still very well be far too close or far away to sustain life.

Even for a solar system that has passed the requirement for having a host star with the right mass (among all of the other parameters), lethal areas are still located in almost its entirety. If too close to such a star, you would then have to worry about a toxic rise in the amount of carbon dioxide in a planet's atmosphere. Causing a planet to trap more heat and to boil away all of its water, this conversion from liquid water to water vapor would then accelerate a runaway greenhouse effect that would produce a surface environment similar to that found on present-day Venus which, having an atmosphere composed of 96% carbon dioxide, reaches *nine-hundred* degrees Fahrenheit. If too far away from such a host star, the much lower temperatures would freeze all of a planet's water, producing a surface environment similar to that of Mars which, with an atmosphere composed of 95% carbon dioxide, gets to *negative two-hundred* degrees Fahrenheit. Therefore, the required location where a planet must reside draws a very fine line through the solar system that, if crossed in either direction, causes life to be impossible. This area, similarly named to that of the previously discussed Galactic Habitable Zone, is called the *Circumstellar* Habitable Zone.

Positioned between Venus (too hot for life) and Mars (too cold for life), Earth is located in this "Goldilocks" region, ninety-three million miles away from the Sun, which is *just right* for sufficient heat, light, and energy, while not boiling away all of its water, freezing all of its water, or positioning it into a tidally-locked state. But, also similar to the Galactic Zone, the total area of the Circumstellar Zone is not completely habitable itself.

This zone is defined as that which could allow for a planet to sustain an abundance of liquid water. With that said, it should be noted that not even *a drop* of liquid water has ever been found on a planet (or a moon) besides Earth. So, this habitable zone only outlines the area around a host star in which liquid water could *potentially* be sustained. Further, within this already significantly narrowed-down area, Gonzalez states that "as you go further out from the sun, you have to increase the carbon dioxide content of the planet's atmosphere. This is necessary in order to trap the sun's radiation and keep water liquid. The problem is that there would not be enough oxygen. . . . It is only in the very inner edge of the Circumstellar Habitable Zone where you can have . . . life. And that is where we are."[26]

To have not only liquid water but also a balance of low enough carbon dioxide levels with high enough oxygen levels, we are talking about a mere five percent move within this zone that would make the habitability of life impossible. This is a perfect example of why Earth, just like our moon, the Sun, and our surrounding planets, also require a nearly perfect circular orbit. It does no good for the habitability of life if Earth orbits the Sun in this zone only part of the time, only to have all of its liquid water to freeze for the rest of the year. Because Earth follows this orbit *all* of the time, and has a composition of 78% nitrogen, 21% oxygen, and less than one percent carbon dioxide, it has just the right atmosphere that is necessary for life.

Now, you would think that having a higher percentage of oxygen would be a good thing. But as the saying goes, you can have too much of a good thing. While an oxygen-rich atmosphere is needed, too much would be lethal. If Earth was composed of even 25% oxygen, we would experience raging fires that would spontaneously combust. On the other hand, it would be impossible to breathe at 15%.

Thus, this eliminates many more planets from contention as potentially being able to sustain life. Even further, having a home that is located within this safe area does not automatically guarantee that a planet *itself* will be safe. One of the many reasons is because, out of those planets that might possibly remain at this point, there would be many which have lost their atmosphere completely and many which have never had an atmosphere at all – let alone one that is even near the necessary composition. And one cause for a terrestrial planet to lose its atmosphere happens to be our next parameter.

Many host stars constantly bombard space and any surrounding planets with large bursts of deadly, charged plasma particles from their upper atmosphere called solar wind. To combat the solar wind (having temperatures of two *million* degrees Fahrenheit and travels at over five-hundred miles per *second*), a planet must meet numerous interior requirements to form what sounds like a weapon straight out of a Sci-Fi movie. When Earth's molten outer core rotates around its solid iron inner core, this generates circulating electric currents which, in turn, creates what is known as a *magnetic field*. This invisible field is essential for life, as it acts as a cosmic shield that deflects these charged particles from Earth. While the vast majority of particles are deflected away, few funnel their way down toward the poles and are able to ever so slightly interact with the upper atmosphere, forming breathtakingly beautiful, multicolored bands of glowing plasma we refer to as *auroras* (the Northern and Southern Lights).

If this magnetic field were to suddenly disappear, not only would significant threats for the entire world's electrical grids, satellite, GPS, and radio communications occur, but life itself would be directly affected with numerous consequences. There are X-Class flares that have more power than millions of hydrogen bombs combined. Solar winds would rip our atmosphere away into space, leaving behind a planet without air or water, and life would also be completely exposed to lethal radiation that would harm our DNA and cause an exponentially higher rate of cancer, neurological disorders, and other horrible illnesses.

Of the planets that are in the already narrowed-down safe zones in already narrowed-down spiral galaxies, many of them lack a magnetic barrier altogether. But, even if a terrestrial planet has a magnetic field, this still does not mean that the planet itself is safe. Such a planet would then have to worry about whether or not the magnetic field that it generates is at the right *strength*. And if it were not for our next example of a parameter, the sustainment of having a magnetic field with the right strength would be in serious jeopardy.

Located between the crust layer and the brittle, uppermost portion of the mantle layer, the lithosphere of Earth is broken into well over a dozen major and minor, constantly moving sections called *plate tectonics*. It is the colliding, rubbing, and separation of these plates that are responsible for the formation of geological features that include the continents, both continental and oceanic mountain ranges, valleys, plains, basins, trenches, and volcanoes – the latter being what we will focus on at the moment.

Besides forming these features and having an effect on Earth's magnetic field, plate tectonics have other jobs that are necessary for life. For example, when two plates collide, one is forced into the deep and increasingly hot mantle. Then, as this lower plate begins to melt, the newly-formed magma rises by intense pressure and finds its impressive escape through explosive volcanic eruptions containing high amounts of dissolved gases that include high concentrations of water vapor, carbon dioxide, and sulfur dioxide. Such gases are crucial to life, as they are what trap energy from a host star and help a planet to retain sufficient heat. Thus, this cycle keeps the composition of gases in our atmosphere in balance.

Just as liquid water is unique to Earth, we have yet to find confirmation of plate tectonics on any other planet. If we ever do come across another planet that shares this phenomenon, though, it would also have to be the right size (with a larger planet comes a thicker crust layer, and with a smaller planet comes a thinner crust layer) in order to avoid deadly consequences. As Earth's crust is roughly half the thickness as the skin is to an apple, it just so happens to be just right to sustain life.

Furthermore, for a planet to have plate tectonics that function and maintain themselves properly, it would need to have an abundance of water within the lithosphere. Thus, as this parameter ties right back to a planet requiring liquid water, this is a perfect example of how all parameters are interconnected for life to be possible.

The level of volcanic activity must be just right as well. If the activity level were too low, this would cause insufficient amounts of water vapor, carbon dioxide, and other gases to be cycled from the interior back to the atmosphere. This limited cycle would then cause the soil to become degraded of its life-sustaining minerals, and the surface to experience a runaway greenhouse effect that would lead to high, uninhabitable temperatures. If the activity level were too great, the Sun would be blotted out by volcanic dust and explosions would destroy all possible life.

As a final example, the mass of a terrestrial planet is also crucially important. Mass is directly proportional to the strength of surface gravity. Surface gravity, like plate tectonics, also has many jobs – three of which we will quickly discuss. First, if a planet's mass was much larger than that of Earth's, the resulting stronger gravity would then cause its atmosphere to retain high, uninhabitable levels of toxic ammonia and methane gas, keeping it close to the surface instead of allowing them to dissipate. If a planet's mass was much lower than that of Earth's, the resulting weaker gravity would form an atmosphere that is significantly thinner than that of Earth's. This would then cause many negative consequences, including its liquid water and internal heat to evaporate and be lost at an uncontrollably rapid rate and for meteorites to strike Earth with great force. Second, if the strength of gravity was too strong, life could never have formed because it would have been crushed. If it was too weak, life could never have formed because it would have been slung off into space. And, third, the strength of gravity is especially evident of working hand-in-hand with plate tectonics to prevent further consequences. Gonzalez continues that a planet "has to be a minimum size to keep the heat from its interior from being lost too quickly. It is the heat from its radioactive decaying interior that drives the critically important mantle convection inside the Earth. If Earth were smaller, like Mars, it would cool down too quickly; in fact, Mars cooled down and basically is dead."[27] On the other hand, he continues, "The bigger the planet, the higher the surface gravity, and the less surface relief between the ocean basins and the mountains. The rocks at the bases of mountains can only withstand so much weight before they fracture. The higher the surface gravity of a planet, the greater the pull of the gravity on the mountains, and the tendency would be toward creating a smooth sphere."

If Earth was a smooth sphere, everything would be completely under water. So a main reason why Earth has land masses to rise above the water is that it has just the right level of plate tectonic activity. We would be in the same situation, or worse, though, if Earth's surface gravity was too weak. To put that statement into perspective, the amount of water we see on the surface does not at all give us the complete picture of just how much the Earth actually contains. The mantle layer, for instance, has vast reservoirs of water within its "transition zone," (located between the upper and lower mantle at 254 to

410 miles below the surface). As National Geographic reports, according to researchers at the Tokyo Institute of Technology, studies estimate this layer could potentially be the home to *five times* the amount of water in all of the oceans, all of the lakes, and all of the rivers on Earth's surface combined![28] If Earth's surface gravity was too weak, it would not have the ability to suppress this water and keep it underground.

SUPER-EARTHS AND UNICORNS

Atheistic scientists are hard at work, frantically trying to find even one more planet that could potentially be habitable to life. And they will perpetuate through means of the media that finding a habitable planet is much easier than it really is. For instance, the examples of headlines below can be quite entertaining once it is obvious the authors purposefully try and deceive the readers.

A Newsweek headline from 2017 reads, "KIC 8462852: Alien Megastructure Star Starts Dimming Again – What Does It Mean?"[29] The star "KIC 8462852," also referred to as "Tabby's Star," has piqued the interest of some scientists simply because its luminosity dims in an irregular fashion as something orbits around it. Yet, for nearly three years, headlines would have us think that not only have we found an alien civilization but an "advanced alien civilization"; and not just a structure but a "megastructure," made up of solar panels "1,500 times the area of the entire Earth." All while, if we read such articles in-depth, they all admit this is pure "speculation," that it is "quite unlikely," it "has nothing to do with aliens," and each study "eliminates the possibility of an alien megastructure."[30][31][32][33] The Newsweek article itself even admits that this is simply playing the headlines-for-attention game:

Ever since KIC 8462852's weird behaviour was discovered, scientists have proposed several hypotheses: a huge family of comets swarming the star; another massive and as-of-yet undiscovered star; KIC 8462852 consuming a planet. But none have been able to fully explain the dimming. A more headline-grabbing proposal was that the dips were the result of an "alien megastructure." . . . Researchers with the Search for Extraterrestrial Intelligence (SETI) looked for radio signals coming from the star's galaxy (which could be a sign of alien life) but failed to find any.

A headline from 2015 reads, "Astronomers find star with three super-Earths."[34] So now the author would have you believe we have found not just one Earth-like planet but three *super*-Earths! Now that is an eye-catching headline. But we quickly see the only "super" thing about these planets are how *super horrible* they are for the habitability of life! Other than having the wrong size, mass, and orbit entirely, among numerous other parameters admits the article, there are also the characteristics of being, "'likely a volcanic world of molten rock. . . very close to the star. The temperature is about [800 degrees Fahrenheit]. . . . Probably the surface is melting . . . kind of a melted lava world with volcanoes . . . not good for life. It was not in the so-called "habitable zone" of its star, and would not have liquid water necessary for life.'"

Another example of a headline reads, "Astronomers Discover a Potentially Habitable Planet Just 14 Light Years Away."[35] Sounds promising, right? Then we read the article and find out its mass is much larger than that of Earth's and is tidally locked to its host star. Another article agrees that it is tidally locked due to its very close proximity to its host star, adding that it "has a mass around 4.3 times that of our planet, and orbits its star every 18 days at a distance of around 10 percent Earth's orbit of the Sun. . . . This changes the circumstances on the surface of the planet substantially. You have one very hot side and one very cool side."[36]

Finally, just something to make us stop and think: in 2015, "Stephen Hawking . . . launched the biggest-ever search for intelligent extraterrestrial life in a $100-million . . . project."[37] How many, say, hungry, homeless families and veterans could be taken care of with wasted money like that? Yet, the grants will keep coming because it is a frantic search for just *something* which will lead to another misleading headline.

Of course, there are plenty of other, even crazier examples that could be discussed. We could bring up how there is a six-figure job for a protector from aliens.[38] But it is all straight out of the imagination of science fiction. After all, just take the fact that light travels at 186,000 miles per second; a light-year is roughly six trillion miles away; and "Tabby's Star," which we mentioned in our first headline example, is more than 1,400 light-years away. Next will surely be the headline of the discovery of a super-duper-crazy awesome-extraordinarily-amazing-Earth that has an abundance of cotton candy and unicorns (and, again, will never mention whether or not it has plate tectonics, a magnetic field, the right atmosphere with any oxygen whatsoever, the right rotation rate, a stable host star of the right kind and mass, etc.) – all while presenting fancy CGI pictures of these planets we have *absolutely no idea* what they actually look like.

Scientists search for planets, and present these CGI pictures, nearly identical to Earth because being on a planet like Earth and having the surroundings that Earth has is exactly the requirement for life to be possible and to be sustained. With that said, we can now tie this fact into what we covered in the previous chapter: the universe began to exist a finite time ago. Thus, the question before us is how, from the very moment of creation, the universe was perfectly fine-tuned for life to eventually form and be sustained on even one planet. Three options are given to this question: physical necessity, chance, or design.

PHYSICAL NECESSITY

When someone discusses *physical necessity*, what they mean is that the values of all parameters *had* to be the way they are; that the universe would not be able to exist otherwise. Therefore, our being able to consciously observe our existence should not come to any surprise. But is this option at all true? No, it is simply not. Craig writes:

> According to this alternative, the universe must be life-permitting. Theprecise values of these constants and quantities could not be otherwise. But is this plausible? Is a life-prohibiting universe impossible? Far from it! It's not only possible; it's far more likely than a life-permitting universe. The constants and quantities are not determined by the laws of nature. There's no reason or evidence to suggest that fine-tuning is necessary.[39]

As philosopher of science, author, and co-founder of the Center for Science and Culture of the Discovery Institute, Stephen C. Meyer states, "There's no fundamental reason why these values have to be the way they are. Yet all of these law and constants conspire in a mathematically incredible way to make life in the universe possible."[40] *Life* is the keyword. Could the universe exist in another way that does not support life? Of course. Could the universe exist in another way that would support life? No. And it cannot be stressed enough that physical necessity also does not work because all parameters are independent of one another; there is not one single parameter that simply set the course for establishing all of the others through some type of cosmic evolutionary process.

Rejecting physical necessity, Richard Dawkins writes, "Physicists have calculated that, if the laws and constants of physics had been even slightly different, the universe would have developed in such a way that life would have been impossible."[41] Elsewhere he writes of the laws and constants that "if they were altered by only modest amounts, the universe would be qualitatively different, and in many cases unsuitable for the development of life."[42]

Davies could not be any clearer when he wrote, "The physical universe does not have to be the way it is: it could have been otherwise."[43] Case closed, and we have not even gone into the fact that physical necessity does not even attempt to explain the origin of the laws of nature nor the Cause behind the creation event! So, since physical necessity is out of the picture, what about option two: chance?

CHANCE

When someone discusses *chance* in this regard, what they are referring to is the naturalistic idea called the "Multiple Universe (multiverse) Theory," or "Many World's Hypothesis." To those who posit naturalistic theories, they believe that nature is doing all the work and obviously does not have the sustainment of life, or actually anything, as an end-goal. If life, then, were to occur, this would simply be an accident that was never supposed to happen. Just as the name implies, this theory states that perhaps our universe is but one of virtually an infinite number of others and, and by ours having every single parameter precisely in place for life to be possible and to be sustained, we just so happen to be in the very universe that accidentally won the cosmic lottery per se. As Hawking has stated, "Were it not for a series of startling coincidences in the precise details of physical law . . . humans and similar life-forms would never have come into being."[44] Similarly, physicist Andrei Linde says, "'We have a lot of really, really strange coincidences, and all of these coincidences are such that they make life possible."[45]

So, where chance fails us with just one roll of the dice, the idea is that perhaps a virtually infinite number of rolls led to why our universe is calibrated just right so that life is sustained. And by what means exactly are all of these universes supposedly being made? By a universe-making machine that continuously cranks out randomly-dialed universe after randomly-dialed universe, of course! If you have ever read the children's book or watched the movie *Cloudy with a Chance of Meatballs*, you cannot help but imagine some silly contraption hovering out there in the cosmos somewhere spitting out universes left and right at the whim.

Now, before we go any further, we should first point out that, by presenting this multiverse explanation, scientists are admitting the option of physical necessity is out of the running; if there are trillions upon trillions of other universes that exist but do not sustain life, they are agreeing that our universe did not *have* to be life-sustaining in order to exist. Thus, by holding to option two, that in turn automatically cancels out option one. But what about this explanation of chance: is it at all plausible that nature itself could form our precise universe and sustain life all by mere chance alone?

As Hawking admitted, the multiverse is "still just a theory. It is yet to be confirmed by any evidence."[46] In an article for the *New Scientist*, titled "When Does Multiverse Speculation Cross into Fantasy?", physicist Mark Buchanan writes that we have "no observational evidence for them."[47] As theoretical physicist John Polkinghorne writes, "People try to trick out a 'many universe' account . . . but that is pseudo-science. It is a metaphysical guess that there might be many universes with different laws and circumstances."[48] In other words, to say this theory is pseudo-science and a metaphysical guess is to say this *is not science at all*. Buchanan continues: "Fantasy is the very word that occurs to many . . . when they hear some of the ideas popular in cosmology. . . In the end, [the multiverse] is not science so much as philosophy using the language of science."⁴⁹ Theoretical physicist Lee Smolin agrees: "The multiverse fails as a scientific hypothesis. . . . We had to invent the multiverse. And thus with an infinite ensemble of unobservable entities we leave the domain of science behind."⁵⁰

Not only do we lack any evidence whatsoever for a multiverse, it has been admitted we will *never* have any evidence. And if there were actually such a thing as a multiverse, all other universes would be subject to completely different laws as those found in our universe and, therefore, would mean that we are forever removed from detection, interaction, measurement, and observation of any kind. Theoretical physicist Carlo Rovelli says these theorists know there is no evidence and no way to ever find any, and are therefore "gasping . . . trying to guess arbitrarily."⁵¹ Writes Tim Folger, science writer and editor of both Discover Magazine and On Earth Magazine, "The multiverse remains a desperate measure ruled out by the impossibility of confirmation."⁵² Cosmologist George F.R. Ellis, writes even if there were such a thing, "The trouble is that no possible astronomical observations can ever see those other universes. . . . All the parallel universes lie outside our horizon and remain beyond our capacity to see, now or ever, no matter how technology evolves. . . . That is why none of the claims made by multiverse enthusiasts can be directly substantiated. . . . We have no information about these regions and never will."⁵³

Another lethal problem with this theory is that, because this machine is supposedly able to perform such incredible feats, it would obviously require having been precisely fine-tuned – being bound to finely tuned laws itself in order to exist, be sustained, operate, and to spit out a continues flow of universes all with their differing, random combinations of laws and other parameters. As Robin Collins, Distinguished Professor of Philosophy and chair of the Department of Philosophy at Messiah College states, "Invoking some sort of multiverse generator as an explanation of the fine-tuning reinstates the fine-tuning up one level, to the laws governing the multiverse generator."[54] And as Davies points out, the multiverse "does not so much explain the laws of physics as dodge the whole issue. There has to be a physical mechanism to make all those universes and bestow bylaws on them. This process will require its own laws, or meta-laws. Where do they come from? The problem has simply been shifted up a level from the laws of the universe to the meta-laws of the multiverse."[55] Of course this does not even touch on the fact that scientists have no clue as to how our unchanging laws came about in the first place, so it is simply illogical to posit the idea that a multiple-universe making machine could just spit out a virtually infinite amount of universes, all with different laws, when we cannot even explain our own!

This leads to yet another lethal problem in that this machine would be bound to space, time, and matter, and would still require a creator outside of space, time, and matter which has all of the qualities ascribed to the Creator we discussed in the previous chapter. Kaku makes this same point: "The question is, 'Where did the multiverse come from?' You could argue . . . you need a god to create the multiverse."[56] So if someone does not want to accept that God is the Creator of one universe, what good does it do to say there are virtually an infinite amount of universes that each require a Creator even more-so? To posit this theory mortally wounds the naturalist's mission to find an explanation for fine-tuning aside from God. Not only is it entirely silly because nothing else which shows purposeful design would make someone think that anything but a designer could be responsible (i.e., a Camaro, a bank, a watch, Mount Rushmore), but it only *helps* the case that God is responsible not only for creation but for its fine-tuning. Whenever something shows evidence of having been made for a purpose, it points us back to a purposeful *designer*. And, as we have seen, the universe is the grandest example of that which obviously requires purposeful design.

PREMISE 3:
THEREFORE, [THE HEAVENS AND THE EARTH] HAVE/HAS A DESIGNER

As one ponders the ever-growing list of cosmic parameters (a list that, according to a 2008 review by Ross, comprised at that time of over four-hundred which must all work together for life to even be possible), from the moment of creation down to the inner core of the Earth, a Designer having the purpose in mind of specifically supporting life is the only reasonable conclusion that can be made.[57] Think of the odds of just the cosmological constant occurring by chance. Then think about two or three parameters each being just right at the exact same time, and so on and so forth. The chain of parameters that sustains our existence is downright amazing.

In his book *The Cosmic Blueprint: New Discoveries in Nature's Creative Ability to Order the Universe*, Davies (an agnostic) writes, "There is for me powerful evidence that there is something going on behind it all. . . . It seems as though somebody has fine-tuned nature's numbers. . . . The impression of design is overwhelming."[58] In his subsequent book, *The Mind of God*, he adds,

> Through my scientific work I have come to believe more and more strongly that the physical universe is put together with an ingenuity so astonishing that I cannot accept it merely as a brute fact. I cannot believe that our existence in this universe is a mere quirk of fate, an accident of history, an incidental blip in the great cosmic drama. . . . Through conscious beings the universe has generated self-awareness. This can be no trivial detail, no minor by-product of mindless, purposeless forces. We are truly meant to be here.[59]

Davies is correct that we can easily eliminate physical necessity and the multiverse theory. Design – and, hence, a Designer – then, is the obvious option; not only because of the irreparable shortcomings from naturalistic explanations but also because design perfectly aligns with all of the facts. George Stanciu, theoretical physicist and Dean Emeritus of Magdalen College, and Robert Augros, professor at Saint Anselm College, in their book *The New Story of Science* write, "A universe aiming at the production of man implies a mind directing it. Though man is not at the physical center of the universe, he appears to be at the center of its purpose."[60] Even Steven Weinberg, the Nobel laureate in physics and an outspoken atheist remarks that "this is fine-tuning that seems to be extreme, far beyond what you could imagine just having to accept as a mere accident."[61] Folger adds:

> Physicists . . . like even less the notion that life is somehow central to the universe, and yet recent discoveries are forcing them to confront that very idea. Life, it seems, is not an incidental component of the universe. . . . In some strange sense, it appears that we are not adapted to the universe; the universe is adapted to us . . . [in] what is often called the "fine-tuning problem" – the baffling observation that the laws of the universe seem custom-tailored to favor the emergence of life.[62]

Even Dawkins himself admits that the fine-tuning of the universe is real and that there is no naturalistic explanation for why that is the case, as it is almost miraculous in his eyes.[63] Professor emeritus of astronomy at Harvard University and senior astronomer emeritus at the Smithsonian Astrophysical Observatory Owen Gingerich adds, "A common sense and satisfying interpretation of our world suggests the designing hand of a superintelligence."[64] As Arno Penzias puts it, "Astronomy leads us to a unique event, a universe which was created out of nothing and delicately balanced to provide exactly the conditions required to support life. . . . The observations of modern science seem to suggest an underlying, one might say, supernatural plan."[65] And as NASA astronomer John O'Keefe stated in an interview, "We are, by astronomical standards, a pampered, cosseted, cherished group of creatures.... If the Universe had not been made with the most exacting precision we could never have come into existence. It is my view that these circumstances indicate the universe was created for man to live in."[66]

With the facts now in hand, this fine-tuning is a troubling revelation to many of these non-believing scientists, as it is very often credited in their eyes as the best argument *for* the existence of God. Says one such scientist, Robert Jastrow, this is "the most interesting development next to the proof of the creation . . . because it seems to say that science itself has proven, as a hard fact, that [the] universe was made, *was designed*, for man to live in. It is a very theistic result."[67] And leading physicist and cosmologist Dr. Frank Tipler adds:

> When I began my career as a cosmologist . . . I was a convinced atheist. I never in my wildest dreams imagined that one day I would be writing a book purporting to show that the central claims of Judeo-Christian theology are in fact true, that these claims are straightforward deductions of the laws of physics. . . . I have been forced into these conclusions by the inexorable logic of my own special branch of physics.[68]

To not follow the evidence where it leads – concluding that the universe was created and finely tuned by the hand of God – would take an immense amount of blind faith. Davies writes in *A Brief History of the Multiverse*: "All cosmologists accept that there are some regions of the universe that lie beyond the reach of our telescopes, but somewhere on the slippery slope between that and the idea that there are an infinite number of universes, credibility reaches a limit. As one slips down that slope, more and more must be accepted on faith, and less and less is open to scientific verification." Again, Davies writes of the multiverse theory that, while it "may be dressed up in scientific language," it is merely a "leap of faith."[69]

For another example of an outlandish theory, Neil deGrasse Tyson thinks the likelihood of the universe being a simulation developed by someone or others far smarter than us "may be very high." He continues: "What would we look like to them? We would be drooling, blithering idiots in their presence." It is never a good thing to view the comment section of any article, but in this case the top comment hit the head on the nail: "This is the guy who doesn't believe in Intelligent Design - but he's willing to buy the idea that the universe is a simulation created by an intelligence many many magnitudes greater than our own. Anybody find this as screwy as I do?"[70] Never mind the fact that such theories do not even attempt to explain a Creator outside of space, time, and matter; they just go to show to what extremes a naturalist will go with a reliance on mere blind faith instead of reason.

CROSSING OPINION

Even though we reasonably eliminated Hinduism from contention in the previous chapter, there is a noteworthy observation to make about that religion in regards to the information we covered within this chapter: Hindus have traditionally believed the Earth is flat, is being supported on the backs of four giant elephants, and these elephants are supported by an even more enormous turtle. Needless to say, no astronaut has ever spoken of seeing a flat Earth or any cosmic animals. This, of course, is opposed to the information that the Bible gives us about the Earth, continuously describing it as circular and that it hangs on nothing in space.[71] Furthermore, taking into consideration all of what religions believe on the topic at hand, our narrowed-down list still remains at three: Christianity, Judaism, and Islam.

With this new information of the fine-tuning of the universe as a whole in mind, what God are we talking about Who would have the purpose of making life as the end goal for the finely tuned universe? While the information found in this chapter does not add further characteristics to the profile of God that we discussed in the previous chapter, though it does add to how vastly powerful, intelligent, purposeful and personal He ultimately is, we are getting closer to answering our first two of four questions we seek to answer: "Where did we come from?" and "Why are we here?"

DOES MANKIND SHOW SIGNS OF DESIGN?

(Part 1)

We have seen from the fields of cosmology and astronomy that the universe as a whole – from the parameters at the moment of creation down to the parameters of planet Earth – has been incredibly fine-tuned. Knowing now how entirely impossible the chance would be for all of the required parameters to be in the right place, at the right time, and work together in just the right way to even potentially have a habitable planet like Earth, we can make yet another step into the fields of both biochemistry and biology to discuss Earth's *most* amazing characteristic. In this chapter we will fill in the blanks of the second and third premises of the Teleological Argument with the topic at hand – mankind:

1. Where there is design, there must be a designer.
2. [   ] have/has design.
3. Therefore, [   ] have/has a designer.

PREMISE 2:
[MANKIND] HAVE/HAS DESIGN

Note that just because the Earth has all of the required parameters in place, that does not at all mean life would automatically just pop into existence here somehow; the parameters would have simply given life the required habitat. But beyond that, we not only exist on Earth but we are carefully sustained to this day.

If a Designer has done all of this – intricately forming a required habitat for mankind in our specific location in the vast universe – then certainly we all, like the universe, our galaxy, our solar system, and Earth itself must have been created for a specific purpose. According to the late geologist, Charles Darwin, and his modern-day followers, our supernatural origin is not the case; we are all just cosmic accidents with no purpose at all. Published in 1859, Darwin would speculate in his signature book, *On the Origin of Species*, that a Designer was not actually necessary for both the creation and the multiplication of all forms of life. While he mostly chose to use the phrase "descent with modification," this speculation has become known today as the Theory of Evolution.

FOOTBALL AND SOUP

Dedicated mostly to the likes of Budweiser Clydesdales, trailer debuts of upcoming summer blockbuster movies, funny babies, or the latest craze of screaming goats, Super Bowl commercials are the prime opportunities for companies to gain the most attention in the least amount of time. After the AFC championship game's infamous "Deflategate" controversy, it was that time again for Super Bowl XLIX (49) between the New England Patriots and the Seattle Seahawks. But instead of using a safe attention-getter like funny babies or, yes, screaming goats, Carnival Cruise Line used in their commercial a speech from President John F. Kennedy in September of 1962. The commercial would go on to highlight a specific excerpt: "I really do not know why it is that all of us are so committed to the sea, except I think it is because . . . we all came from the sea. . . . We are tied to the ocean. And when we go back to the sea – whether it is to sail or to watch it – we are going back from whence we came."[1] We all came from the sea? We are tied to the ocean? What exactly was President Kennedy referring to in reference to the relationship between mankind and the sea?

It is a grossly unknown fact that Darwin never formally states how he thought life first came into existence. Instead, he writes that "Science as yet throws no light on . . . [the] origin of life."[2] Now, you would think for a book ironically titled *On the Origin of Species* that it would consist of a very well thought out explanation as to how life first came to exist! While Darwin's idea of an origin story is absolutely nowhere to be found, the starting point of the book was simply a theory for what he thought could have happened long *after* life was *already* present on Earth.

Like a toddler exaggerating a story about, say, how high they can jump, or how a fisherman talks about the supposed monster that got away, Darwin did not stop there; he would go on to state that every form of animal life and plant life that has ever existed also descended from a mystery first life form. As author Raymond Barber writes of this theory, "Once upon a time – nobody knows when – at some given place – nobody knows where – a speck of protoplasmic substance – nobody knows what – came into existence – no one knows how – over a period of time – no one knows how long. From that one speck of protoplasm there developed – and no one knows how – all the forms of life in the animal and [plant] world."[3] This would mean that the likes of penguins, giraffes, crape myrtles, tulips, fungus, potatoes, and mankind all supposedly share this same, ancient, mystery ancestor.

That is a pretty bold statement coming from a guy who admitted that science as a whole did not have the slightest clue about the formation of the first life form! In fact, it was not until nearly twelve years later in a letter to a colleague that Darwin would speculate a very brief idea on the matter of how the first form of life may have originated. Referred to as evolutionary abiogenesis, he believed that the first life form was a one-celled amoeba that may have been produced on the primitive Earth, roughly three billion years ago, in what he said could have been – while not exactly a huge sea – a "warm little pond, with all sorts of ammonia and phosphoric salts, light, heat, electricity, etc."[4]

In other words, Darwin believed that if such a pond had possibly existed that contained a specific brew of chemicals and environmental ingredients – often termed the "Primordial Soup" – then perhaps a first life form could have been produced within it. Then, as soon as this first life form was produced, it could begin replicating itself over and over again through the reproductive means of binary fission to make even further forms of primitive creatures. Therefore, it was from a pond of soup that mankind, along with the plethora of millions upon millions of animal and plant species that have ever called Earth home, supposedly gained their eventual rise to life.

Of course, this was total speculation on Darwin's part. Nevertheless, he would posit that with these replicated life forms inhabiting this pond, a process known as "natural selection" would become the mechanism that would eventually take over and drive evolution in order to populate the Earth with continually new, unique species; when populations within each species were exposed to different environmental conditions, natural selection was theorized to select the characteristics (such as size and color) among them which are better suited – more "fit" – for a higher chance towards both survival and reproduction. These selective changes would then weed out the less beneficial characteristics from the gene pool within each species. Thus, over a considerably lengthy period of time, slight modifications within each species would eventually produce these new species.

Darwin constantly pained that this process, occurring long after life was already on Earth, would not be a quick one: "As natural selection acts solely by accumulating slight, successive, favorable variations, it can produce no great or sudden modifications; it can act only by short and slow steps."[5] And as these incremental changes would ever so slowly lead to genetic mutations and cause a variety of creatures within each species to diverge over billions of years, this process would eventually lead to entirely new *classes*: single-cellular life evolving into multi-cellular life, multi-cellular life into fish, fish into amphibians, amphibians into reptiles, reptiles into mammals, and so on.

Being comprised of only one sketch, readers can view Darwin's thoughts of this gradual process in *On the Origin of Species*. Termed the "Tree of Life," he illustrates his idea for the history of life by placing our supposed shared ancestor (the one-celled amoeba) at the base of the tree, with the tree's limbs, branches, and twigs representing the growing divergence of multitudes of newly formed species and classes made possible by the gradual process of natural selection so that, as you move down from the very top of the tree to its base, you can see today's great diversity of life being interconnected through common descent all the way down to the most primitive life of the distant past.

This phylogenetic metaphor of a sketch is now one of the world's most famous illustrations, as the theory of evolution has taken a foothold in academia from the grade school level to courses at the world's most prestigious colleges. Further, federal laws have even been influenced by this theory. In 1981, for instance, a lawsuit – *McLean v. Arkansas Board of Education* – was filed against the Balanced Treatment for Creation-Science and Evolution-Science Act which required the balanced teaching of both evolution and creationism within public schools in Arkansas. The law was overturned in favor of evolution and stated that creationism was not science. While this ruling was not universally applicable for the entire country, nevertheless, it did have considerable influence on further court rulings. In 1987, a lawsuit – *Edwards v. Aguillard* – was filed against a similar law – this time by the state of Louisiana – which also required the balanced, side-by-side teaching of both evolution and creationism. However, this time around, the case was brought before the United States Supreme Court where it was ultimately stated that the teaching of creationism was to be prohibited in all public schools throughout the entire country and that only evolution was allowed to be taught as supposed true science.

This theory has also influenced societal opinion. For example, according to a recent U.S. Religious Landscape Survey by Pew Research Center, only 19% of Americans say that humans have not evolved.[6] Therefore, those who deny evolution hold to a position that is viewed by a convinced majority as being archaic, irrelevant, backward, and in direct opposition to the advancement of modern-day science. This can even be seen in popular entertainment. Take, for instance, the hit sitcom, *Friends*, where the character Phoebe Buffay-Hannigan – a ditzy massage therapist and part-time guitarist at the Central Perk coffee house – states to the character Ross Geller – a college educated, evolution-believing paleontologist – that she does not believe in evolution:

Ross: (In utter disbelief) Evolution is scientific fact. Like, like, like the air we breathe. Like gravity. . . . How can you not believe in evolution?

Phoebe: I dunno. Look at this funky shirt!

Ross: I have studied evolution my entire adult life. Okay, I can tell you, we have collected fossils from all over the world that actually show the evolution of different species. Okay? You can literally see them evolving through time.

Phoebe: Look, cannot we just say that you believe in something and

I don't?

Ross: No, no . . . we cannot.

Phoebe: Are you telling me that you're so unbelievably arrogant that you cannot admit that there's a teeny tiny possibility that you could be wrong about this?

Ross: There might be a teeny, tiny, possibility.[7]

Ross sounds a whole lot like the late Richard Dawkins who, being the world's most popular Darwinist up to his death, wrote in his book *The Greatest Show on Earth*, "Evolution is a fact. Beyond reasonable doubt, beyond serious doubt, beyond sane, informed, intelligent doubt . . . . The evidence for evolution is at least as strong as the evidence for the Holocaust. . . . It is the plain truth that we are cousins of chimpanzees, somewhat more distant cousins of monkeys, more distant cousins still of aardvarks and manatees, yet more distant cousins of bananas and turnips."[8] *Time* magazine concludes for its readers that Dawkins is entirely correct, that evolution can explain everything about the formation of life: "Charles Darwin did not want to murder God, as he once put it. But he did."[9]

With all of this support behind the theory of evolution by the courts, supposed modern academia, and societal opinion, the scientific facts must be *overwhelmingly* in its favor – right? Well, to those who hold that seemingly obvious conclusion, what we are about to cover will surprise you. So, to geek out for a second and quote Captain America, as he once said prior to defeating a large number of assailants inside an elevator: "Before we get started, does anyone want to get out?"[10]

TWO TYPES OF EVOLUTION

At this point, it is absolutely crucial for us to define the two types of evolution. Yes, there are two types.

Most people would define it broadly as "change over time." If this were all that evolution pertained to, there would be no controversies and no need for any kind of debate between Darwinists and Creationists. After all, as it is easily seen throughout reproduction, we can all agree that those within a single species are related through descent with slight changes. Or just go to any dog park and you will see a great variety of characteristics. In fact, dog breeders commonly choose specific dogs to potentially have the desired offspring. Take the Jack Russell Terrier, the Labrador Retriever, the Miniature Australian Shepherd, the Siberian Husky, the Spitz, and the Dachshund "wiener dog" as examples; the incredible variety in characteristics between these dogs alone is abundantly clear.

It is important for us to understand it is a solid fact that, like these examples, there *are* short-term variations in characteristics through reproduction over time. This obvious type of "evolution," which should really just be referred to as common sense, is categorized as *micro*evolution. But microevolution is completely different compared to the long-term *macro*evolution of one species evolving into another species and so on (e.g., man evolving from chimpanzees) that Darwinists claim and that is discussed all throughout *On the Origin of Species*. Darwinists very rarely make the slightest distinction between the two types. Instead, they combine them, stating that if we simply imagine an extrapolation of what microevolution could do over an extended period of time, that is supposed "proof" for what natural selection has done since life first formed.

So, if someone were to ask you personally if you believe in evolution, the first thing you should ask them is, "What is your usage of that term?" Obviously, if the two types of evolution had been broken down and explained within the questionnaire of the Pew Research Center analysis, many would have seen that variety of characteristics through means of *micro*evolution does not at all provide a description of how *macro*evolution is defined, and the statistical findings would have shifted away from a belief in *macro*evolution to a significant degree. Thus, by failing to make a distinction between the two types, the public is duped into believing small changes in organisms is proof that all organisms have slowly but surely evolved from a supposed one-celled ancestor.

Nevertheless, even with the two types of evolution differentiated, that does not answer the question of whether macroevolution is true. With that said, we can now move on, using the "very best evidence for macroevolution" along the way to see how it has held up throughout the many years of scientific advancement.

OBSERVING HAECKEL'S EMBRYOS

"Ontogeny recapitulates phylogeny," stated German zoologist Ernst Haeckel. What he meant by in this statement was that he believed human embryos and other vertebrate animals all pass through identically-looking stages of evolution upon conception. This was his theory of recapitulation. In 1866, he would go on to publish side-by-side sketches that depicted this in three stages of embryologic development among eight vertebrates (fish, salamander, turtle, chicken, pig, cow, rabbit, and human embryos) as support for his theory. It was these illustrations from Haeckel which Darwin would rely heavily on when writing later editions of *On the Origin of Species*.

Haeckel illustrated that, as each of these examples moved through subsequent stages, all of them were strikingly similar early-on in development and would then become more and more dissimilar with the passing of time. To Darwin, this transition showed exactly what he himself had predicted with his theory of macroevolution – organisms were vastly *similar* to their ancient ancestor, and developed through means of natural selection to become vastly *dissimilar* species and classes after a considerably lengthy period of time. In other words, each stage of development was supposedly an observable means by which we could see the lengthy process of macroevolution take place before our very eyes and proof that all animal life can be traced back to a common ancestor. As Haeckel put it, "Embryonic development is a short and rapid re-run, or recapitulation, of evolution," similar to watching a movie play from beginning to end on the fasted fast-forward setting.[11]

Darwin would quickly classify the developmental stages of vertebrate embryos as "by far the strongest single class of facts in favor" of his theory.[12] Did Darwin jump the gun on making such a conclusion? Were these developmental stages *really* such strong "facts" towards his theory? Well, among other major ones, three critical points need to be covered before we can reach our own conclusion about Haeckel's work among vertebrate embryos.

First, what Haeckel was attempting to pass off as the earliest developmental stage is actually a stage that belongs in the middle. He left out the actual earlier stages because, if you were to compare embryos in the stages that come earlier, they look vastly dissimilar. It is actually in the middle stage that they are *most* similar (though, still not too similar at all), and then towards the end they look vastly dissimilar again. Instead of these embryos developing in the fashion of Darwin's "Tree of Life" (from similarity to dissimilarity based on universal descent from a common ancestor), they develop in a manner that embryologists refer to as "the developmental hourglass" (from dissimilarity to similarity to dissimilarity). This, of course, is a complete contradiction with Darwin's theory of macroevolution and shows zero signs of the sharing of a common ancestor from the distant past.

Second, Haeckel cherry-picked the animals for his study. Says Molecular biologist Jonathan Wells, Haeckel,

Only shows a few of the seven vertebrate classes. For example
. . . four are mammals, but they're all placental mammals. There
are two other kinds of mammals that he did not show, which are
different. The remaining four classes he showed – reptiles, birds,
amphibians, and fish – happen to be more similar than the ones he
omitted. He used a salamander to represent amphibians instead of
a frog, which looks very different. So he stacked the deck by picking
representatives that come closest to fitting his idea – and then he
went further by faking the similarities.[13]

That is right; the third and most obviously important point to discuss is that Haeckel's sketches are, says Darwinist and embryologist Michael Richardson, "one of the most famous fakes in biology."[14] He states elsewhere: "This is one of the worst cases of scientific fraud. It is shocking to find that somebody once thought was a great scientist was deliberately misleading. It makes me angry. What he did was to take a human embryo and copy it, pretending that the salamander and the pig and all the others looked the same at the same stage of development. They do not. These are fakes."[15] Darwinist and biologist Stephen Jay Gould adds that the sketches were the "academic equivalent of murder."[16] Elsewhere he states: "Haeckel had exaggerated the similarities by idealizations and omissions," and that "in a procedure that can only be called fraudulent," Haeckel "simply copied the same figure over and over again. . . . Moreover, Haeckel's drawings never fooled expert embryologists, who recognized his fudging right from the start."[17]

In reality, the sketches did not by any means give even a close representation of how the *actual* embryos of his examples look. This can be seen for yourself by observing real photographs of actual embryos, such as those taken by Richardson and a team of international experts in 1997 during a study of comparative embryology, published in the journal *Anatomy and Embryology*, which completely exposes the lies which Haeckel was trying to pass off as truth.

In all actuality, this blatant dishonesty has been known since Haeckel's contemporaries (notably, Wilhelm His Sr., professor of anatomy at Leipzig University) exposed him for being a fraud shortly after the publishing of his sketches. Yet, note that we say these sketches *are* fakes and not *were* fakes because, even though the sketches were easily found to be forms of deliberate propaganda, as Haeckel himself would admit, and the claim that "ontogeny recapitulates phylogeny" is blatantly false, the sketches *are still* stated in textbooks all around the world today as fact! As Richardson states, "I know of at least fifty recent biology textbooks which use the drawings uncritically."[18] And as Gould adds, these sketches have "entered into the most impenetrable and permanent of all quasi-scientific literatures: Standard student textbooks of biology. . . . We do, I think, have the right to be both astonished and ashamed by the century of mindless recycling that has led to the persistence of these drawings in a large number, if not a majority, of modern textbooks!"[19]

OBSERVING DARWIN'S BLACK BOX

Let us look back at this idea Darwin had that life may have originated from a single-celled amoeba. He wrote of the human body that if it consists in any way complexity "which could not possibly have been formed by numerous, successive, slight modifications," his theory of macroevolution "would absolutely break down."[20] And with this observation made, Darwin provided his (confident) criterion which, if such examples were ever found to exist, would be enough to conclude that his theory is false.

Named to the National Review's 100 most important non-fiction works of the twentieth century, biochemist Michael Behe's book, *Darwin's Black Box*, is one of the most elite critiques used against Darwinian evolution today. Made obvious by its title, Behe goes on to discuss what scientists refer to as a "black box" – the term used when describing something they view as interesting to observe but do not have the slightest clue how it ultimately functions. For many of us, this would be, say, a modern computer or cell phone; we may understand how to use them to a great extent, but we have absolutely no idea how their internal workings actually function. To Darwin, the cell was an example of a mysterious "black box."

Around the time *On the Origin of Species* was released, anyone who viewed a cell under a microscope would have been quick to conclude that it looked very similar to just a blob of Jell-O (Thomas Huxley, "Darwin's bulldog," in 1869 and Haeckel in 1905 described it as a "homogeneous globule of plasm") and, therefore, its inner workings must be incredibly simple.[21] Since observational equipment at that point was not nearly strong enough for us to see inside of a cell, we could not even begin to have an educated understanding as to what it was truly made of or how it ultimately performed functions. But with the continual advancement in magnification, the secret world of the cell was slowly but surely unlocked by a whole new field of science in the form of biochemistry.

Now, with our modern 2D and 3D electron microscopes (whereas your average light microscopes in an average chemistry classroom may view a slide under 100x magnification, just grasp the fact that we can now easily see inside of a cell at 500,000x magnification!) and our overall biotechnological understanding, scientific discoveries have completely assured us that life at the cellular level is *far* more complex than any form of modern technology and is absolutely teeming with many examples of micro machine-ran organs, systems, and processes that fit perfectly with Darwin's ultimate criterion. In fact, Frank Sherwin, professor of human physiology and anatomy, medical microbiology, parasitology, general biology, and cell biology rightly compares the cell to an interdependent city:

> The cell is the most detailed and concentrated organizational structure known to humanity. It is a lively microcosmic city, with factories for making building supplies, packaging centers for transporting the supplies, trucks that move the materials along highways, communication devices, hospitals for repairing injuries, a massive library of information, power stations providing usable energy, garbage removal, walls for protection and city gates for allowing certain materials to come and go from the cell.[22]

The comparisons do not stop there. For example, Walter Bradley, distinguished professor of engineering at Baylor University, states that a cell is compared to,

> A high-tech factory, complete with artificial languages and decoding systems; central memory banks that store and retrieve impressive amounts of information; precision control systems that regulate the automatic assembly of components; proofreading and quality control mechanisms that safeguard against errors; assembly systems that use principles of prefabrication and modular construction; and a complete replication system that allows the organism to duplicate itself at bewildering speeds.[23]

And Behe gets in on the fun and adds his own words. He states of the inner workings of a cell that,

> Life is actually based on molecular machines. They haul cargo from one place in the cell to another; they turn cellular switches on and

off; they act as pulleys and cables; electrical machines let current flow through nerves; manufacturing machines build other machines; solar-powered machines capture the energy from light and store it in chemicals. Molecular machinery lets cells move, reproduce, and process food. In fact, every part of the cell's function is controlled by complex, highly calibrated machines.[24]

Upon viewing the complexity by which cells are the building blocks of bodily tissues, organs, and overall body plans, Behe describes that life at such a microscopic level is "irreducibly complex" (IC). What is meant by IC is that we are made-up of organs, systems, and processes that each require many finely calibrated, independent, interworking parts to be fully formed, in the right places, at the right times, in the right shapes, in the right spatial relation, etc., in order for them to perform functions. In every instance, if *even one* part is not present or does not work together simultaneously with all of the other parts, the entire entity does not function; in other words, they are *interdependent*.

Purely as an easy-to-understand example, Behe illustrates that even a simple, traditional mousetrap is IC. Composed of just five integral parts (i.e., a base, catch, spring, hammer, and holding bar), each part is matched and stapled in just the right configuration and spatial relationship for their specific jobs to interwork with the others parts. If any part is either missing or is present but does not interwork, though, the function of the mousetrap cannot be performed, and zero mice will be killed. Therefore the function of a mousetrap cannot be performed without all of the parts present and working together in the right configuration and at the exact same time; it is all or nothing. Or take a car as another, more complex example: you could not go very far if you did not have the interdependent cooperation of an engine, wheels, a steering wheel, and so on and so forth.

Because natural selection is theorized only to modify something if it *already functions*, and because a traditional mousetrap cannot function until all of the parts are available and interwork, a mousetrap or a car could not be functional at all if built in a step-by-step, piece-by-piece, non-package deal manner similar to the "numerous, successive, slight modifications" required by macroevolution. So, upon observing even our example of a mousetrap, it is clear that the intricacy of this considerably simple example is in direct opposition to Darwin's criterion.

Of course, those are just man-made concepts used for illustrations. We must now ask if there are any organs, systems, and processes that make-up the human body that, like the mousetrap or a car, also could not have been built in the step-by-step manner of natural selection. The answer is a clear yes. Thanks to our gains in scientific understanding, we know there are a vast number of biological systems in our bodies that, besides not being able to have been built step-by-step, are infinitely more complex than a mousetrap and so on. In the same fashion, if any of our organs, systems, and processes are either missing parts or parts are present but do not interwork, the whole system will cease to perform its function. Let us, then, take a quick look at three such biological examples of IC.

THE BACTERIAL FLAGELLUM

Appearing very similar to that of an outboard motor on a boat, the bacterial flagellum, discovered in 1973, is a whip-like structure that can be found providing movement for certain bacterial cells such as Escherichia ("E.") coli bacteria. It is composed of more than fifty interworking parts that include a rotor, O-rings, a stator, propeller, universal joint, bushings, drive shaft, forward gears, reverse gears, mounting disks, water-cooled and acid-driven motor, signal transduction circuitry-based sensory components that inform it both when and where it needs to move in a bidirectional manner, and many others that function similar to an outboard motor – just in a much, *much* more efficient and complex way. With our modern advancements in mind, our technology is nowhere close to that of the flagellum, as Harvard University biophysicist Howard Berg deemed it "the most efficient machine in the universe."[25]

This bacterial motor is only one-millionth of an inch in diameter, and you would imagine its size would cause its speed to be considerably low. On the contrary, though, its rotary propeller moves at a rate of 100,000 revolutions per minute (rpm) and can then completely stop and instantly begin to move in another direction at this full speed within just *one-quarter of one spin*![26] This is the equivalent of a six-foot-tall person swimming at 60 miles per hour (mph)![27] In fact, the flagellum is so efficient that it is an absolute marvel to modern scientists, as they are continually discovering more of its roles and still trying to fully understand all of their intricate capabilities.

Seeing how all of its parts must be present, formed in the right places and at the right time, and have the right interactions with one another to intricately interwork in a specific, complex configuration to function at all, while also being able to perform both self-assembly and self-repair, the bacterial flagellum could not have been formed by the "numerous, successive, slight modifications" of macroevolution. Therefore, as our first biological example successfully meets Darwin's criterion, this, along with our discussion on the findings from embryological development should be more than enough for someone to conclude that the theory of macroevolution is false. Nevertheless, let us continue with our next, more relatable example of IC that has saved your life on many occasions.

BLOOD CLOTTING

When you get a cut on your skin, platelets quickly clump together and form a small clot in the form of a scab by releasing twelve proteins called "coagulation factors" (i.e., fibrinogen, prothrombin, tissue thromboplastin, ionized calcium, proaccelerin, proconvertin, antihemophilic factor, plasma thromboplastin component, Stuart-Prower factor, Plasma thromboplastin antecedent, Hageman factor, fibrin-stabilizing factor) to stop the bleeding. While we take this process completely for granted and assume that it is not very complicated, it is actually a highly complex process that, like the mousetrap, the car, and the bacterial flagellum, is just one step away from not functioning. Occurring in the very specific order of a long series of cascading chemical reactions, clotting a cut requires all of these clotting factors to be present, to be in the right places and at the right time, and to have the right interactions with one another to intricately interwork in a specific, complex configuration to function at all. If just one of these steps are not present, or is present but does not interact correctly with the others, the function of blood clotting will not occur, you will continue to bleed out, then faint, and eventually die.

Even if all of the factors are present as needed, since the entire chain reaction has to be intricately regulated in order to perform just right, there are even further problematic scenarios that could take place. First, if blood clotting takes too long, infection would be the last thing on your mind as you would soon be dead. Second, you would die if a scab does not cover your entire wound. Third, you would die if a clot did not form in the right location and, instead, completed its formation at another part of your body such as your heart or your brain. And fourth, you would die if, instead of just your specific wound being treated, your entire bloodstream congealed.

While we could lay out every intricate step in great detail, the whole process is much too complex to do so. We *can*, though, state that this process, like the mousetrap, the car, and the bacterial flagellum, *has to be* a package deal; all of the parts must be fully formed, all at once, to then intricately work together and be regulated as needed for the process to work. Darwin's theory that these parts could ever form by the "numerous, successive, slight modifications" of natural selection simply would not ever work. You can just imagine the supposed first life forms all dying out because they had no way to stop any bleeding!

With that, we have our second biological example that successfully meets Darwin's criterion. Even though these two examples suffice in covering our point of discussion and helping someone conclude that the theory of macroevolution is false, their amazing complexity absolutely pales in comparison to our final biological example of IC.

THE EYE-BRAIN RELATIONSHIP

Even with limited knowledge in his time to really delve into scientific studies, Darwin himself would admit about his own theory that it definitely had problems. For instance, he admits, "To suppose that the eye, with all its inimitable contrivances for adjusting the focus to different distances, for admitting different amounts of light, and for the correction of spherical and chromatic aberration could have been formed by natural selection, seems, I freely confess, absurd in the highest degree."[28] In a letter to a Harvard professor in 1860 he would later go on to say, with possible pun intended, "The eye to this day gives me a cold shudder."[29] Similarly, it is making Darwinists tremble even more-so today. So, what are some of the characteristics that make eyes such special bodily organ systems that they draw such awe from modern-day Darwinists and the father of macroevolution himself?

A highly sophisticated digital camera that we will never be able to completely understand nor be able to ever build – this is an acceptable, but still extremely limited, analogous way to describe the human eye. Containing forty individual parts between the two, each having their own unique structures, the inner workings of the eye are nothing short of being completely breathtaking. Take, for instance, just the sensory lining of the eye called the retina. With eleven different layers, the retina is required to perform all of the jobs within each layer to receive optical images through the lens and convert them into electronic signals to then be sent to the visual cortex – the part of the brain that controls sight – via the optic nerve. This process is aided by three types of roughly 135 *million* specialized light-sensitive photoreceptor cells (called rods, cones, and ganglion cells) which transmit these electronic signals at a rate of roughly one and a half *billion* per second.

And that is just *one* part. Macroevolution not only must explain the formation of the retina and all of its interworking layers but how all of the individual parts of the eye (e.g., the pupil, iris, cornea, lens) and their unique structures formed at the exact same time and in the same relational manner to perform their functions. If you have 99.9% of an eye, you are blind; as with any examples of IC, it *must* be a package deal. Obviously, the theory that these parts could have been formed by the "numerous, successive, slight modifications" of natural selection would not work. We have already seen (no pun intended) how Darwin himself feels about the complexity of the eye; how he conclusively made his observation even when based on the world's incredibly lacking scientific understanding from the mid-1800s!

Further, add to this complexity the fact that we have not one but two interworking eyes that share this amazing complexity. Furthermore, add to this complexity the fact that both eyes must also interwork through means of another individual part – the optic nerve – with the brain – yet another irreducibly complex organ. A section of the brain called the visual cortex then interprets the electronic signals as black and white, color, depth perception, contrast, etc.

Using an analogy, this eye-brain relationship through means of the optic nerve would be the equivalent of a keyboard not being plugged into a computer. Just as there is zero input to a computer without it being connected to a keyboard, eyes cannot transmit electronic signals for sight without being connected to the brain. Therefore, both of these complex organs, similar to the mousetrap, the car, the bacterial flagellum, and blood clotting, *have to be* a package deal; all of their parts must be present, fully formed in the right places and at the right time, and have the right interactions with one another to intricately interwork in a specific, complex configuration in order to function at all. Of course, keep in mind that even if two eyes interworked with the brain as required we would still need to meet other crucial requirements – such as having the biological system in place for blood clotting. After all, having two eyes that interwork with a brain would be pretty useless towards survival when there is no way of getting around bleeding to death!

A BROKEN THEORY?

It would take entire volumes of books to even begin to grasp the IC of the eye-brain relationship. While the eye is, in fact, an amazing example, it is just one more of the many examples that we could discuss in regards to the total inner-workings of the human body. The relationship between two eyes and the brain is a perfect example of how our bodies are made up entirely of highly complex, micro machine-ran organs, systems, and processes that must then all work in harmony to perform life's functions as a whole. It would take an incredible leap of faith to believe that any one of them could possibly have been formed by the "numerous, successive, slight modifications" required by the theory of macroevolution, let alone all of them together. Yet, this is exactly what is continually being taught and accepted throughout the entire world about the formation of the human body. As Behe writes, "The idea of Darwinian molecular evolution is not based on science. There is no publication in the scientific literature that describes how molecular evolution of any real, complex, biochemical system either did occur or even might have occurred."[30]

Having discussed these three biological examples that successfully meet Darwin's criterion, along with our discussion on the findings from embryological development, this information should be more than enough for anyone to reasonably conclude that, using Darwin's words, the theory of macroevolution "absolutely breaks down." Yes, this information should be more than enough to conclude that macroevolution is false, but is there a way to see firsthand whether or not that is truly the case?

OBSERVING THE FOSSIL RECORD

Richard Dawkins writes that macroevolution should explain the development of millions of uniquely complex species by "breaking the improbability up into small, manageable parts . . . inch by million-year inch."[31] Therefore, the formation of completely different species and entirely new classes by means of natural selection, if true, should be very evident when uncovering fossils.

Since, according to Darwin, the process of natural selection would have taken a significant amount of time to accomplish such feats, the fossil record should house a significant abundance of many creatures in their between-species and between-classes transitional forms (e.g., a fish growing legs and a reptile growing wings). Thus, having been nearly one hundred and sixty years since the release of *On the Origin of Species*, we must ask ourselves if the gradual formation of Darwin's Tree of Life actually corresponds with the reality of what the fossil record tells us.

To begin with, as geologists study what is housed within the stratum (distinguishable layers of sedimentary rock) on and beneath the Earth's surface, it is obvious that an amazing phenomenon has been found to have taken place in our distant past. While hundreds of millions of fossils have been discovered thus far, none of them, surprisingly, has come from the most ancient layers; what paleontologists call the Pre-Cambrian stratum. In fact, this stratum bears nothing whatsoever but thousands upon thousands of feet of lonely rocks. What makes eyes widen even more-so, though, comes from the Cambrian stratum.

As we move up from these thousands of feet of nothingness, we then come across an *abrupt* abundance of fossils. But this mother lode is not comprised of simple forms of early life in their earliest stages of evolution; they are of *fully developed creatures* from nearly *all of the major animal groups we see today*. This discovery has been termed "The Cambrian Explosion" and "Biology's Big Bang," as life had suddenly burst onto the scene.

Therefore, the record clearly shows that there are *no* fossils showing a linkage among, for example, fish transitioning into amphibians, amphibians into reptiles, reptiles into mammals and, you guessed it, monkeys into cavemen and then into modern-day humans. Animals and humans alike appeared suddenly and did not evolve gradually over time like the Darwinist would have you believe. Of course, these geological findings are in direct opposition to gradual macroevolution through means of natural selection and give us all the proof we need that the likes of Darwin and Haeckel were dead wrong.

As T.S. Kemp, lecturer and curator of zoological collections at the Oxford University Museum of Natural History writes, "Organisms appear for the first time in the fossil record already fully evolved" and these findings are "not at all" what you would expect to find by following Darwin's Tree of Life.[32] Biochemist Michael Denton states, "Darwinism is claiming that . . . all the organisms which have existed throughout history were generated by the accumulation of entirely undirected mutations. This is an entirely unsubstantiated belief for which there is not the slightest evidence whatsoever."[33]

In fact, Darwin himself was fully aware of this explosion of fossils that showed no evidence for any previous progression of macroevolution ever occurring. This is why he admits in *On the Origin of Species*, "Why then is not every geological formation and every stratum full of such intermediate links? Geology assuredly does not reveal any such finely graduated organic chain, and this, perhaps, is the most obvious and gravest objection which can be urged against my theory."[34] Darwin said, "These difficulties and objections may be classed under the following heads: first, why, if species have descended from other species by fine gradations, do we not everywhere see innumerable transitional forms? Why is not all nature in confusion, instead of the species being, as we see them, well defined?"[35]

The only way Darwin hoped that he could maneuver around these findings was by throwing an idea out there that would outlive him: supposedly, he said, later archaeological discoveries would vindicate his theory as truth. So how has this idea faired?

Horrendously. In fact, the only "transitional" fossils that have ever been "found" turned out to be nothing but deliberate hoax after deliberate hoax. Take the "Piltdown Man" for instance:

> Charles Dawson, a British lawyer and amateur geologist, announced in 1912 his discovery of pieces of a human skull and an apelike jaw in a gravel pit near the town of Piltdown, England. . . . Dawson's announcement stopped the scorn cold. Experts instantly declared Piltdown Man (estimated to be 300,000 to one million years old) the evolutionary find of the century. Darwin's missing link had been identified. Or so it seemed for the next 40 or so years. Then, in the early fifties . . . scientists began to suspect misattribution. In 1953, that suspicion gave way to a full-blown scandal: Piltdown Man was a hoax. Radiocarbon tests proved that its skull belonged to a 600-year-

old woman, and its jaw to a 500-year-old orangutan from the East Indies.[36]

That is not all of it. On top of this finding, the microscopic analysis also found that the jaw teeth had been deliberately filed to make them look more humanlike and that all of the remains had been stained with acids and solutions in order to create the appearance of extensive aging.[37]

As another example, Lee Strobel gives details of his fascination as a child reading about the "Java Man" in his *World Book Encyclopedia*. He writes:

> With his sloping forehead, heavy brow, jutting jaw, receding chin and bemused expression, he was exactly what a blend of ape and man should look like. . . . The encyclopedia confidently described how Dutch scientist Eugene Dubois, excavating on an Indonesian Island in 1891 and 1892, "dug some bones from a riverbank." Java man, which he dated back half a million years, "represents a stage in the development of modern man from a smaller-brained ancestor." He was, according to Dubois, *the* missing link between apes and humans. And I believed it all. I was blithely ignorant, however, of the full Java man story. "What is not so well known is that Java man consists of nothing more than a skullcap, a femur (thigh bone), three teeth, and a great deal of imagination," one author would later write. In other words, the lifelike depiction of Java man, which had so gripped me when I was young, was little more than speculation fueled by evolutionary expectations of what he *should* have looked like if Darwinism were true. As a youngster beginning to form my opinions about human evolution, I wasn't aware of what I have more recently discovered: that Dubois' shoddy excavation would have disqualified the fossil from consideration by today's standards.

Or that the femur apparently did not really belong with the skullcap. Or that the skull cap, according to prominent Cambridge University anatomist Sir Arthur Keith, was distinctly human and reflected a brain capacity well within the range of humans living today. Or that a 342-page scientific report from a fact-finding expedition of nineteen evolutionists demolished Dubois' claims and concluded that Java man played no part in human evolution. In short, Java man was not an ape-man as I had been led to believe, but he was "a true member of the human family."[38]

Or take, for instance, the "Archaeoraptor." A report in 2000 by *U.S. News & World Report* stated of this archaeological find that,

> Imaginations certainly took flight over *Archaeoraptor Liaoningensis*, a birdlike fossil with a meat-eater's tail that was spirited out of northeastern China, "discovered" at a Tucson, Arizona, gem and mineral show last year, and displayed at the National Geographic Society in Washington, D.C. Some 110,000 visitors saw the exhibit . . . millions more read about the find in November's *National Geographic*. Now, paleontologists are eating crow. Instead of "a true missing link" connecting dinosaurs to birds, the specimen appears to be a composite, its unusual appendage likely tacked on by a Chinese farmer, not evolution.[39]

Wells adds, "'A Chinese paleontologist proved that someone had glued a dinosaur tail to a primitive bird. He created it to resemble just what the scientists had been looking for. There was a firestorm of criticism – the curator of birds at the Smithsonian charged that the society had become aligned with "zealous scientists" who were "highly biased proselytizers of the faith" that birds evolved from dinosaurs.'"[40]

This hoax brought attention to illegal fossil deals conducted in China, where it is a big operation done mostly by thousands of poor farmers just looking to make money. Obviously the better, more intriguing specimens bring higher amounts of money – some reaching tens of thousands of dollars – so fakes are being made better and better and sold all the time. Not surprisingly, this illegal operation is not only still going but is only growing in size. Luis Chiappe, director of the Dinosaur Institute at the Natural History Museum of Los Angeles County describes it as the "paleontological parallel of the construction of the Great Wall of China."[41]

Over the one hundred and sixty year stretch since the release of *On the Origin of Species*, we have come to find out that the Cambrian Explosion was even more abrupt than we had previously thought. Dawkins states of the Cambrian strata, "It is as though [the fossils] were just planted there, without any evolutionary history. Needless to say . . . this has delighted creationists."[42] Evolutionist Steven J. Gould, arguably the most influential evolutionary biologist of the twentieth century, states that the fossil record is an "embarrassment" for evolutionary theory.[43] Colin Patterson, evolutionist and senior paleontologist at the prestigious British Museum of Natural History, replied to an inquiry from a reader of his book *Evolution* as to why he had not shown one single photograph of a transitional fossil in it: "I fully agree with your comments on the lack of direct illustration of evolutionary transitions in my book. If I knew of any, fossil or living, I would certainly have included them. You suggest that an artist should be used to visualize such transformations, but where would he get the information from?"[44] He continues, "'Gould and the American Museum people are hard to contradict when they say there are no transitional fossils. . . . You say that I should at least "show a photo of the fossil from which each type of organism was derived." *I will lay it on the line—there is not one such fossil.*'"

All of the facts run completely counter to what Darwin theorized. There should be a vast array of transitional fossils to easily vindicate his theory. Yet, there are . . . zero. So, all of the drawings found in textbooks about embryonic development and all of the museum displays showing gradual evolution through means of natural selection are all false advertising for evolution; they cannot be backed up by one measly fossil when there should be more than one could count.

Small, *micro* changes in characteristics do not eventually accumulate and lead to large, *macro* changes as we continue up the hierarchy of different species, genus, family, order, and class. This is precisely because of genetic limitations. For example, no matter how dogs are bred, due to the restraints of genetic limits, the offspring will forever remain as . . . dogs. Or, take fruit flies for instance. As a fruit fly can lay over 500 eggs at one time, and the entire life cycle from egg to adult is less than ten days, we can observe and even intelligently induce various mutations for many generations per year and, therefore, somewhat directly observe whether or not macroevolution is taking place. Ever since the early 1900s, what have we found? Wells writes: "Although interference may introduce deformities, the basic endpoint of development never changes. If they survive, fruit fly eggs always become fruit flies, frog eggs always become frogs, and mouse eggs always become mice. Not even the species changes. Every embryo is somehow programmed to develop into a particular species of animal."[45] He continues, "No matter what we do to a fruit fly embryo, there are only three possible outcomes – a normal fruit fly, a defective fruit fly, or a dead fruit fly. Not even a horsefly, much less a horse."[46] Intelligent scientists, with all of our modern-day understanding and advancements, and the specific goal in mind to manipulate fruit fly embryos in this fashion, cannot dream of ever getting beyond genetic limitations. So why would one think that the unintelligent, blind, purposeless process of natural selection could accomplish such a feat? Yet, Darwin's Tree of Life is still described throughout textbooks for all ages across the world as being, as Ross from *Friends* put it: "scientific fact. Like, like, like the air we breathe. Like gravity."

With all we have covered, you can clearly see there is no evidence for the worldview of the Darwinist. It gets even worse from here, as we can now look at yet another problem – actually, the *most lethal* problem – for macroevolution that Darwin and everyone else was not remotely aware of at the time *On the Origin of Species* was released.

ON TO THE MOST LETHAL PROBLEM

The most lethal problem for macroevolution has nothing at all to do with whether or not every form of plant and animal life is related to a common ancestor. Therefore, it also has nothing to do with either the fossil record or how natural selection could possibly form irreducibly complex organs, systems, and processes in a gradual, step-by-step manner. While those are all critical problems for macroevolution, the most lethal problem has to do with the building of the very first life form.

Getting straight to the point, Darwin was just flat-out wrong in saying natural selection formed a Tree of Life that contained very "simple" life at its base and increasing complexity as it branched out at the top. Of all the critical problems for macroevolution that we discussed and could discuss, the main reason we know Darwin was wrong is because modern science has clearly shown that a cell is light-years beyond the complexity that Darwin and his colleagues ever could have thought.

In fact, even the "simplest" life today (i.e., bacterial cells) require vast amounts of information to even form, let alone function. According to Michael Denton, even the smallest bacterial cell is "a veritable microminiaturized factory containing thousands of exquisitely designed pieces of intricate molecular machinery, made up altogether of 100 thousand million atoms, far more complicated than any machine built by man and absolutely without parallel in the non-living world."[47] This was made abundantly evident, nearly 100 years after the release of *On the Origin of Species*, when in 1953 a team of molecular biologists and physicists (James Watson, Francis Crick, Maurice Wilkins, and their colleague Rosalind Franklin) made the 1962 Nobel Prize-winning discovery of the molecular structure of DNA (deoxyribonucleic acid).

Found almost entirely in the nucleus of every cell, with a small portion in each cells' mitochondria, DNA easily performs the most complex function of life. Besides gaining a new understanding of heredity and hereditary diseases, in particular, the discovery of the structure of DNA was met with such high praise because the secret as to how the genetic makeup of a human being is built had been revealed as being in the form of *instructional code*.

In fact, this code, composed of four chemical building blocks called nitrogenous based (i.e., guanine, cytosine, adenine, and thymine) which scientists represent with an abbreviated genetic alphabet consisting of the four letters *G*, *C*, *A*, and *T*, is identical to a language. An alternating pattern of sugar-phosphate molecules, the two strands that make-up the backbone of entire DNA molecules are held together by these four bases within a structure, looking much like a spiral ladder, referred to as a double helix. Hydrogen bonds are then responsible to form the rungs of this ladder by ordering these bases – "G" bases are always paired with "C" bases, and "A" bases are always paired with "T" bases – in a specific manner. To illustrate how this process works, a tiny portion of a person's instructional code for, say, having hazel-colored eyes would have a uniquely ordered sequence of chemical letters: it would be something on the lines of ATGCGCTACGATCGTA and so on in a much, much more lengthy sequence. Whereas the English alphabet, for instance, consists of twenty-six letters used to form words and communicate messages, it is the arrangement of these four letters (bases) which determines the unique genetic instructions for how each living thing overall is to be constructed.

For those having a familiarity with computer programming, you know that using differing combinations of characters is the exact same way in which a programmer instructs a computer what to do. Of course, DNA does not just store information, it also processes it; hence why the founder of the technology company Microsoft, Bill Gates, stated that "Human DNA is like a computer program but far, far more advanced than any software ever created."[48] In fact, programmers study DNA to learn better ways to develop more advanced technology.

Capable of storing billions of times more data, having faster computing speeds, and being vastly more compact and efficient than conventional silicon-based microprocessors, DNA-based microprocessors are the "next big thing" in the upcoming generations of supercomputers. One single gram worth of DNA could store roughly 489 *billion* gigabytes worth of information – "enough for all the data held by Google, Facebook and every other major tech company, with room to spare!"[49] Further, DNA molecules are so long and chock-full of encoded information that they could never fit inside of a cell without being tightly and perfectly coiled inside of a chromosome. So long, in fact, that Dawkins states that the specified, complex information stored within the DNA of a one-celled amoeba would be equivalent to 1,000 sets of *Encyclopedia Britannica*.[50] To illustrate this to the highest degree, if you were to stretch out just one strand of DNA it can reach nine feet in length. If you were to extrapolate that statistic out with your estimated 37.2 trillion cells (a very conservative number, as many estimates reach between *70 and 100* trillion cells) in the average human body, our DNA would reach to the Sun up to 759 times, to the moon up to 307,270 times, and around the circumference of the Earth up to 2,788,708 times!

Thus, the only difference between the instructional code of a computer (binary code) and DNA is that, while DNA uses a series of four letters in a chemical alphabet to enter instructional code, lines of binary code are entered by using differing sequences of the numbers "0" and "1", for example, the actual way to write the word "Hello" in binary code is "01001000 01100101 01101100 01101100 01101111." So as with the English alphabet, binary code, or any other language, the four chemical letters that make-up DNA molecules are carriers of specified information in the exact same way to compose meaningful sequences which intricately form a person's entire instructional blueprint.

With that said, how exactly does this lead to the most lethal problem for macroevolution? Well, because even the most basic form of life requires this vast amount of genetic information found within its DNA in order to have the instructions on how to form, the obvious question is how this information originated. As Paul Davies states, "We need to explain the origin of this information, and the way in which the information processing machinery came to exist."[51]

DOES MANKIND SHOW SIGNS OF DESIGN?

(Part 2)

OPTION ONE

There are two options that attempt to answer how this information originated. Starting with the first option – evolution – the modern-day Darwinist would claim that life supposedly generated spontaneously from nonliving chemicals.

First of all, we hear a lot about this so-called warm little pond, or "Primordial Soup," of chemicals that supposedly were on the primitive Earth before life originated. Before we discuss whether or not life could form from nonliving chemicals, is there absolutely any evidence that such ponds could be habitable for the production of life, or that they ever even existed?

To answer the first part of that question, the answer is *no*. It has been proven time and time again that factors such as (but not limited to) pond leakage, ultraviolet photodissociation due to a lack of an ozone layer, and the oxygen-ultraviolet paradox would never have allowed the timeframe for which life could be produced (more on this timeframe later). As Hugh Ross explains the oxygen-ultraviolet paradox, for instance, and answers the second part of the question as well:

> Earth never had a prebiotic soup nor any kind of prebiotic mineral substrate. Physicists now know why earth never could have possessed any prebiotics. . . . If the environment of earth at the time of life's origin contained any oxygen, that oxygen would immediately and catastrophically shut down prebiotic chemistry. On the other hand, if earth's environment . . . contained no oxygen, ultraviolet radiation from the sun would penetrate earth's environment to a sufficient degree as . . . catastrophically shut down prebiotic chemistry. Either way, earth never could have naturalistically possessed any prebiotics.[1]

Further, take the Miller-Urey test of 1953 for instance. Biochemists Stanley Miller and Harold Urey performed an experiment to see if organic compounds could be spontaneously produced with the environmental conditions thought to be most optimal for the production of life on the primitive Earth (e.g., an abundance of ammonia, hydrogen, methane, and water vapor). Of course, it was later shown the test was highly invalid because Earth barely had any of those gases besides perhaps water vapor. Once you run an experiment with the conditions most likely to have been present on the primitive Earth you get, as Wells states, "Formaldehyde! Cyanide! . . . In my lab at Berkeley you could not even have a capped bottle of formaldehyde in the room, because the stuff is so toxic. You open the bottle and it fries proteins all over the place, just from the fumes. . . . The idea that using a realistic atmosphere gets you the first step in the origin of life is just laughable. . . . Do you know what you get? Embalming fluid!"[2]

The scientific significance of the Miller-Urey experiment, says Bradley, "is zilch."[3] He would go on to say, "'Even Miller, some forty years after his famous experiment, said in a great understatement to *Scientific American*: "The problem of the origin of life has turned out to be much more difficult than I, and most other people, envisioned."'[4] Nevertheless, it is the results found with the conditions that Miller and Urey used which speaks volumes on the fact that life could never form from non-living chemicals.

In using the most optimal conditions possible, Miller and Urey produced a tiny number of simple, non-living amino acids. And this was not a breakthrough by any means whatsoever because, unlike what Darwin thought (a cell is very simple so it would not be difficult at all to create life from nonlife), the gap between non-living amino acids and even the most basic life form is of *incalculable distance*; even if the environmental conditions were the most optimal ones which Miller and Urey used, in a warm little pond, by hydrothermal vents, or wherever, and a virtually infinite amount of time was available on top of that, life would *still* never emerge. As Wells states,

> The gap between nonliving chemicals and even the most primitive living organism is absolutely tremendous. . . . Let me describe it this way. Put a sterile, balanced salt solution in a test tube. Then put in a single living cell and poke a hole in it so that its contents leak into the solution. Now the test tube has all the molecules you would need to create a living cell, right? You would already have accomplished far more than what the Miller experiment ever could. . . . The problem is you cannot make a living cell. There's not even any point in trying. . . . No biologist in his right mind would think you can take a test tube with those molecules and turn them into a living cell. Even if you could accomplish the thousands of steps between the amino acids in the Miller tar . . . and the components you need for a living cell – all

the enzymes, the DNA, and so forth – you're still immeasurably far from life. . . . The problem of assembling the right parts in the right way at the right time and at the right place, while keeping out the wrong material, is simply insurmountable.[5]

So with such tests, even when intelligence was directly involved with the specified task of trying to create even the most basic form of life, scientists cannot get anywhere close. Bradley adds to this some reasons as to why it is so difficult to create *even one single protein* of what all is required to form even the most basic, one-celled organism from non-living materials:

> Essentially, you start with amino acids. They come in eighty different types, but only twenty of them are found in living organisms. The trick, then, is to isolate only the correct amino acids. Then the right amino acids have to be linked together in the right sequence in order to produce protein molecules. . . . And there are a lot of other complicating factors to consider. For instance, other molecules tend to react more readily with amino acids than amino acids react with each other. Now you have the problem of how to eliminate these extraneous molecules. . . . So you'd have a lot of other chemical material that would gum up the process. Then there's another complication: there are an equal number of amino acids that are right- and left-handed, and only left-handed ones work in living matter. Now you've got to get only these select ones to link together in the right sequence. And you also need the correct kind of chemical bonds – namely, peptide bonds – in the correct places in order for the protein to be able to fold in a specific three-dimensional way. Otherwise it won't function. . . . And, remember, that's just the first step. Creating one protein molecule doesn't mean you've

created life. Now you have to bring together a collection of protein molecules . . . with just the right functions to get a typical living cell. . . . In living systems, the guidance that's needed to assemble everything comes from DNA. Every cell of every plant and animal has to have a DNA molecule. Think of it as a little microprocessor that regulates everything. DNA works hand-in-glove with RNA to direct the correct sequencing of amino acids. It is able to do this through biochemical instructions – that is, information – that is encoded on the DNA. The making of DNA and RNA would be an even greater problem than creating protein. These are much more complex, and there are a host of practical problems. . . . Frankly, the origin of such a sophisticated system that is both rich in information and capable of reproducing itself has absolutely stymied [a situation or problem presenting such difficulties as to discourage or defeat any attempt to deal with or resolve it] origin-of-life scientists.[6]

According to Stephen Meyer, the odds at the most optimal conditions for nature to produce the incredibly intricate chain of roughly 150 amino acids through a covalent peptide bond to form merely one functional protein is at least one part in 10^{164}.[7] Further, mathematician and astronomer Fred Hoyle estimated the odds at the most optimal conditions for nature to produce the entire, even more intricate, chain of roughly three to five hundred protein molecules necessary for merely one of the simplest cells to be at least one part in $10^{40,000}$.[8] Hoyle then uses the analogy of these odds being the equivalent of a tornado going through a junkyard and fully assembling an operational Boeing 747 aircraft.[9]

Further, DNA contains the uniquely detailed instructional code as to how, how often, in what amounts, when, and where to build protein molecules and ultimately cells; proteins being long chains of amino acids which are attached to one another by peptide bonds, and properly arranging the four chemicals letters instructs the cell on how to build differing sequences of amino acids, which are the building blocks of protein molecules; and protein molecules are responsible for replicating DNA within new cells. Thus, as none of these can exist in any way on their own and must be simultaneously formed to depend on each other and function mutually, this is a chicken-and-egg paradox that evolutionary abiogenesis will never be able to explain. Meyer adds:

> This issue has caused all naturalistic accounts of the origin of life to break down, because it's *the* critical and foundational question. If you cannot explain where the information comes from, you have not explained life, because it is the information that makes the molecules into something that actually functions. . . . Darwinists admit that natural selection requires a self-replicating organism to work. Organisms reproduce, their offspring have variations, the ones that are better adapted to their environment survive better, and so those adaptations are preserved and passed on to the next generation. However, to have reproduction, there has to be cell division. And that presupposes the existence of information-rich DNA and proteins. But that's the problem – those are the very things they're trying to explain! In other words, you've got to have a self-replicating organism for Darwinian evolution to take place, but you can't have a self-replicating organism until you have the information necessary in DNA, which is what you're trying to explain in the first place.[10]

Of course, Hoyle's analogy does not go nearly far enough. This is not just because evolution cannot explain how nature produces even the simplest cell, but since the worldview is in line with the false belief that the universe created itself, evolution also cannot explain how any materials – non-living chemicals, the Earth itself, or anything whatsoever – even got here in the first place! When intelligence creates, say, a mousetrap, the parts are already made; in the cellular world, on the other hand, the parts to create life were not just floating around, somehow knowing how to form and function together on their own.

In the same way, evolution cannot explain the origin of genetic information necessary to build the first life or any life because the whole theory behind the wild idea of natural selection is that it only happens to organisms *that already have genetic information*; if there is nothing to "select," there is zero natural *selection* occurring. This, then, means there is no possibility of natural selection "breaking the improbability up into small, manageable parts . . . inch by million-year inch" as Dawkins states. Therefore, evolution must be a theory of chance. And as Dawkins himself admits, if evolution is a theory of chance, because of what we have discussed about the odds of life forming from non-living chemicals, "It is grindingly, creakingly, crashingly obvious that . . . it could not work."[11] Microbiologist Michael Denton adds, "The complexity of the simplest known type of cell is so great that it is impossible to accept that such an object could have been thrown together suddenly by some kind of freakish, vastly improbable event."[12] And Dean Kenyon, Professor Emeritus of Biology at San Francisco State University concludes, "No longer is it a reasonable proposition to think that simple chemical events could have any chance at all to generate the kind of complexity that we see in the very simplest living organism. We have not the slightest chance of a chemical evolutionary origin for even the simplest of cells with the new knowledge that has accumulated."[13]

Of course, on top of all we have discussed on parameters, this information about the formation of even the simplest form of life makes the chance of any life being somewhere out there in space to be much lower than it already was. When we say life elsewhere, or articles say scientists are still searching for *alien life*, what is meant by that is specifically microbial life; not little green men. There will never, ever be even microbial life found elsewhere. But an ironic, entirely wretched note is that if scientists ever found microbial life in space it would be heralded as life on the front page of every major print – yet, a baby from conception to its due date is commonly heralded as *not* a life (and in the next chapter we will see that some even believe babies should not even be considered a person until a certain amount of time has passed even *after* having been born!).

Origin-of-life scientists have abandoned chance theories and, thus, Darwinism is bankrupt beyond measure. Writes Swedish biologist and embryologist Soren Lovtrup in his book *Darwinism: The Refutation of a Myth*, "'I suppose that nobody will deny that it is a great misfortune if an entire branch of science becomes addicted to a false theory. But this is what has happened in biology. . . . I believe that one day the Darwinian myth will be ranked the greatest deceit in the history of science. When this happens, many people will post the question: "How did this ever happen?"'[14]

Dr. Colin Patterson, senior paleontologist at the British Museum of Natural History, stated in his keynote address at the American Museum of Natural History in New York City:

> One morning I woke up and . . . it struck me that I had been working on this stuff for twenty years and there was not one thing I knew about it. That's quite a shock to learn that one can be misled so long. . . . For the last few weeks I've tried putting a simple question to various people and groups of people: "Can you tell me anything you know about evolution, any one thing, any one thing that is true?" I tried that question on the geology staff at the Field Museum of Natural History and the only answer I got was silence.   I tried it on the members of the Evolutionary Morphology Seminar in

the University of Chicago, a very prestigious body of evolutionists, and all I got there was silence for a long time and eventually one person said, "I do know one thing – it ought not to be taught in high school." . . . I think many people in this room would acknowledge that . . . you've experienced a shift from evolution as knowledge to evolution as faith.[15]

Meyer sums it up nicely: "We've learned a lot about biology since the Civil War. Evolutionists are still trying to apply Darwin's nineteenth-century thinking to a twenty-first century reality, and it is not working. Explanations from the era of the steamboat are no longer adequate to explain the biological world of the information age."[16] And writes double Ph.D. William A. Dembski, known for his extensive work with specified complexity,

> Darwin was like a magician performing far enough away from his subjects that he could dazzle them – until somebody starts handing out binoculars. Darwin's idea was a good trick while it lasted. But with advances in technology as well as the information in life sciences (especially molecular biology), the Darwinian magic gig is now up. It is time to lay aside the tricks – the smokescreens and the handwaving, the just-so stories and the stonewalling, the bluster and the bluffing, and to explain scientifically what people have known all along, namely, why you cannot get design without a designer.[17]

As Kenyon adds, "This new realm of molecular genetics [is] where we see the most compelling evidence of design on the Earth."[18] And as Behe writes, "'The result of these cumulative efforts to investigate the cell – to investigate life at the molecular level – is a loud, clear, piercing cry of "design!"'[19] Thus, this leads us to our second option and third premise.

PREMISE 3:
THEREFORE, [MANKIND] HAVE/HAS A DESIGNER

Making the concluding that a Designer is the best explanation for reality is not made simply because the naturalistic theories held by atheists do not suffice. Instead, it is a conclusion based on a house built brick by brick with well-reasoned, scientific evidence. In fact, this is a conclusion held by Dawkins himself.

In regards to The Cambrian Explosion and the complete lack of life evolving "inch by million-year inch," for instance, Dawkins writes in his very next sentence that, "Only God would essay the mad task of leaping up the precipice in a single bound."[20] He states in his book *The Blind Watchmaker*, "The only alternative explanation of the sudden appearance of so many complex animal types in the Cambrian era is divine creation."[21]

James Tour, professor at Rice University's Department of Chemistry and Center for Nanoscale Science and Technology who was awarded "Scientist of the Year" in 2013 and among the "50 Most Influential Scientists in the World Today" since then states that, with our modern day understanding of the cell, he stands "in awe of God because of what he has done through his creation. Only a rookie who knows nothing about science would say science takes away from faith. If you really study science, it will bring you closer to God."[22]

Now, there is one more thought that we have yet to cover. With that said, let us dig deeper into the specific code of DNA to bring home the point that mankind has an obvious Designer.

EXPLOSION IN A PRINTING PRESS

What is something that is *always* required to convey specified, complex information? An *intelligent mind*.

Imagine you and your kid are walking along the ocean shore looking for shells and sand crabs and you take notice of the ripples in the sand. In regards to how they were formed, what would you automatically conclude about the ripples? Of course, they were formed by the ocean waves. Now, contrast that observation with something you come across as you both continue walking: a drawing in the sand with the words "Ricky loves Lucy" written inside of a heart. What would you automatically conclude this time? Of course, unlike the ripples in the sand, the drawing was formed by an intelligent mind. Soon thereafter, you get a text message on your phone: "Are you on your way home yet?" And after sending your reply, you take one last look at the view and see something in the sky that was not there earlier: the phrase "LUCY WILL YOU MARRY ME?" These are two more instances of an intelligent mind.

You pull into your driveway and notice two things: to the left is a giant, jump-in-worthy pile of leaves, and to the right is the phrase written with leaves "fall is here." Which would you conclude was potentially caused by the wind and which would you conclude definitely was caused by an intelligent mind? While it is most likely that the pile of leaves was made by someone (after all, the rake was propped up nearby), the wind at least *could have* caused them to be there, but there is absolutely no denying that an intelligent mind made the phrase written with leaves. You then walk into the kitchen to see that "Please do the dishes for your sweet wife" has been written in Scrabble letters and placed on the counter next to the sink. Do you assume that the cat got into the bag of letters which you thought were safe up high, or do you audibly sigh a few times and just go ahead and do the dishes? If you know what is good for you, you had better give credit that a very, *very* intelligent mind composed that request and not leave it to chance!

It is funny because chance is exactly how the popular message of Darwinism would explain such examples of obvious intelligibility, as it is believed that information can be formed *without* intelligence. Similar as to how the beginning and initial formation of the universe, the fine-tuning of the universe, and mankind's eventual rise from a common ancestor is approached by the popular message of atheism and Darwinism alike using chance as their supposed explanation, chance is used yet again to also try and explain the formation of information within DNA; in other words, the drawings of a heart and three words in the sand could have been formed by the ocean waves, and the words "LUCY WILL YOU MARRY ME?" in the sky could have been formed by odd cloud formations in the area. Oh and let us not forget about that text message; it definitely could have been typed and sent by your dog, using the contact's phone to reach you, because it was about time for their afternoon walk!

Speaking of animals, to illustrate the popular Darwinian viewpoint that information can supposedly arise by chance alone, a theory – the "Infinite Monkey Theorem" – was presented stating that a number of monkeys, if given enough time, could eventually type all of the works of Shakespeare, without error, by mere chance of correctly striking all of the letter, number, punctuation, and space keys as needed. To test the legitimacy of this theory, with the aid of a financial grant from The British National Council of Arts, a group from the University of Plymouth performed an experiment in cooperation with the Paignton Zoo Environmental Park in England. By placing a computer into a primate enclosure and giving them access to just the keyboard, the researchers were curious to test the literary output of the six monkeys (Elmo, Gum, Heather, Holly, Mistletoe, and Rowan) that had taken part in the experiment. And after a month of observing their output, lead researcher Mike Phillips records that the monkeys initially tried to destroy the keyboard with a rock but then found interest in "defecating and urinating all over the keyboard."[23] Ultimately the monkeys did eventually produce five pages of text, but no words were made as the majority of the text was a repetition of the letter "S."

To say with a straight face that you actually think monkeys could complete such a task, that is just as bad or even worse as saying that an explosion in a printing press could form an entire dictionary! That experiment was obviously a silly waste of both time and taxpayer dollars from the start because, while nature can produce repeated patterns such as ripples in the sand, salt crystals, and snowflakes, we all know that absolutely anytime we see intelligibility we can *always* rightly conclude that an intelligent mind must be behind it.

Because it consists of specific *messages* on how to build unique lives, DNA is not at all like repeated patterns of ripples and such that do not produce messages. Meyer gives further insight into this fact:

> If all you had were repeating characters in DNA, the assembly instructions would merely tell amino acids to assemble in the same way over and over again. You wouldn't be able to build all the many different kinds of protein molecules you need for a living cell to function. It would be like handing a person an instruction book for how to build an automobile, but all the book said was "the-the-the-the-the-the." . . . Chemical evolutionary theorists are not going to escape this. The laws of nature, by definition, describe regular, repetitive patterns. For that reason one cannot invoke self-organizing processes to explain the origin of information, because informational sequences are irregular and complex. . . . If you study DNA, you will find that its structure depends on certain bonds that are caused by chemical attractions. For instance, there are hydrogen bonds and bonds between the sugar and phosphate molecules that form the two twisting backbones of the DNA molecule. However, there's one place where there are *no* chemical bonds, and that's between the nucleotide bases, which are the chemical letters in the

DNA's assembly instructions. In other words, the letters that spell out the text in the DNA message don't interact chemically with each other in any significant way. Also, they're totally interchangeable. Each base can attach with equal facility at any site along the DNA backbone. . . . Each individual base, or letter, is chemically bonded to the sugar-phosphate backbone of the molecule. That's how they're attached to the DNA's structure. But – and here's the key point – *there is no attraction or bonding between the individual letters themselves.* So there's nothing chemically that forces them into any particular sequence. The sequencing has to come from somewhere else. . . Clearly, the cause comes from outside the system. And that cause is *intelligence*.[24]

Frank Turek adds to this line of thought: "The laws of chemistry explain why ink binds to paper, but they do not account for the order of the letters that make the message on the paper. . . . The same is true for your iPod. . . . The music has to be created by an intelligent being, converted into digital code, and then programmed into the iPod. . . . Likewise, for you to work at all, an intelligent being had to provide you with your own genetic program."[25] Thus, making an inference to the best explanation, this leads us to the conclusion that, from the creation of the universe, its fine tuning all the way down to the depths of the Earth, and life itself, an intelligent Designer with the purposeful intent of creating and sustaining life is responsible for our existence.

Reiterating Bill Gates' quote again that, "Human DNA is like a computer program but far, far more advanced than any software ever created," we must point out the obvious that, of course, Microsoft or any other technology company uses intelligent minds to make computer programs. Thus, just as a book is traced back to an intelligent mind which is an author, a newspaper is traced back to an intelligent mind which is a journalist, binary code is traced back to computer programmers, and so on, it is entirely reasonable to conclude that the instructional code within the DNA of each and every human being must be traced back to an intelligent mind "far, far more advanced" than our own.

The whole thought process of believing chance could ever account for such signs of intelligibility gets even sillier once you realize, when it comes to the information that is encoded within DNA, we are not dealing with a capacity of information which similarly amounts to two names drawn in the sand, a phrase that is written with Scrabble letters, an entire dictionary, or even all of the literary works of Shakespeare. As the amount of specified, complex information in even a one-celled amoeba, says Dawkins, is the equivalent to 1,000 complete sets of the *Encyclopedia Britannica*, and with the mind-blowing statistics of the length that the average human's DNA would stretch in-full, the question one must ask is, "If even a brief, specified message is always traced back to an intelligent mind, how could anyone *ever* think that the encoded information within each and every strand of DNA should not also be traced back to an intelligent mind?"

NO FOOT IN THE DOOR

This puts Darwinists in a tight corner. Dawkins himself agrees that life not only seems planned but "meticulously planned."[26] So how do he and others think they can bypass this? He adds that the "results of natural selection overwhelmingly impress us with the appearance of design as if by a master watchmaker" and that these results of natural selection "impress us with the illusion of design and planning."[27] He also wrote, "Biology is the study of complicated things that give the appearance of having been designed for a purpose."[28] Another Darwinist, Crick, expressed a similar thought as Dawkins: "Biologists must constantly keep in mind that what they see was not designed, but rather evolved."[29]

Those quotes, especially from Crick, sound very desperate; they sound like the titular character in *The Wizard of Oz* upon being caught in a lie and trying to cover it up, saying, "Pay no attention to that man behind the curtain!"[30] So why give a warning to people to ignore the obvious signs of intelligibility? Why continue on believing in a theory that is so obviously false? You can clearly see how much more those who do not believe in God must rely on faith (faith without reason) than religious people do with their faith (with reason). After all, to not follow all of the evidence where it leads and conclude that the universe seems designed because it *is* designed is to say, "If it looks like a duck, swims like a duck, and quacks like a duck . . . then it must be a hippopotamus!" The only logical conclusion is that life and the whole universe "appear" so "meticulously planned" and "designed for a purpose" because . . . it really *is* planned and designed for a purpose. So why not just admit that?

It is simply because they *do not want there to be a God*. Thomas Nagel, professor of philosophy and Law Emeritus at New York University, states this plain as day:

> I speak from experience, being strongly subject to this fear myself: I want atheism to be true and am made uneasy by the fact that some of the most intelligent and well-informed people I know are religious believers. It's not just that I don't believe in God and, naturally, hope that I'm right in my belief. It's that I hope there is no God! I don't want there to be a God; I don't want the universe to be like that. My guess is that this cosmic authority problem is not a rare condition and that it's responsible for much of the scientism and reductionism of our time. One of the tendencies it supports is the ludicrous overuse of evolutionary biology to explain everything about human life, including everything about the human mind. . . .

This is a somewhat ridiculous situation.[31]

No matter what, their unreasonable worldview of a world without God will never let them have an unbiased look at the facts; they conclude beforehand that God does not exist simply due to a heart issue and not an intellectual issue. Dawkins even admits this: "[Our] philosophical commitment to materialism and reductionism is true."[32] (We will get more into the definitions of materialism and reductionism in a later chapter, but for now, just know that they are simply synonyms for atheism). Similarly, Harvard University biologist Richard Lewontin admits this as well and goes even farther with the admission that nonbelievers must go along with the worldview of atheism no matter what scientific facts say otherwise:

> Our willingness to accept scientific claims that are against common sense is the key to an understanding of the real struggle between science and the supernatural. We take the side of science in spite of the patent absurdity of some of its constructs, in spite of its failure to fulfill many of its extravagant promises of health and life, in spite of the tolerance of the scientific community for unsubstantiated just-so stories, because we have a prior commitment to materialism. It is not that the methods and institutions of science somehow compel us to accept a material explanation of the phenomenal world but, on the contrary, that we are forced by our a priori adherence to material causes to create an apparatus of investigation and a set of concepts that produce material explanations, no matter how counterintuitive, no matter how mystifying to the uninitiated. Moreover that materialism is absolute for we cannot allow a divine foot in the door.[33]

Did you catch that? Lewontin admits that Darwinists believe in theories that are "against common sense" simply because of their preconceived philosophical bias. As physicist and information theorist Hubert Yockey writes, "The belief that life on earth arose spontaneously from nonliving matter, is simply a matter of faith in strict reductionism and is based entirely on ideology."[34] "No wonder atheists are sporting billboards asking us to "imagine…no religion." When science, far from disproving God, seems to be pointing with ever-greater precision toward transcendence, imagination and wishful thinking seem all that is left for the atheists to count on."[35]

There is no evidence for macroevolution, and Darwinists know it; they just cannot fathom the thought of letting God get His "foot in the door" and ruining their religion of atheism (more on the *why* of this fact in a later chapter). And it *is* a religion. Michael Ruse, professor of zoology and philosophy at Florida State University, was the leading anti-creationist philosopher in the *McLean v. Arkansas Board of Education* we mentioned earlier to see whether or not if both sides (God and evolution) could be taught alongside one another in public schools. In the trial, he and other Darwinists denied that evolution was a religion. Yet, he wrote in a 2000 article for the *National Post* that, "Evolution is promoted by its practitioners as more than mere science. Evolution is promulgated as an ideology, a secular religion. . . . I am an ardent evolutionist and an ex-Christian, but I must admit that . . . *evolution is a religion. This was true of evolution in the beginning, and it is true of evolution still today.*"[36]

What atheists are doing is not allowing even the thought of God to be an option and, therefore, are not looking at the facts objectively; they rule God out even before looking at the evidence. Thus, by atheists philosophically ruling out intelligence design beforehand, such a strong, preconceived bias based on feelings alone is not science at all. States Turek:

Atheists such as Peter Atkins and Lawrence Krauss assert that it's "intellectually lazy" to say that God or some unknown designer did it.... First of all, scientists who are open to intelligent causes are not ceasing to look for natural causes. They're looking for natural causes just like anyone else. Nor are they merely plugging in God because they have not found a natural cause.... They have positive evidence that intelligence was involved.... These scientists are simply maintaining that we shouldn't rule out the possibility of intelligence beforehand because then you're assuming what you're trying to prove — you're mandating a materialistic cause regardless of what the evidence looks like. Why be afraid of following the evidence where it leads? After all, only a bad detective argues, "There cannot be a murderer in the basement because I'm afraid to look there."[37]

Of course, not following the evidence wherever it leads and hating the evidence because it seems to lead directly to God is not something unique for atheism in regards to macroevolution alone. When it comes to the beginning of the universe, atheists will not dare admit that God is responsible. As Hawking wrote, for instance, "Many people do not like the idea that time has a beginning, probably because it smacks of divine intervention."[38] Einstein desperately wanted the universe to be eternal so that he could try and bypass a Creator, dismissing the evidence and calling it "irritating" because it had "theological implications." Eddington stated, "Philosophically, the notion of a beginning . . . is repugnant to me. . . . I should like to find a genuine loophole." And as Vilenkin said, "With the proof now in place, cosmologists can no longer hide behind the possibility of a past-eternal universe. There is no escape, they have to face the problem of a cosmic beginning."

Those who hold to naturalistic explanations of the world will not even consider the thought of God getting in the way of their religious ideology and having anything to do with their lives. In other words, no matter what evidence may be staring them right in the face, they will simply look away and shield their eyes and ears to avoid the implications of there really being a Creator and Designer of the universe. An atheist will run with anything whatsoever to hide their eyes from the possibility of God – even scissors (sarcastic gasp!).

This hiding of eyes from God has even led to the harassment and firing of many well-meaning, esteemed college professors and others by presenting how bankrupt such atheistic theories are and even by doubting them. Dean Kenyon, Professor Emeritus of Biology at San Francisco State University, for instance, who we have recently quoted, was removed from the classroom due to merely presenting the facts about problems with Darwinism. Turek states:

> Many scientists who doubt Darwin and merely suggest intelligent design is possible have been the victims of ideological witch-hunts for questioning atheistic orthodoxy. They've been harassed, denounced, and fired. If you doubt the secular religion of materialistic science, you risk being charged with heresy! There is another reason why Darwinism and materialism turn out to be science stoppers. Dissent is not tolerated. The problems with the unguided molecules-to-man version of evolution are legion, so why is it taboo to question it? Why is Richard Dawkins calling anyone who disbelieves in evolution or believes in creation "ignorant, stupid or insane" or perhaps even "wicked?" Why is Lawrence Krauss calling an esteemed colleague a "moron" for correcting Krauss's obvious error? Why are intelligent design theorists harassed, denounced, and fired? Because nature is objective, but too often the people interpreting it are not. They have other agendas.[39]

Dawkins would also state, "You cannot be both sane and well educated and disbelieve in evolution. The evidence is so strong that any *sane, educated* person has got to believe in evolution" [emphasis added].⁴⁰ And evolutionary biologist Ernst Mayr stated in a 2000 issue of *Scientific American*, "No *educated* person any longer questions the validity of the so-called theory of evolution, which we now know to be a simple fact" [emphasis added].⁴¹

So, if Darwin's theory "is a fact," has evidence that is "at least as strong as the Holocaust," people are "ignorant, stupid, or insane" if they do not believe it, and "any sane, educated person has got to believe" in it, one must ask the obvious question: if macroevolution is supposed to be such an overwhelmingly true slam dunk of a theory, then where is *any* real evidence? If evolution is true, then why do textbooks have forged data? That would be like saying lizards are real and then showing pictures of Godzilla! The fact is that there is not any evidence; every point leads directly to a Creator and Designer.

HOW THE WORLD'S MOST NOTORIOUS ATHEIST CHANGED HIS MIND

Atheists: the only people dedicated to fighting what they swear does not exist. Neil deGrasse Tyson also makes the observation that the idea behind atheism is silly. After all, there is not a name for people who gather to talk about why they do not like golf or skiing (it can be supposed that those who talk about why they do not like golf could call themselves a*tee*ists, abiding to their *tee*ology, and those who talk about why they do not like skiing could call themselves a*skii*sts!).⁴²

Dawkins once said that, "Faith is the great cop-out, the great excuse to evade the need to think and evaluate evidence."⁴³ He adds: "Faith, being belief that is not based on evidence, is the principal vice of any religion."⁴⁴ Since atheism should instead be called *faith*eism, how ironic that he is ultimately talking about himself and his fellow atheistic colleagues who hold so blindly to the religion of atheism!

Dawkins is just plain wrong in saying you cannot be an educated believer in God. Jeffrey Burton Russell, historical and religious scholar and Professor Emeritus of History at the University of California, Santa Barbara writes, "If it were true that Christianity and science were incompatible, there would be no Christians who were respected scientists. . . . About forty percent of . . . scientists are practicing Christians, and many others are theists of other kinds. Fewer than thirty percent are atheists."[45] Max Planck, the Nobel Prize-winning physicist considered to be the founder of quantum theory, and one of the most important physicists of all time, wrote, "There can never be any real opposition between religion and science; for the one is the complement of the other. . . . And indeed it was not by accident that the greatest thinkers of all ages were deeply religious souls."[46]

This last-resort-tactic of name calling is a logical fallacy called an *ad hominem* attack; merely an attempt to belittle the messenger when they themselves cannot disprove the message of the messenger. After calling theists ignorant, stupid, insane, and so on, what are they going to say next, quotes from the movie *Monty Python and the Holy Grail*: "Your mother was a hamster and your father smelt of elderberries"? With all of the name calling flying around, you would think that saying there is zero evidence for evolution makes you out to be a murderer! If atheists could offer a naturalistic explanation they would, but they cannot defend their empty, bankrupt positions and instead resort foaming out the mouth while belittling those who dare even to mention God.

Atheism stops science. So why should this dangerous indoctrination of our youth persist; simply to protect the insecurities of childish, anti-scientific, anti-common sense atheists who cannot stand even to fathom the mere thought that there could possibly be a God? Note that *not one time* did we mention scriptures of any kind when discussing our science-based chapters;

so how could a single word be claimed as controversial and not fit for the classroom at any level? At this point, do you not think it is quite inconceivable that evolution is taught as not having any flaws whatsoever and intelligent design cannot even be mentioned?

Why do we not simply present all of the facts and let our youth decide? Even Darwin himself wrote that, "A fair result can be obtained only by fully stating and balancing the facts and arguments on both sides of each question."[47] A poll of college students shows that 84% believe, "Teachers and students should have the academic freedom to discuss both the strengths and weaknesses of evolution as a scientific theory."[48] Remember that Pew Research poll, where it stated 60% of Americas believe in evolution? What would that poll look like if those who took it had similar information presented to them such as that we have discussed? If both sides of the issue were presented and allowed the public to make their own conclusions that would be entirely reasonable. W.R. Thompson, a leading evolutionary scientist who was asked to write the Introduction to the 1956 edition of *On the Origin of the Species*, wrote of the success of hiding the fact that evolution is bankrupt:

> There is a great divergence of opinion among biologists . . . because the evidence is unsatisfactory. . . . It is therefore right and proper to draw the attention of the non-scientific public to the disagreements about evolution. But some recent remarks of evolutionists show that they think this unreasonable. This situation, where scientific men rally to the defense of a doctrine they are unable to define scientifically, much less demonstrate with scientific rigor, attempting to maintain its credit with the public by the suppression of criticism and the elimination of difficulties, is abnormal and unwise in science.[49]

However, even the hardest of hearts who have once been considered the most hardcore of all atheists can eventually throw their hands up, release their past philosophical bias and denial, and come to the firm conclusion that God is the only reasonable explanation. And some do so publically, a prime example of who many of you know well is Antony Flew.

Before Dawkins, Harris, Hawking, Hitchens, or any of the other well-known atheists came along into popularity, Flew was by far the most influential and famous intellectual atheist of the twentieth-century. Teaching at Oxford and other major universities, writing tens of books, and having penned the most widely reprinted philosophical publication of the last half of the twentieth-century, all while being a leading champion for atheism and a strong critic of creationism, it was very clear where Flew stood when it came to the existence of God. Then, something incredible happened.

In 2004 Flew made the headline-making announcement that he had converted from being a staunch atheist to a firm believer in God. Having defended atheism for so long, it was obvious that something significant had led him to this decision. In fact, in his book *There Is a God: How the World's Most Notorious Atheist Changed His Mind*, he affirms that it was his research into the modern-day scientific understanding of DNA which was a prominent game changer that he could not avoid. He writes: "DNA material has . . . shown, by the almost unbelievable complexity of the arrangements which are needed to produce life, that intelligence must have been involved in getting these extraordinarily diverse elements to work together. . . . The enormous complexity by which the results were achieved looks to me like the work of intelligence."[50] He further adds that his conclusions were based on a lifelong decision in philosophy to "follow the argument no matter where it leads."[51]

As Flew made it over the hump of atheism, DNA was not the only push but simply the *final* push that ultimately helped lead him to this conclusion. In fact, he gave credit also to the creation of the universe and its exquisite fine-tuning as further evidence for God. He adds:

I now believe that the universe was brought into existence by an infinite intelligence. I believe that this universe's intricate laws manifest what scientists have called the mind of God. I believe that life and reproduction originate in a Divine source. Why do I believe this, given that I expounded and defended atheism for more than half a century? The short answer is this: This is the world picture as I see it that has emerged from modern science.[52]

ANSWERING THE QUESTION OF OUR ORIGIN

Throughout all of our science-based chapters, whether the conclusions are from experts who are believers or from experts who are nonbelievers, it is a fully agreed upon fact that space, time, and matter all came into existence at the same moment a finite time ago. Further, it is a fully agreed upon fact from these experts that the universe itself, our galaxy, our solar system, and Earth is just right for life to both exist and to be sustained. And, speaking of life, mankind itself is the very best evidence of a master Designer at work. It is only by fully taking into account the topics we have discussed that one can reasonably reach the conclusion that God is the *only* explanation. Thus, from the telescope to the microscope, by taking these investigative, objective steps, we have taken Flew's reasonable approach of simply following the evidence wherever it leads.

Since it is reasonable to believe that God purposefully fine-tuned the universe at the moment of creation, and if He also purposefully fine-tuned our galaxy, our solar system, and Earth in a way that shows we are uniquely special to the point Davies says it is unavoidable that we are "truly meant to be here," then it would also be reasonable to believe that God also purposefully fine-tuned mankind to be unique creations as well. This, then, answers our first of four questions about life overall that everybody seeks: our origin is not from any evolutionary process but, instead, is from the purposeful hand of God. We are truly *meant* to be here.

Life is not just a cosmic mistake. Since God purposelessly created and fine tuned us and an intricate habitat for us to exist, it is highly implied from a scientific standpoint that God created and designed each and every one of us to have a unique purpose in life. This means that we are on the reasonably direct path of finding in this chapter the answer to our second of four questions: what is our purpose in life? Before we get there, though, let us first see how hopelessly depressing both our identity and "purpose" are within the worldview of atheism.

OUR IDENTITY AND OUR PURPOSE ACCORDING TO ATHEISM

It is impossible for there to be a creation without a Creator. But for the sake of discussion and pretending for a moment that it could be possible, the universe and everything in it would clearly be due to an accident that was never, ever meant to happen. This means that those who desperately hold to theories that attempt to do away with God can never escape the fact that the universe would have no end-goal for life and, thus, no room whatsoever for objective identity and purpose.

In regards to the first implication that our identity is dire within the worldview of atheism, arguably the most influential paleontologist of the twentieth century George Gaylord Simpson states of mankind that the universe "did not have him in mind."[53] Carl Sagan proclaimed mankind was simply an accident; "a mote of dust in the morning sky."[54] Hawking stated we are "such insignificant creatures."[55] And physicist Victor Stenger remarks, "Humanity developed by accident, contradicting . . . that humans are special."[56] Within the worldview of atheism, they are absolutely right. And the situation gets even worse.

In regards to the second implication that we have no purpose within the worldview of atheism, Dawkins states, "The universe that we observe has no design [and] no purpose."[57] Krauss, at the 2009 conference of the Atheist Alliance International, states: "We are more insignificant than we ever imagined. . . . We constitute a one percent bit of pollution in [the] universe. . . . We are completely irrelevant."[58] Says evolutionary biologist Jerry Coyne: "People like me don't worry about what it's all about in a cosmic sense, because we know it is not about anything. . . . Being an atheist means coming to grips with reality. . . . We're going to die as individuals, and the whole of humanity . . . is going to go extinct. . . . So you just deal with it."[59] Writer of literary classics such as "The Adventures of Tom Sawyer" and "The Adventures of Huckleberry Finn," Mark Twain wrote,

> A myriad of men are born, they labor and sweat and struggle for bread. They squabble and scold and fight. They scramble for little mean advantages over each other. Age creeps upon them. Infirmities follow. Shames and humiliations bring down their prides and their vanities. Those they love are taken from them, and the joy of life has turned to aching grief. The burden of pain and care and misery grows heavier year by year. At length, ambition is dead. Pride is dead. Vanity is dead. Longing for release is in their place. It comes at last – death, the only unpoisoned gift earth ever had for them. And they vanish from a world where they were of no consequence, where they achieved nothing, where they were a mistake and a failure and a foolishness, where they have left no sign that they have existed; a world which will lament them a day and

forget them forever. And then another myriad takes their place, and copies all they did, and goes along the same profitless road, and vanishes as they vanished, to make room for another, and another, and millions of myriads to follow the same arid path through the same desert and accomplish what the first myriad and all the myriads that came after it accomplished – nothing.[60]

William Provine, a scholar of the history of evolutionary biology and professor of biological sciences at Cornell University straightforwardly adds to this bleak, hopeless view of life in a debate with University of California, Berkeley's Phillip Johnson: "Let me summarize my views on . . . modern evolutionary biology . . . and I must say that these are basically Darwin's views. There are no gods, no purposes, no goal-directed forces of any kind. There is no life after death. . . . There is no . . . ultimate meaning to life."[61] And philosopher, Nobel laureate, and world-renowned atheist Bertrand Russell wrote succinctly of a life without God that it is "purposeless" and "void of meaning."[62] He continues:

> Man is the product of causes which had no prevision of the end they were achieving; that his origin, his growth, his hopes and fears, his loves and beliefs are but the outcome of accidental collocations of atoms; that no fire, no heroism, no intensity of thought and feeling, can preserve an individual life beyond the grave; that all the labors of the ages, all the devotion, all the inspiration, all the noonday brightness of human genius, are destined to extinction in the vast death of the solar system, and that the whole temple of man's achievement must inevitably be buried beneath the debris of a universe in ruins.[63]

Atheism says, because there is no such thing as a distinction for mankind, we are no more important than any other forms of life. Time plus chance plus matter does not equal objective identity. Therefore, says the atheist, our identities are nothing more than being mere accidental freaks of nature. As Jean-Paul Sartre, one of the twentieth century's foremost militant atheists, stated of a full realization of the implications that atheism has on our identity, "It was true, I had always realized it – I had not any "right" to exist at all. I had appeared by chance, I existed like a stone, a plant, a microbe. I could feel nothing to myself but an inconsequential buzzing. I was thinking . . . that here we are eating and drinking, to preserve our precious existence, and that there's nothing, nothing, absolutely no reason for existing."[64]

As far as purpose goes, time plus chance plus matter does not equal objective identity, either. While many of us may think we have purpose in our daily pursuits (e.g., a personal concern for healthy longevity, animal rights, alleviating pain and suffering, world travel, obtaining knowledge, making the environment cleaner, or believing we have a form of immortality that is based on being remembered by other people), how could anyone truly hope to believe there is actually any purpose to his or her lives that is not based merely on our subjective desires? In the end, our constant efforts to try and create purpose will make no difference whatsoever. Our families, friendships, careers, hobbies, interests, and any other means by which we fill our daily lives will all be in vain. For us to live believing otherwise would simply mean that we have been fooled by self-delusion – as Sagan puts it: "Our imagined self-importance."[65]

Is this a brutal view of mankind? Sure it is. But, as a list of quotes from atheists admitting these implications from their own mouths could continue for miles, it is entirely consistent with how atheists *must* view the world. And this honesty is the kind of information that is being taught, especially to our youth, in schools and throughout cultures all across the world.

With that in mind, no wonder that suicide rates are at an all-time high all across the board, rising by 24% from 1999 to 2014 alone![66] According to the Centers for Disease Control and Prevention (CDC), suicide rates have risen sharply to the point that they make up more deaths than motor vehicle accidents.[67] This is an extremely disheartening statistic because, on top of the fact there are a multitude of failed attempts, suicides themselves are "vastly underreported," says Julie Phillips, professor of sociology at Rutgers University.[68] While this is disheartening news of reality, is it really that surprising? After all, who could help but feel worthless and hopeless after hearing from supposedly trustworthy, respected scientists that we are accidents and our lives have zero real significance?

In the eyes of atheism, our lives are like a flame: they flicker for just a fleeting moment and then die forever. Even having the status of "pollution" in our dying universe goes away at the grave. It is clear that, when one tries to answer the questions of where we come from and why we are here without any reference to God, they have failed miserably in trying to kill God and, instead, have only killed themselves in the process.

CROSSING OPINION

Anyone who has spoiled rotten pets experiences something daily: once they cannot convince you to give them their fifth snack for the day, they put on the "look how cute I am" act to try and fool someone else in the house. While animals are simply satisfied with a full belly, mankind (while we do have fun at buffets!) has a unique perception of eternity and a desire for significance. Atheism cannot explain this nor satisfy our fervent desire to know the answers in regards to our identity and ultimate purpose in life. But God can.

Thus, before we can go into any detail about how mankind is viewed by God, we must first ask *which* God would have the purpose of creating and sustaining unique, complex life as the end-goal for the finely tuned universe. And at this point in our overall investigation, the information we have covered in both our previous chapter and this chapter simply adds to how vastly powerful, intelligent, purposeful, and personal God ultimately is. Therefore, our list of world religions remains at three: Christianity, Judaism, and Islam.

Though scientific evidence alone does not get us all the way to proving the existence of a particular God, it has, however, got us all the way to proving the existence of *some* God that is consistent with the Christian God. Let us, then, see what the God of the Bible, as opposed to atheism, has to say about our identity and ultimate purpose in life.

OUR IDENTITY ACCORDING TO THE GOD OF THE BIBLE

To find the answer to the question of why we are here, we do not have to search very far at all. In fact, the very first verse in the very first chapter of the Old Testament begins giving us insight: "In the beginning God created the heavens and the earth."[69] The chapter goes on to describe that God then created light, the sky, land, sea, vegetation, the Sun, the moon, the stars, marine animals, birds, land animals, and on the sixth day He created mankind; as God the Father communicated with Jesus and the Holy Spirit: "'Let us make mankind in our image, in our likeness, so that they may rule over the fish in the sea and the birds in the sky, over the livestock and all the wild animals, and over all the creatures that move along the ground.' So God created mankind in His own image, in the image of God He created them; male and female He created them.'"[70] From the very words of the God of the Bible we see that mankind is specially made in His image to be unlike any other forms of life.

This, then, fits perfectly with the scientific evidence that unavoidably shows the universe was created with specifically mankind in mind.

It should also be noted that the Bible states God created all life forms fully developed; there was absolutely no macroevolution involved in creation. Therefore, God's Word matches perfectly with how the fossil record shows the sudden appearance (the "Cambrian explosion") of remains from only fully developed life forms and gives zero hints of any macroevolution taking place whatsoever. With these facts in mind, we can now move on to an example of a verse which speaks volumes of God's intimacy towards mankind.

In chapter two of the book of Ephesians, we find that God uses a very interesting term when He describes mankind: "For we are His workmanship."[71] If you refer back to the original language that Ephesians was written (Greek), you can see that the word for *workmanship* directly translates to the word *poem*. This implies we can literally view our DNA as a vast, uniquely arranged poem within each and every of one our cells! Therefore, in God's view, this means that we are not only His creations, but are His epic, masterful poems which clearly display that He, as stated in the book of Acts, is the Author of the text of life Who took the intricate time and the heartfelt care to uniquely form and fine-tune us to be, well . . . us.[72]

This would be scientific confirmation of what King David expressed in the book of Psalms: "For you created my inmost being; you knit me together in my mother's womb. I praise you because I am fearfully and wonderfully made; your works are wonderful, I know that full well."[73] This is also confirmation of what God told the prophet Jeremiah: "Before I formed you in the womb I knew you."[74] To God, Who "knows the number of the stars and calls them each by their names" and Who takes daily care of even the birds, you are "far more valuable to Him than they are!"[75] How clearer could it possibly get that all human life, even *before* conception, is infinitely and uniquely precious in the eyes of God?

God values your existence as the individual person you are. No one is ever, ever an accident. Each and every one of us, regardless of our age, skin color, intelligence, or physical defects are a heartfelt poem of the Creator and Designer of the entire universe. How amazing is that? So for those of us who struggle every single day with problems of self-image, eating disorders, depression, anxiety attacks, and an overall feeling that you are completely worthless, it cannot be stressed enough that you, personally you, are the purposeful creation of the God who loves you more than any words or actions could ever hope to describe; Who wants you to know all that truly matters is what *He* thinks of you.

Like how all snowflakes are unique from one another, and how no one shares your unique fingerprints, no one else has *your* unique DNA. And in the same fashion that we are unique creations, God also has a purpose for each of our lives that only we can uniquely accomplish.

OUR PURPOSE ACCORDING TO THE GOD OF THE BIBLE

You hit the snooze button twelve times, finally stumble to the shower, have a few cups of what we think is fancy coffee while reading the newspaper, go to our dreaded job that is always too cold, do some errands mostly for cat food your cat thinks is fancy, make it home in time to choke down a burnt cheesy pita from the microwave, and then hopefully get eight hours of sleep in before doing it all again the next day. As we go round and round the hamster wheel of the monotonous daily grind, what ultimate purpose in life can be found?

Surely our purpose in life involves us getting that fat paycheck, having a model as a spouse, being on a billboard and on TV, having rock-hard abs, living in a gated community where every house down to its shrubbery looks

CROSSING OPINION

identically like an uninviting dentist's office, and simply living comfortably and being happy overall in our personal bubble – right? Oh, and how could we forget about having that perfect photo taken of our perfect, cookie-cutter family where we all feel the need to wear matching white and khaki clothes on the beach because that is just what everyone does on the "short-term, dopamine-driven feedback loops . . . destroying how society works" called social media.[76] All of that and more is exactly what is promoted all around us, but none of it can deliver us our ultimate purpose in life.

Take King Solomon of Israel, for instance. He had everything (and more) that anyone could ever hope to obtain. And in his lifetime of trying to seek-out what could bring him purpose (e.g., wealth, power, status, vocation, property, hobbies, entertainment, humanitarianism, relationships, and so on) he ultimately concluded that all of his pursuits were vanity. From the words of Solomon himself, as he reflected back on his past: "All that my eyes desired I did not refuse them. I did not withhold my heart from any pleasure. . . . But as I looked at everything I had worked so hard to accomplish, everything was meaningless, a chasing after the wind. There was nothing to be gained under the sun."[77] Most of us believe that if we had even close to what King Solomon had, *then* we could be content. But in reality, while we may find temporal contentment from these things, they turn out to be nothing but distractions that attempt to keep us from being alone with our thoughts, asking, "Is this all there is to life?"

We do not have to just take Solomon's word for it; look around at those who supposedly "have it all." When they get to what is considered the "top of the world," they are amazed to find out that, instead of an abundance of happiness, they only acquire an empty bag full of holes. This can clearly be seen in the lives of those who suddenly get rich, for instance, by means of inheritance, earning it through a rookie sports contract, or winning it in a state lottery. As comedian Rodney Dangerfield told Johnny Carson when asked if his wealth made him happier, "Money don't mean nothin.' You're the same guy, you know? . . . Suddenly, I'm depressed."[78] In fact, it is far too common that, after experiencing what they thought would finally satisfy their lives failed and gave them a punch-in-the-gut realization that psychologists term the *Sudden Acquired Wealth Syndrome*, their lives go on a downward spiral of substance abuse and, much too frequently, suicide.

Ladies, Solomon had all of the jewels that the world could offer and had so much gold that he himself caused silver to devalue! Fellas, Solomon also had 700 wives and 300 mistresses! The Bible clearly teaches that nothing in this world apart from God will ever take you one step closer to accomplishing the purpose in life for which you were created and designed. The Apostle Paul was very well-off himself before becoming a Christian. He learned this the hard way, stating of his possessions and status: "I consider them *garbage*, that I may gain Christ" [emphasis added].[79]

After all, if we were purposefully created and designed, then only the Creator and Designer knows exactly for what purpose. Think of it like a painting that everyone has an opinion about, yet the painter meant for it to portray a specific metaphor. It does not matter what the opinions may be because there is only one truth as to what the painter intended. In the case of mankind being poems, while many have their own opinions about the matter, it does not really matter because there is a truth as to what the Creator and Designer intended in regards to our ultimate purpose in life.

This is a reminder of a TV commercial that aired a few years back about a man who has just finished a long, treacherous journey, topping a snow-covered mountain to visit a hermit-guru. "You may ask one question," says the guru. After a short pause for dramatic effect, the man asks, "What tire category should I choose to get the most comfortable ride?"[80] It was a funny commercial, because you expect a much more serious question to be asked. But, in reality, asking that question is the same as asking someone about our ultimate purpose in life. It would just be their subjective opinion.

We all continually long for something more than mere material existence. In our hearts, we are well aware that there just has to be more to life than the here-and-now. This is precisely because it is the truth! God the Father, as Solomon wrote, "has set eternity in the human heart."[81] It makes perfect sense, then, why nothing of Earth can bring us ultimate purpose; Earth was never meant to be our permanent home. Therefore, being found pertaining to aspects that have an eternal scope rather than merely temporal, Jesus summarizes into two aspects exactly why we were created: "Love the Lord your God with all your heart, with all your soul, and with all your mind. This is the greatest and most important commandment. The second is like it: love your neighbor as yourself."[82]

In regards to the first aspect, our purpose cannot be accomplished simply by accepting Jesus as the risen Savior, but also by trusting that His words have not only His but also our best, eternal interests in mind. When we slowly but surely begin to do that – seek to learn about Him, spend intimate time with Him in His Word, have a steady prayer life, and grasp that He will direct our paths and provide us with everything that we will ever need, as His disciples, we will come to find that His promises are immensely fulfilling. As Jesus says, "Come to Me, all of you who are weary and burdened, and I will give you rest. Take my yoke upon you and learn from Me, for I am gentle and humble in heart, and you will find rest for your souls."[83] The fourth-century philosopher, Augustine, was right when he wisely observed, "Our hearts are restless, until they can find rest in you."[84]

The second aspect is later reiterated in the book of Philippians, "Do nothing out of selfish ambition or vain conceit, but in humility consider others as more important than yourselves. Each of you should look not only to your own interests but also to the interests of others."[85] In other words, it is not enough for we ourselves to find this rest in God; we must tell others about how to find it as well.

This is a reminder of a parabolic song that author and speaker Ravi Zacharias once highlighted in a speech. Called "Desert Pete" by The Kingston Trio:

> It is about a man going through the desert, and he has got bottles of water all over strapped to him. But he keeps drinking and drinking and drinking until the water is gone. . . . He suddenly sees a pump. And he sees a tin can wrapped around it. And inside the tin can a note [saying], "Dear traveler, do not despair, there is plenty of water . . . Just follow the directions. Borough down about a foot deep into the sand . . . and you will find a bottle of water. It should be full. . . . Do not drink it, because you've already tried to work the pump and the pump was dry. Pour the water gently into the cylinder of the pump and keep priming it and the suction system will start working. It will bring out all of the water you . . . need. Refill the bottles that you have got and do not forget to fill up that one bottle for the person to pass by next."[86]

Zacharias continues: "It is a parable of life. You are walking through a desert; your choice is to consume your life upon yourself and soon be empty again or to put your hands into the hands of the living God who gives you that living water so that you will not thirst again. And when you find that living water, you become an instrument . . . to give that nourishment to everyone else who passes by."

We may worry about things such as animal rights and the environment. We may desire things like world travel and obtaining knowledge. We may work at jobs that seem so mundane and those that we genuinely despise but know they simply bring home a paycheck for our families. Regardless of how our days are filled, with the scientific evidence reviewed and the answers from the God of the Bible in mind, the mystery and misery of simply not knowing as to why we are here in the first place are gone. That itself is comforting to the highest degree.

Not only is our ultimate purpose in life to know God, but also to make Him known; telling everyone about His resurrection and what it means eternally for them and their families. To make Him known, everybody on Earth can accomplish that purpose in a vastly unique way because we all have unique gifts and, most importantly, unique personalities that are embedded deep within our unique DNA. Thus, starting in our unique place within our own families and branching out, no matter if you are the owner of a body shop or a mechanic shop, an assistant for an eye doctor, a carpenter, a massage therapist, a writer, or a precious child who wants to become an engineer, an architect, or a doctor to help other people, we all can come together and uniquely let the world know, as Jesus says, "Whoever believes in me . . . out of their heart will flow rivers of living water."[87]

FROM THE TELESCOPE TO THE MICROSCOPE

We can be rest assured that we are not accidental freaks of nature. Our identity and purpose as God describes them is not an opinion; that is where the historical evidence and scientific evidence clearly leads.

Not only do we have eternity set in our hearts to let us know there must be something beyond life on Earth, but we also know in our hearts that, just by taking a look at and sensing the world around us, there must be a God. As the book of Romans says, "From the creation of the world, God's invisible qualities – His eternal power and divine nature – have been clearly observed in what He made. As a result, people have no excuse for not knowing God."[88]

DOES MANKIND SHOW SIGNS OF DESIGN? (PART 2)

While it may take many of us a while to finally surrender and throw our hands up to trying to find identity and purpose through worldly pursuits, there is absolutely nobody who can honestly say they do not know there is a God. This is becoming *even more* of an obvious fact as our scientific advances continue and mankind uncovers and learns further details about God's incredible creation. Take, for instance, a story that Zacharias once shared about physician and geneticist Francis Collins while they were both guest speakers at Johns Hopkins University:

> Before I spoke, [Francis Collins] spoke. And he showed a slide on the screen. The left side of the screen was exposed; the right side covered. And he showed a magnificent stained glass window [with] thousands of pieces in this brilliant design. . . . Then he uncovered the right side to show something even more spectacular. He said, "Do you know what you are looking at now? . . . A vertical section of the human DNA." The audience just gasped at it. . . . He did not say anything. He took a guitar and sang after that. Brilliant response. . . . It was only worship that could express at that point.[89]

We can all be wonderstruck at creation. Says author Eric Metaxas, in his aptly titled book *Miracles*, "Reason and science compel us to see what previous generations could not: that our existence is an outrageous and astonishing miracle. . . . It is something to which the most truly human response is some combination of terror and wonder, of ancient awe and childhood joy."[90] With combined observations from the farthest reaches of the telescope all the way down to the farthest reaches of the microscope, we can praise Him: "You are the Maker, Creator, Master Designer of Heaven and Earth. You saw the future and made me. You had a plan before my birth. So shape my life by Your design. You are the Maker, Creator, Master Designer of Heaven and Earth."[91]

6

MORALITY AND CONSCIOUSNESS

(Part 1)

Whether or not you accept that our identity and purpose as seen through the eyes of the God of the Bible is true, it is certainly easy for us all to agree that to love your neighbor as yourself is always better than doing wrong towards one another. But think about that observation for a moment; just *why* exactly is it that each and every one of us feels this strong moral obligation that we should do right rather than wrong?

As we continue our overall investigation, now by discussing the topic of ethics (i.e., the study of the general nature of morals and of the specific moral choices to be made by a person), we move our way into finding the answer to our investigation's third question: "How should we live?" As we have done in the science-based chapters, we must split our discussion into three flowing premises – this time in what is referred to as the *Moral Argument*:

1. Every law has a lawgiver.
2. There is an objective moral law.
3. Therefore, there is an objective moral lawgiver.

PREMISE 1:
EVERY LAW HAS A LAW GIVER

This premise is undeniably true. For example, we know that every watch cannot exist without there first being a *watchmaker*, that every command cannot be made without there first being a *commander*, that every prescription cannot be made without a *prescriber*. In the same way, there can be no such thing as a law without there first being a *lawgiver* who makes it. While this first premise is undeniable (and justifies such a short discussion on it!), our second premise, on the other hand, will take a considerably longer amount of time to cover the points that must be made.

PREMISE 2:
THERE IS AN OBJECTIVE MORAL LAW

The cultural divide goes against our second premise by considering morality to be subjective rather than objective. Similar to what we discussed in our first chapter about, say, preferences in ice cream flavors, according to polling done in 2016 in the U.S. by The Barna Group, 74% of those between ages 18 and 34 (compared to 48% of older generations) seem to think that moral views are something which may be "true for you but not true for me."[1]

But does this culturally dominant philosophy that moral views must be seen through a subjective lens actually correspond with reality? Well, we must first ask ourselves to imagine what the world would look like if morality were subjective and what would follow if we were to embrace and carry out that moral philosophy to its conclusions.

We would find ourselves in a world where we had absolutely no ground by which we could stand to label *anything* said or done as being objectively right or as being objectively wrong. Therefore we could never, for instance, condemn murder and rape. After all, while they may not be "true for you," such actions would simply be personal preferences that were morally "true" for those that decided on committing them – like an ice cream flavor preference! Further, we could never praise actions such as kindness and humility. After all, who could say being kind and humble was morally right compared to murder and rape?

If morality were truly a matter of preference, we could never justify a reason to argue that there was an actual moral difference between love and hate, freedom and slavery, or life and murder. In short, we could not condemn terrorists such as Al-Qaeda, nor praise conveyors of peace such as Mother Teresa, or vice-versa, since there would no longer be any binding moral distinctions. Says Francis J. Beckwith, professor of philosophy at Baylor University, "The moral relativist has a difficult time explaining moral progress, moral reformation, and clear-cut cases of moral saints and moral devils."[2] Thus, in any attempt to pass a moral judgment onto something we did not agree with, we would ultimately be left with conflicting *opinions* where neither view held any more valid weight than another person's views.

The serial rapist, pedophile, necrophiliac, and murderer Ted Bundy is an example of someone who fully embraced this philosophy of subjective morality and lived it out to its conclusions. In a recording between him and one of his many victims before he raped and murdered her, Bundy stated,

> I learned that all moral judgments are "value judgments," that all value judgments are subjective, and that none can be proved either "right" or "wrong." I even read somewhere that the Chief Justice of the United States had written that the American Constitution expressed nothing more than collective value judgments. Believe it or not, I figured out for myself – what apparently the Chief Justice

could not figure out for himself – that if the rationality of one value judgment was zero, multiplying it by millions would not make it one whit more rational. Nor is there any "reason" to obey the law for anyone, like myself, who has the boldness and daring – the strength of character – to throw off its shackles. . . . I discovered that to become truly free, truly unfettered, I had to become truly uninhabited. And I quickly discovered that the greatest obstacle to my freedom, the greatest block and limitation to it, consists in the insupportable "value judgment" that I was bound to respect the rights of others. I asked myself, who were these "others"? Other human beings, with human rights? Why is it more wrong to kill a human animal than any other animal, a pig or a sheep or a steer? Is your life more than a hog's life to a hog? Why should I be willing to sacrifice my pleasure more for the one than for the other? . . . Let me assure you, my dear young lady, that there is absolutely no comparison between the pleasure that I might take in eating ham and the pleasure I anticipate in raping and murdering you. That is the honest conclusion to which my education has led me.[3]

Of course, Bundy soon felt the repercussions of his moral philosophy, being incarcerated, receiving two death sentences, and finally being executed by means of Florida's electric chair in 1989. Polly Nelson, a member of Bundy's defense team to whom he openly confessed as being the culprit behind the gruesome rape, murder, and dismemberment of over one-hundred men and women, said of Bundy that he "was the very definition of heartless evil."[4] Whereas a monster like Bundy tried to justify his horrifying actions with moral subjectivism, we all internally understand there is, in fact, *a real moral distinction* between right and wrong in the world.

As an example, we all grasp the fact that an act such as slavery is morally wrong. If someone were to say, "If you do not like slavery, then just do not own a slave," we would have every right to be outraged at that person's logic which was derived from having embraced the philosophy that morality is merely subjective. We know that slavery is wrong, not because the vast majority of people do not find it to be an act of their liking, but because it is *objectively* wrong to degrade and enslave another person! However, if one were to hold to the view that morality is subjective, by what basis could one ever hope to condemn slavery as actually being wrong? After all, slavery would just be a person's preference. So who would someone be to push their subjective preference towards slavery onto someone else?

Thus, while most people *think* they believe morality is subjective, the vast majority do not actually prescribe to that worldview. They could easily be shown that their truly held positions are the exact opposite, and that is a main point to this discussion: we *all* know morality is not based on subjective preferences. Nevertheless, the worldview of moral subjectivism itself still needs to be further dismantled if we are to find thoroughly reasoned answers for our premises.

OBJECTION 1: TRUTH CHANGES OVER TIME

Hands down, the most common objection raised to argue for moral subjectivism is that truth changes over time (i.e., "There were views in the past which are not morally true for people today, so moral truth is subjective"). To someone who raises this objection, states Norman Geisler and Frank Turek:

> They confuse what *is* with what *ought* to be. What people *do* is subject to change, but what they *ought* to do is not. . . . For example, when discussing a moral topic like premarital sex or cohabitation, you often

hear people in support of it say something like, "Get with it, this is the twenty-first century!" as if current behaviors dictate what's right and wrong. To illustrate the absurdity of [this subjective] reasoning, you need only to turn the discussion to a more serious moral issue like murder, which also occurs much more frequently in America today than it did fifty years ago. How many [who believe morality is subjective] would speak in support of murder by asking us to "Get with it, this is the twenty-first century!"? That's where their reasoning takes them when they confuse what people do with what they ought to do.[5]

Time-based change to moral truth is the same approach taken by people when they commonly state, "We used to believe Earth was flat, but now we know that it is round. See, truth changes over time!" The obvious problem behind that view is the failure to understand the difference between *belief* and *truth*. While some people in the distant past held to the flat-Earth view (though, not many, because all you had to do to find the truth was view a lunar eclipse), common sense tells all of us that Earth has *always* been round. It would not have mattered if every single person believed Earth was flat, the truth was always there. Personal beliefs about Earth's shape changed, but the unchanging *truth* was discovered thanks to a better scientific understanding. In the exact same way, what people may *do* in regards to morality may change, but what we *ought* to do does not change; subjective opinions may vary but objective truth never will. Again, this can be seen with slavery. While it once was accepted by groups of people in the U.S., for instance, the truth has always been that slavery is wrong. Truth cannot change over time because truth, by definition, is *unchanging*.

OBJECTION 2: CULTURES SHOW SOME SIGNS OF DIFFERING VIEWS ON MORALITY

The second most common objection raised among those who hold to moral subjectivism is the view that, since there are cultures throughout the world that hold some differing moral beliefs, this is proof that morality is subjective. But, just as with the first objection, the logic behind this objection is also seriously flawed and can easily be refuted in many ways.

Beckwith refers to an excellent example of a differing view between India and the U.S. to highlight the faulty logic of this objection.[6] He rightly states that, while most Americans eat meat that from cows, the vast majority of people in India do not and, instead, deeply revere them as being sacred. Now, at first glance, this seems like an obvious moral difference between the core values of those in India and the core values of those in the U.S. But that is not the case. The reason why the vast majority of people in India do not eat meat from cows has absolutely nothing to do with moral values; it is due to their religious belief that cows may contain the reincarnated souls of their deceased loved ones and fellow man. Obviously, the vast majority of Americans do not hold to this religious belief, and beef is a significant part of what many of our meals are based around. Therefore, what appears to be a moral difference is actually a moral agreement; while each culture may have different beliefs towards the sacredness of cows and whether or not they contain the souls of reincarnated humans, the real matter boils down to the fact that both cultures know it is objectively wrong to eat Grandma! Cultural differences in morality are simply a perception problem and not a problem of objective facts. This is the equivalent to different cultures driving on different sides of the road – while some permit driving on the left and others permit driving on the right, no culture says we can drive on any side we prefer, weaving and crashing into one another for the fun of it!

STEALING DONUTS

There is no such thing as a subjective moral preference. There are acts in the world which have always been and will always be objectively wrong for everyone – such as murder, rape, slavery, child abuse, theft, and racial discrimination – and there are acts which are objectively right for everyone – such as love, kindness, charity, kindness, humility, and justice. The reason being? It is inescapable that we all have a moral law written on our hearts that, while we may not listen to it from time to time, makes the moral rightness and wrongness of actions self-evident facts about reality to all people, at all times, and in all places. Sean McDowell writes:

> Moral choices are personal in the same way as when you take a science test: you take the test and you are given an individual grade. There is a right answer to each question . . . you may get it right, or you may get it wrong. But your mere choosing does not make your answer right; the correct answer exists independently of your choosing it. . . . We do not invent morality, any more than we invent the length of a day. We cannot make lying right, and we cannot make murder good. We are not free to create our own values, and we are not free to create our own truths. We are free to reject truth, just as we are free to obey or disobey moral laws. Similarly, we do not invent the law of gravity, but we are free to disregard it, to jump off a building and believe we can fly. But our mere disregard for the truth does nothing to change truth itself. We do not *create* truth, we *discover* it.[7]

Therefore, by appealing to the *unchanging* standard of the moral law, every person on Earth can transcend the limits of mere opinions of individuals to, instead, objectively identify when something is either morally right or morally wrong. This is how we can ultimately judge the actions of, say, Mother Teresa and those of Al-Qaeda. C.S. Lewis stated well:

> The moment you say that one set of moral ideas can be better than another, you are, in fact, measuring them both by a standard, saying that one of them conforms to that standard more nearly than the other. But the standard that measures two things is something different from either. You are, in fact, comparing them both with some Real Morality, admitting that there is such a thing as a real Right, independent of what people think.[8]

And, yes, even the Nazis or a homegrown serial killer like Ted Bundy knew well and good that their heinous crimes were morally wrong before ignoring that inner knowledge. This is evident because they went through a process of dehumanizing their victims in an attempt to justify their crimes.

Even after showing the faulty logic behind each of these common objections to an objective standard of morality, what if someone *still* concludes that morality is merely subjective? Well, the way you can quickly find out what another person truly believes about morality has nothing to do with what they think, what they say, or even with their actions; it is with their *reactions*. One way to do this is by figuring out something they care about, tell them that it can be treated subjectively, and then sit back for the show. Take this true story (about a fake story to make a point) told by philosopher J.P. Moreland as a prime example:

> Years ago I met a young man who claimed to [believe morality was subjective].... I found out that he cared deeply for the environment. I then told him that four of my buddies and I had a monthly routine:

We would each contribute 50 dollars to a [pool of bets], buy a 100-gallon vat of sulfuric acid, drive to a local lake, dump in the acid, and see how many dead fish floated to the surface. The person whose guess was closest to the number of dead fish won... Well, you could see the blood vessels popping on his neck. He was enraged. I noted that from his body language, it seemed that he thought our monthly practice was, well, *wrong*.[9]

Another way to personally put someone to the reaction test is by briefly treating them unfairly and then seeing what happens. Take this next story, again by Moreland, as an example:

One afternoon . . . at the University of Vermont [a] student began to espouse . . . "Whatever is true for you is true for you and whatever is true for me is true for me. If something works for you because you believe it, that's great. But no one should force his or her views on other people since everything is [subjective]." . . . I thanked the student for his time and began to leave . . . On the way out, I picked up his small stereo and started out the door with it. "Hey, what are you doing?" he shouted. . . . "You can't do that," he gushed. "Well .. maybe you meant to say [you] ought not do that because you are stealing my stereo. Of course, I know from our previous conversation that this isn't what you mean. I happen to think it's permissible to steal stereos . . . Now I would never try to force you to accept my moral beliefs in this regard because, as you said, everything is [subjective] and we shouldn't force our ideas on others. But surely you're not going to force on me your belief that it's wrong to steal your stereo."[10]

MORALITY AND CONSCIOUSNESS (PART 1)

Try cutting in line in front of someone who believes morality is subjective and see what happens. Further, try breaking a promise, not fulfilling a contractual obligation, or try and steal their glazed donut. Although these people may *think* they believe morality is based on preferences as they give lip service to their position from a safe distance away, once it is revealed how they react when it is personally inconvenient, they quickly show their inconsistencies with living out the worldview.

This is a reminder of a particular comic strip of Calvin and Hobbes. Calvin, an adventurous six-year-old boy says to Hobbes, his real-only-to-him stuffed tiger, "'I don't believe in ethics anymore. As far as I'm concerned, the ends justify the means. Get what you can while the getting's good – that's what I say! Might makes right! The winners write the history books! It is a dog-eat-dog world, so I'll do whatever I have to, and let others argue about whether it is "right" or not.'" At that time, Hobbes pushes Calvin in the mud. Shocked and angry that he had just been treated unfairly, Calvin replies: "Heyy! Why'd you do that?!? . . . I did not mean for everyone, you Dolt! Just me!"[11]

Every single time someone reacts that something is wrong or unfair, they are affirming the existence of objective morality. After all, if everything is subjective, then by what binding basis could we ever get upset at anyone for treating us in similar ways? Nothing could ever truly be wrong or unfair and, if you are going to live by the worldview of moral subjectivism, you would simply have to allow someone to pour acid in ponds and, to steal your treasured items, and so on. That worldview is undeniably unlivable.

While we may not listen sometimes, *we all know* how to discern right from wrong. No matter where your location is on Earth, there is an objective moral law that is self-evident, that is true for everyone, and from which we cannot escape. So the question before us now is not whether there *is* an objective moral law, but *from where* it comes from.

THE SOCIAL CONTRACT THEORY

The first of three "candidates" that gets presented in an attempt to provide a foundation for objective morality is referred to as the *social contract theory*. This popular suggestion presents the claim that objective morality originates from the majority-rule agreement within each society from all around the world. Thus, what each society decides as being morally acceptable and morally repulsive is deemed as part of its unique, objective moral code. Again, according to polling done in 2016 in the U.S. by The Barna Group, this is the belief held by 70% of those between ages 18 and 34, compared to 62% of older generations.[12]

It should be noted that Richard Dawkins, who as of recently has come to admit that he believes in objective morality, is a prominent advocate of this theory. In his book *A Devil's Chaplain*, he clearly presents his supporting position by writing that, "Deciding what is ethical . . . is a matter for individuals and for society."[13] In his book *The God Delusion*, he describes that the social contract is theorized as an effort for moral improvement; in some cases by enacting so-called progressive legislation. He then refers to the continuous change in consensus in regards to morality with the German term *Zeitgeist*, meaning "spirit of the age": "Some of us lag behind the advancing wave of the changing moral *Zeitgeist* and some of us are slightly ahead. . . . The whole wave keeps moving. . . . Of course, the advance is not a smooth incline, but a meandering sawtooth. . . . But over the longer timescale, the progressive trend is unmistakable and it will continue."[14]

In an interview from *byFaith* magazine, when asked what defines morality, Dawkins continued, "Moral philosophic reasoning and a shifting zeitgeist. We live in a society in which, nowadays, slavery is abominated, women are respected, children cannot be abused—all of which is different from previous centuries. . . . If you travel anywhere in the Western world, you find a consensus of opinion which is recognizably different from what it was only a matter of a decade or two ago."[15]

The first problem with this theory is obvious: if each society can simply "vote on" what they think is morally right and wrong at any given time, that "truth" can change many times. In claiming that societies are the source for objective morality, this is an attempt for those who hold this position to have their cake and eat it at the same time. It simply cannot be said that societies form an *unchanging* moral code when at the same time the majority-rule consensus of societies are, by definition, meant to be in a continual process of *change* over time in an effort for moral improvement! This theory, then, is nothing more than a glorified form of moral subjectivism that moves the difference in opinion from being between two or more people to being between two or more societies.

Second, if societies are changing their views to reach moral improvement, this means that there must be an objective moral law that we all know must be reached. So, as it is something outside of majority-rules opinion, a social contract does not form this moral law.

Third, shared opinion, no matter how decisive, does not form objective truth. Supposedly creating objective truths based on opinion is like the illustration we discussed in chapter one about the elementary school show-and-tell: you cannot decide the gender of a puppy by voting!

Fourth, if objective right and wrong are decided merely by the majority-rule of each society, then by that logic it would always be morally wrong for someone to speak out against that shared consensus. Therefore, every minority position, even things such as seeking to end slavery and segregation or any examples of moral improvement that is contrary to the prevailing currents within a given society, would be immoral by definition and would cause the very act of moral reform to be blatantly impossible. In that case, virtuous reformers such as Jesus, Gandhi, and Martin Luther King Jr. would all be characterized as immoral.

Fifth, just because a value is shared does not somehow automatically make it morally right. Again, just think about slavery; societies for most of human history have had a shared view that people could enslave other people, but that shared opinion did not make slavery morally right. Or consider the immensely sickening acts that were done by the Nazis under the leadership of the dictator Adolf Hitler; just because the majority of the German people at that time supported the Nazi Party, the majority-rules opinion did not make those acts morally right. This leads us to the sixth glaring problem.

If the ever-changing majority-rule within each society is the source of morality, then how could we ever hope to have the basis to objectively judge the actions of other societies as being objectively wrong when we disagree? While we may not *like* certain actions, that would just be our shared opinion competing against their shared opinion.

When two or more individuals believe that morality is merely subjective, and their differing moral views clash, there is no final arbiter that is above the two opinions saying which view is correct. In the *exact same way*, when the shared opinions of two or more societies clash with one another, there is no arbiter above them either. In other words, how could we say what the likes of Hitler, Joseph Stalin, or Mao Zedong (who between them were responsible for the deaths of well over an estimated 100 *million* people) were wrong when, in fact, the majority of those who they ruled over supported them? Dawkins was asked this very question: "Absolutely fascinating. What's to prevent us from saying Hitler was not right? I mean, that is a genuinely difficult question."[16]

Absolutely *ridiculous* is more like it! Not only did Hitler and the Nazis initiate World War II, and not only did they cause the mass extermination of at least thirteen and a half million Jews, Russians, Poles, Catholic priests, Jehovah's Witnesses, effeminate homosexuals, prisoners of war, physically and mentally handicapped, and others of all ages during the Holocaust, they conducted excruciatingly painful and lethal experiments on the concentration camp prisoners. These included, but were not limited to, freezing people alive in order to find an effective treatment for hypothermia, forcing people to drink seawater in order to test various methods of making it safe to drink, bone-grafting experiments, testing pharmaceuticals in dangerous and lethal ways, being subjected to chemicals such as phosgene and mustard gas in order to test possible antidotes, sterilization experiments on young girls, injecting sodium hydroxide into the wombs of young girls, having healthy limbs amputated, shock experiments, excessive blood transfers in order to test if it would change the subjects in any way, draining lethal amounts of blood, testing what kind of offspring would come from brother and sister pairs and other forms of incest, children having chemicals injected into their eyes in order to see if they would change color, children being injected with lethal germs to see how their bodies would react before a long and agonizing death, sewing the bodies of twins together for the fun of making them conjoined, injecting the hearts of twins with chloroform, and being subjected to the removal of their internal organs. There is no doubt the known outcome of these and other experiments, as the laboratories were built next to crematoriums. On top of all of this, countless were buried alive and starved to death, and the young boys would be strangled, crushed and gnawed to death by their attackers all while being brutally raped.

It is mind-blowing to think how someone with such obvious intelligence as Dawkins would state it is a "genuinely difficult question" whether or not what Hitler and the Nazis did was morally right or morally wrong. But his confession that societies cannot condemn other societies for what they find as morally wrong gives you a taste of what one is forced to believe to consistently maintain the social contract theory and, thus, moral subjectivism. Further, another similar confession was made in a debate between William Lane Craig and atheist physicist Bernard Leikind:

Craig – I'd like to know, on an atheistic, naturalistic worldview . . . why is our set of values which abhor slavery superior to any other cultures which adheres to slavery? Why characterize this as a moral improvement rather than just a difference?

Leikind – The reason I think it's a moral improvement is that all of us have things to offer, and slavery denies large numbers of people the chance to achieve everything they have to offer to us.

Craig - Why are you imposing our values on [a society that adheres to slavery]?

Leikind – Oh, I'm not criticizing them for having slaves. That's their society. The point I am making is that there is no place where it's written in stone, "Here are the moral values by which we should all live for all time."

Craig – So, you cannot really condemn slavery on an atheistic, naturalistic worldview, can you?

Leikind – No, I do. I think slavery is a bad thing.

Craig – But is not that just an expression of your own socio-cultural situation that you were born in?

Leikind – That's right.

Craig – So it doesn't have any objective sort of validity.

Leikind – No. It comes from our society. . . . That's the way morals are created. . . . And I would say, if you believe that you have some set of objective moral values, I would say, "Well, why should I believe that you have them?"

Craig – You don't think that you can tell that we ought to love a child rather than torture and sexually abuse a child?

Leikind – I think that's a good idea to love a child.

Craig – But one is not morally different from the other?

Leikind – No, I think that they're morally different.

Craig – On what basis do you make that value judgment?

Leikind – I think it's bad to inflict suffering and harm on other people

Craig – Why is that wrong on a naturalistic worldview? The Nazis thought it was alright to do that to Jews.

Leikind – That's because morals are created by societies.

Craig – On the one hand, you want to make value judgments like… slavery was *abhorrent*, we have *improved* morally over this other culture, the Nazis were *wrong*. And, yet, on the other hand, out of the other side of your mouth, you're affirming moral relativism. You have no transcendent anchor for these values and, hence, you're lost in a sea of socio-cultural relativism.

Leikind – You're correct.[17]

Just like Dawkins, Leikind is suppressing the truth that the social contract theory is just a bunch of bologna. To hit the point home, the remaining example is from a debate between Frank Turek and president of the American Atheists from 2010 to 2018, David Silverman:

Silverman – There is no objective moral standard. We are responsible for our own actions.

Turek – Responsible to who?

Silverman – To ourselves and to our society.

Turek – Which society? Mother Teresa's or Hitler's?

Silverman – The society in which we live. Yes, this is not an easy question.

Turek – So at Nuremberg then we really had no right to convict the Nazis for obeying their government.

Silverman – We as a world society judge our criminals, and we judge them as we see fit.

. . .

Turek – So you're saying we just judge them based on our preference…

Silverman – Yes. It's an opinion.

Turek – Well, if it's just an opinion . . . if there is no objective morality . . . we have no real way to condemn the Nazis for what they did.

Silverman – The hard answer is you're correct. The hard answer is it is a matter of opinion.[18]

Of course, since Silverman admitted that the social contract theory is not a foundation for objective morality, "Condemning them as a society" is just another way of saying, "We may not like the actions of the Nazis, but it is just our opinion against theirs." Turek continues:

> That's why when [Silverman] appealed to society as his moral standard, I asked him, "Which society? Mother Teresa's or Hitler's?" "Society'" is just a collection of humans, and one collection may assert different moral positions than others, which is why we had World War II in the first place! . . . [Silverman] acknowledged it was a "hard answer" to say that the Nazis were not really wrong. But it's only hard because he's suppressing his most basic moral intuitions. He's refusing to call evil what it's in order to maintain his atheism. Objective moral values are not hard to know. For some, they are just hard to accept.

Stating that morality is subjective, and that we can still somehow objectively condemn other societies for what their shared opinion says is acceptable, is yet another attempt to have cake and eat it at the same time. Add this to the fact that Silverman was born into a Jewish family himself, and you can see just how ridiculous the extent is to which some will go to consistently maintain the position that morality is created by societies.

To say that societies of the world can simply decide for themselves what is morally right is a mere extension of the non-binding view, "That may be true for you but not for me." This view plagues the minds of young people today. To see a prime example of this worldview in action, let us take a stroll back to an instance when the social contract theory was famously raised and directly tested in the court of law during World War II.

Held in the city of Nuremberg, Germany, the Nuremberg trials were a series of thirteen military tribunals made by the World Court of the Allied forces between 1945 and 1949 for the purpose of ultimately prosecuting Hitler's Nazi war criminals for the extensive list of monstrous crimes against humanity. During their defense, the lawyers for the Nazis argued that nobody from another society (e.g., the U.S., Britain, and so on) could come in and judge their actions when they were morally acceptable to a majority of shared opinion in the nation of Germany at the time of the war. (It should be noted that hardly any of the general public in Germany knew what was actually going on at concentration camps, as video shows people taking tours once the war was over, smiling and waving upon going in and puking and crying uncontrollably upon leaving). Noted lawyer, professor, and author John Warwick Montgomery describes their argument: "The most telling defense offered by the accused was that they had simply followed orders or made decisions within the framework of their own legal system, in complete consistency with it, and that they, therefore, could not rightly be condemned because they deviated from the alien value system of their conquerors."[19]

Judging and prosecuting the Nazis was never a dilemma, as the court saw right through the defense's argument that morality is based from society to society. The World Court ultimately ruled that we all know there is a higher morality that is above and beyond individual and societal beliefs and that the Nazis simply deviated from what they internally knew to be morally right from morally wrong. Appointed by President Harry S. Truman as the chief prosecutor representing the U.S., Supreme Court Justice Robert H. Jackson phrased this internal knowledge as "the law above the law." In the end, justice was served and the Nuremberg trials became regarded as a crucial precedent for the rulings of later hearings of genocide and other crimes against humanity.

Merely scratching the surface of the vast multitude of problems that it is faced with, the social contract theory *clearly* is not the objective standard that tells each and every one of us what is morally right and wrong. Acts such as child abuse, slavery, rape, and murder are more than socially taboo; they are *moral abominations* and we do not need a social contract to know those intrinsically obvious facts! To have a foundation for objective morality we need an unchanging standard that is beyond man, but the social contract theory leaves us with 7.7 *billion* opinions from around the world. Thus, this candidate is clearly not the source by which the World Court appealed. Could it be, then, that our next candidate is the true foundation?

THE THEORY OF EVOLUTION

Of course, the answer is a big, fat *no*. In previous chapters, we have seen there is zero scientific credibility for the theory of evolution, along with its horrible ramifications about our supposed lack of identity and purpose in life. Therefore, what is discussed from here on out about evolution is merely in the hypothetical arena to show that it could never, ever, adequately bring about objective morality.

With that said, how Darwinists theorize we have morality today is based on the idea that, as our ancient, human ancestors developed throughout history and the process of natural selection would "pick and choose" behavioral traits that were more conducive towards survival and reproduction than others, a behavioral code was constructed and placed on our genes parallel with the physical evolution of our species. As Darwinist and Harvard biologist E.O. Wilson writes of this dual process: "In the course of evolutionary history genes predisposing people toward cooperative behavior would have come to predominate in the human population as a whole. Such a process repeated through thousands of generations inevitably gave rise to moral sentiments.[20]

So, in short, nature supposedly gave us our sense of right and wrong to preserve the human race, and these certain behavioral patterns that have been genetically determined over time for aid in our continued existence are what we refer to today as morality. But as was the case with the social contract theory, the source for objective morality somehow being the theory of evolution is also ripe with many, many examples of glaring problems.

First of all, evolution is theorized as a continually changing process. This brings up the implication that morals must also mutate and evolve along with our genetic codes, meaning that acts such as murder, rape, theft, and selfishness all have the potential to be considered as good acts in the future. Since evolution is theorized as a continually changing process, this means that, as with the social contract theory, by its very definition, evolution cannot be the *unchanging* standard for objective morality by which everything is measured.

Second, our moral principles, or "moral sentiments," we all know that we should abide by (e.g., do not commit acts of murder, rape, theft, and selfishness) having been passed down by our ancient ancestors just does not make any sense. After all, if nature gave us morality simply as an aid towards the survival and reproduction of the human race, both of those goals would have been achieved best by *not* abiding by these moral principles.

Murdering the weak and handicapped, for example, would have aided in the survival of the fittest by both freeing up precious resources they were using and by enhancing the gene pool. Also, unfaithfulness and rape clearly would have aided in increasing the amount of reproduction. Therefore, it is obvious that natural selection would have chosen behaviors such as these to flourish instead. Yet, across all societal lines, we know that such behaviors are morally unacceptable.

Third, why would we assume that our ancient ancestors would have even cared about the long-term survival of the species as a whole? Why would they have ever considered the survival of the species as more important than the survival of themselves and their loved ones? Common sense says that individuals and people groups would have *competed* instead of cooperated.

To this day, people can easily gain advantages and prosper simply by *not* cooperating with others. In brutal, primitive times, this would include stealing from rivals, being selfish towards them, raping them, and even murdering their young to ensure fewer rivals in the future. Of course, natural selection would have found such behaviors favorable towards survival and reproduction and would have favored them to flourish for future generations. Yet, again, these are examples of behaviors that we all know are morally unacceptable. This, then, leads us to a fourth glaring problem.

Why should people *not* murder, rape, steal, be selfish, and so on? The quick reply by Darwinists would be that it harms others when we behave in those ways. But that reply would presuppose we *ought* to be concerned about the welfare of others. The Darwinist would then say that a concern about the welfare of others is important for the survival of our species. But that reply presupposes we *ought* to care about whether or not our species survives. So how does evolution explain this moral oughtness?

The answer is that it cannot explain why someone is morally obligated not to murder, rape, steal, be selfish, and so on. If it were possible, that would assume an ultimate goal – survival – for evolution. But because evolution is a nonintelligent, blind, purposeless process, an end-goal is precisely what evolution, by definition, does not have! If evolution were true, the most that chemistry and biology could answer would be what *does* survive, not what *ought* to survive. Therefore, even though it is obvious that behaviors such as these could aid in the overall survival of our species, evolution can never explain why we *ought* not to behave in those ways.

After all, it was Darwin himself who asked that very question in his book *The Descent of Man*: "Why should a man feel that he ought to obey one instinctive desire rather than another?"[21] And his answer? Well, he completely dodges his own question. Rather, he subsequently resorts to saying that man simply acts on our "more persistent instincts" and continues by adding onto that thought: "The wish for another man's property is, perhaps, as persistent a desire as any that can be named."[22] Again, this does nothing to answer how we *ought* to behave. Darwin is saying evolution could only ever explain what behavior *does* get obeyed instead of what behavior *ought* to be obeyed. By Darwin's own logic that theft could be justified in evolutionary terms of survivability simply because it is a strong urge, then murder, rape, and selfishness could also be justified. But we all know such behaviors are morally unacceptable and we *ought* not to do them! Darwinism cannot explain that moral obligation and leaves us with no basis for determining which urges to follow. With so much talk about survival, the argument that evolution presents, ironically, does not survive.

Now, before they come to a dead end, there is a final reply which is commonly given by Darwinists to try and answer the questions of why we ought to be concerned about the welfare of others and the survival of our species. As we will see, it also fails miserably, but it is definitely worth noting here because it leads us to a fifth glaring problem for the theory.

"Because humans have value," they say. Seriously? That is quite interesting because, if evolution were true, the event of any life form coming from a "warm little pond" would be a cosmic fluke that was never meant to happen. Therefore, as we have discussed, all life forms would be entirely void of both purpose and worth. So, since all life forms would be accidental by-products if they came from this same, unintelligent, blind, random, purposeless process, why think that mankind is somehow specially endowed with any objective moral value when compared to any other species? Yet, we treat humans as though we are unique and are innately worthy of moral obligation. Even more interesting, though, is the fact that consistent Darwinists themselves do not even try to hide the moral ramifications of mankind not having any intrinsic value whatsoever if evolution were true. Just take a look at these examples of quotes from the heaping pile of others that could be listed.

Ingrid Newkirk, the co-founder of PETA, stated, "A rat is a pig is a dog is a boy."[23] Dawkins, speaking of cows going to the slaughter house, stated that, "When I pass one of those lorries with little slats and see fearful eyes peering out, I think of the railway wagons to Auschwitz" (Auschwitz being a network of concentration camps during to the Holocaust).[24] Philosopher James Rachels, speaking about mentally handicapped people in the context of the Darwinian worldview, wrote in his book *Created from Animals: The Moral Implications of Darwinism*, "The natural conclusion, according to the doctrine we are considering [Darwinism], would be that their status is that of mere animals. And perhaps we should go on to conclude that they may be used as non-human animals are used – perhaps as laboratory subjects, or as food."[25] Peter Singer, decamp professor of bio-ethics at Princeton University, has even went so far as to say a human newborn baby is of *less* value than "the life of a pig, a dog, or a chimpanzee."[26] His shocking statement did not stop there, as he continued by saying that a baby should not even be considered a person until after he or she has lived for thirty days and that "killing a newborn baby is never equivalent to killing a person."[27] He also says that parents should allow physicians to murder disabled babies by putting them through the long process of death by means of starving them and injection.[28]

What is even more sickening is the fact that these disturbing, Darwinian inspired thoughts about infanticide was and still is nothing new among those who share that worldview. One might think that such quotes are cherry-picked, but nothing could be further from the truth! Countless other Darwinists who have also publically expressed such commonly-viewed thoughts includes, for example, philosopher Michael Tooley, who stated babies have no moral right to live because they do not, "Possess . . . the concept of a self as a continuing subject of experiences and other mental states."[29] American University philosophy professor Jeffrey Reiman has asserted that babies do not, "Possess in their own right a property that makes it wrong to kill them."[30] And, says molecular biologist, geneticist, and zoologist James D. Watson in regards to birth defects, "Because of the present limits of such detection methods, most . . . are not discovered until birth. If a child were not declared [a person] until three days after birth, then all parents could be allowed the choice. . . . The doctor could allow the child to die if the parents so choose."[31]

As horrible as it would be, for instance, to use mentally handicapped people "as laboratory subjects, or as food," Darwinists cannot give an objective answer as to why we *ought* not to do that. Even the horrendous, abhorrently gruesome experiments of the Nazis cannot be condemned by Darwinists because there is not an objective moral standard in the context of a Darwinian worldview. Further, why limit infanticide (murder) to just three or thirty days and not three or thirty weeks, months, or years? After all, murder at any age cannot be condemned by Darwinists because, again, there is not an objective moral standard in the context of a Darwinian worldview. It is only when you come to realize that humans are viewed as nothing more than animals within this worldview that you can understand the thought processes behind such outrageous beliefs.

As we have touched on in previous chapters, the theory of evolution claims that humans evolved from molecules to man over a period of billions and billions of years, with one of our intermediate steps being monkeys. What we have not touched on thus far is that the theory goes one step further. In Darwin's opinion, this descent from monkeys implies that some races of humans have descended further away from them on the evolutionary scale than have other races. It was widely viewed that blacks evolved from the less intelligent gorillas, Asians from the more intelligent orangutans, and whites from the most intelligent chimpanzees.[32] In fact, Darwin in his book aptly entitled *The Descent of Man*, considered his own white race as being much more advanced than races with darker skin whom he categorized as being "lower organisms," "savage," and "degraded," among plenty of other racist characterizations.[33]

His prejudice was evident as he continued in *The Descent of Man*: "At some future period, not very distant as measured by centuries, the civilised races of man will almost certainly exterminate and replace throughout the world the savage races."[34] In a letter to his colleague W. Graham he stated, "The more civilized so-called Caucasian races have beaten the Turkish hollow in the struggle for existence. Looking to the world at no very distant date, what an endless number of the lower races will have been eliminated by the higher civilized races throughout the world."[35]

While Darwin was not the first person to submit biological arguments for racism, his works, more-so than any other, significantly fueled the rise and attempted justification of lethal racism. The staunch evolutionist Stephen Jay Gould even wrote of this fact that, "Biological arguments for racism may have been common before 1859, but they increased by orders of magnitude following the acceptance of evolutionary theory."[36] The theory also fueled the rise and attempted justification of oppression and even genocide.

As the historical record shows, immediately after their rise to power, the Nazi party abundantly showed their committed support of the Darwinian worldview. In fact, just prior to World War II, the Nazi party passed a law of compulsory sterilization for those in Germany who were considered mentally or physically handicapped. In doing so, several hundred thousand were sterilized (nearly one percent of the entire population of Germany). The Nazis then went one step further and began the involuntary euthanasia (murder) of tens of thousands of physically and mentally handicapped Germans. And these acts, of course, are considered to historians as the stepping stones to the full-blown Holocaust of World War II. It was then that Hitler himself, also greatly influenced by Darwinian evolution, used the theory as a justification for the Holocaust in the attempted advancement of the so-called Aryan "master race" and extermination of the dehumanized "inferior races." In his book *Mein Kampf*, he wrote the following about the hierarchy of superior and inferior races based on their higher and lower stages of evolution:

> If nature does not wish that weaker individuals should mate with the stronger, she wishes even less that a superior race should intermingle with an inferior one; because in such cases all her efforts, throughout hundreds of thousands of years, to establish an evolutionary higher stage of being, may thus be rendered futile. . . . But such a preservation goes hand-in-hand with the inexorable law that it is the strongest and the best who must triumph and that they have the right to endure. He who would live must fight. He who does not wish to fight in this world, where permanent struggle is the law of life, has not the right to exist.[37]

Hitler would have argued that the Holocaust was the logical outworking of evolutionary theory and that he was simply following good steward of Darwinian evolution to ensure the survival of the strong and the total elimination of the weak. This fact was also made evident in the Nazi propaganda films that were spread to the masses in an effort to conform Germany to the theory of evolution. One video, for instance, upon showing a disfigured handicapped person, stated, "Mankind has sinned frightfully against the law of natural selection. We have not just maintained life unworthy of life, we have even allowed it to multiply! The descendants of these sick people look . . . like this person here!"³⁸ And even before Hitler and the Nazi Party took control, Darwinism had already greatly influenced the public opinion as a whole in Germany to have a dehumanizing prejudice towards certain races. One instance that stands out was a cover from a popular magazine which portrayed German soldiers who had captured an African man from the French forces and was taking him, a "gorilla," to a famous man's zoo collection.³⁹

Now, here is the question at-hand: if killing the weak helps improve the human species and its overall survival, according to evolution, how can we say that Hitler and the Holocaust was really wrong? By more than a subjective opinion, why should not the likes of the Nazis have been the ones to survive if they made a case for being the fittest to do so? Evolution cannot tell us this answer because, again, it could only describe what *does* survive as opposed to what *ought* to survive.

With the later regimes such as Mao, Stalin, and Lenin in mind, is it really any wonder that these dictators were responsible for millions upon millions of deaths when their worldviews supported ethnic superiority and devalued human life overall from the start? Their views did not at all conflict with the Darwinian worldview; instead, they were entirely consistent with its moral implications that the strong should survive by seeing to it that the weak were eliminated at any cost.

Such beliefs towards a hierarchy within the human race have even made their way into children's biology textbooks. As made famous by the Scopes "monkey trial," the controversial textbook – George William Hunter's *A Civic Biology: Presented in Problems* – *is a particularly well-known example. For instance, one among other racist sections reads,*

> At the present time there exist upon the earth five races or varieties of man, each very different from the other in instincts, social

customs, and, to an extent, in structure. These are the Ethiopian or negro type, originating in Africa; the Malay or brown race, from the islands of the Pacific; the American Indian; the Mongolian or yellow race, including the natives of China, Japan, and the Eskimos; and finally, the highest type of all, the Caucasians, represented by the civilized white inhabitants of Europe and America.[40]

The book then goes on to suggest placing people with certain handicaps and undesirable traits into asylums and separating them by gender to prevent them from reproducing offspring whose traits would become "parasitic" to the higher evolution of the human race. It should be duly noted that asylum was the second proposal, as the first proposed course of action was to "kill them off to prevent them from spreading." Of course, the *racist and eugenics (*a movement wanting to control human reproduction to improve the human species*)* ideology sections such as these were scrubbed from subsequent editions of the textbook before ultimately finding its home in the library of Congress. So, if you want to see the unaltered version, you will also have to do some digging.

It should also be duly noted that the lead attorney who defended the textbook and Darwinian evolution as a whole in the Scopes trial was a committed Darwinist named Clarence Darrow. Darrow was a prominent supporter of infanticide who was not shy to publically share his evolution-inspired beliefs, such as the proposal that it would be beneficial to the survival of the fittest humans if society would, "Chloroform unfit children. Show them the same mercy that is shown beasts that are no longer fit to live."[41]

If the fact that such blatantly racist remarks were expressed in children's textbooks as being based on scientific truth does not hit close enough to home, then it may be of assistance to be informed that in the early 1900s, villages of African pygmies – full of "evolutionary inferior natives" as they were characterized – were slaughtered by the tens of thousands. Their bodies were mutilated in order to be sent to British and American museums in the Darwinist's hopes of finding evidence of "missing links" to show the transitional evolution from apes to humans (the Smithsonian Institution in Washington alone holds the remains of over 15,000 people from various races).[42] Not only were the bones of great interest, but also fresh skins to provide stuffed displays. This is what happens when you go against true science, in which genetics plainly shows we are all equals and that the only difference between races is mere skin pigmentation.

Of course, we must ask how anyone could ever claim to be from a "higher race" when we could stoop so low and act so evil as to treat fellow humans in such dehumanizing ways. Since the racist, hate-filled, purposeless, and valueless worldview of Darwinian evolution has continued to infiltrate our schools, our entertainment, and our societies as a whole to erode at the sanctity of life ethic, it really is no shocking matter that we still attempt to justify such blatantly evil acts, not only with babies that would be born with definite handicaps, or even possible handicaps, but with perfectly healthy babies, simply because they are selfishly considered as possible inconveniences to our own, non-aborted lives.

In agreement that evolution has led to this continued erosion of human value, whether it be the act of abortion murdering supposedly inconvenient humans or the act of aiding in the killing of elderly humans who rack up expensive medical bills and supposedly do not contribute to society, says history professor Nick Kemp at Collingwood College, Camberley, Surrey, "We should be . . . cautious of underestimating the importance of evolutionary thought in relation to the questioning of the sanctity of human life."[43] Speaking of the sanctity of life, the view that humans are special and sacred, Singer writes that evolution "gave what ought to have been its final blow."[44] Darwinism leaves us with no basis for why we ought not to copy nature and destroy those who are considered weak and costly; there are no moral restraints within the Darwinian worldview.

As you can see, as far as evolution goes, humans are considered being no different than any other animal besides being highly evolved (some races more-so than others), and any thinking to the contrary would simply be a biased observation based on a speciesist illusion. But humans *are* different than animals, and one of the main ways we know this to be a solid fact is because humans, uniquely, are moral agents.

To illustrate, for example, a dog may look at a bowl of food in front of him and think, "There's a lion behind my food, but I won't go near it because I don't want to get eaten." But no dog could look at another dog and think, "She's beautiful, but I'll wait until marriage."[45] That is a reminder of an episode of *The Tonight Show with Jay Leno* from a few years ago. "Headlines" was an all-time fan favorite segment done by comedian Jay Leno every Monday, highlighting funny articles and advertisements in print that were mailed in by viewers. One article in particular was about two suspects who were charged with check forgeries. Now, that does not sound too funny, until you see that the accompanied picture of the two "suspects" were accidentally that of two dogs (with hilariously fitting mischievous, up-to-no-good faces)![46] The article got a big laugh from the audience. Why? Because we all know not only that dogs cannot forge signatures but that they are not at all morally responsible for their behaviors.

Dogs also do not set up the likes of doggy courts and doggy jails to seek judgment and punishment for those who steal bones. They could not care less, because animals have zero moral obligations towards one another. Further, professor of philosophy at the University of Rochester and ethicist Richard Taylor observes, "A hawk that seizes a fish from the sea kills it, but does not murder it; and another hawk that seizes that fish from the talons of the first hawk takes it, but does not steal it – for none of these things is forbidden."[47] If evolution were true and humans are just other animals, why do we consider our actions differently than the actions of dogs, hawks, and so on? We would have to view human behavior in the exact same way because, since murder, rape, theft, selfishness, and so on occur all the time in the animal kingdom, such actions could not be considered as morally wrong. Yet, humans are obligated to spend billions upon billions of dollars each year seeking justice for wrongs done to one another. But, observes crime scene investigator J. Warner Wallace,

> Why would *any* human feel obligated toward another human when we do not recognize moral obligations toward other forms of life on the planet? We seldom hesitate to exterminate the rodents and insects in our homes, and we feel no moral obligation toward the weeds growing in our garden. What, from a naturalistic perspective, gives us the right to consider *humans* differently? . . . Imagine . . . a superior race of aliens from another planet invades Earth with the goal of enslaving humans for their own selfish purposes. . . . In a scenario such as this, would we (as humans) have a right to complain? After all, we have a history of using horses, hunting dogs, oxen, and a variety of other species in a similar way. How could we argue against such treatment by a species as superior to us as we are to other forms of life on this planet?[48]

Even further, if evolution were true, it would make no difference how we acted. After all, since we are all ultimately going to die soon anyway, it would be entirely foolish to jeopardize your short time here by not looking out solely for your own self-interests. Yet, we all know in most cases that our personal desires directly contradict the acts we are obligated to do. This is precisely because humans know we are not animals but, uniquely, are moral agents.

THE FINAL POINT ON EVOLUTION

While the previous five problems are damning for evolution being the source for objective morality (on top of the fact that science has already shown that evolution is entirely false), there is a sixth problem that we need to discuss. And it is a quite lengthy problem that requires plenty of background information, as it leads directly into our next topics of discussion – consciousness and the afterlife.

MORALITY AND CONSCIOUSNESS

(Part 2)

Evolution cannot be the standard for objective morality because of the fact that evolution is a *material* (physical) process. Morality is entirely *immaterial* (non-physical). Not to be confused with its popular usage of referring to a concern for obtaining material possessions such as money, houses, cars, etc., *materialism* (also referred to as physicalism) in a philosophical sense is the Darwinist's belief system that only physical things exist. Materialism is essential to their worldview and is the only system of thought they have in their quiver. As we have discussed in previous chapters, though, the Cause and Designer of the universe *must* be immaterial and, therefore, we already know that materialism is wrong. Nevertheless, any attempt by one who holds to this belief that everything in the universe consists of and has been caused by materials alone would be, as we will see, to contradict themselves in the process.

MATERIALISM

Frank Turek recalled a presentation's Q&A in which he had a discussion with an audience member named Michael. Turek writes, "Since I had argued that a spaceless, timeless, immaterial God created the universe, Michael put me on the spot by asking me if I knew of anything other than God that was spaceless, timeless, and immaterial:

Michael: Can you please explain to me how something can exist without time, space, or matter to exist out of? And if you can explain how that is possible, can you please demonstrate it?
Frank: Sure, the laws of logic we are using right now. They are outside of time, outside of space, and they are not made of material.
Michael: I would argue that the laws of logic really don't exist then.
Frank: So you're saying that they *do* really exist.
Michael: No.
Frank: Yes, you're saying they do.
Michael: How am I saying they do?
Frank: Because you're using [a law of logic] right now to say that I'm wrong."[1]

    Turek is giving an illustration here of how it was easy to point out Michael's faulty and self-defeating argument when it came to denying the laws of logic. You cannot deny the laws of logic and yet use the laws of logic at the same time to reason that the laws of logic do not exist!

    In the same way, anyone who believes in materialism cannot argue in favor of materialism in any fashion because that would be using the laws of logic – entities, like morality, that are universal, self-evident, unavoidable, independent of human invention, discovered, spaceless, timeless, unchanging, and *immaterial* – in an attempt to reason that nothing *immaterial* exists! Turek continues about the laws of logic: "They are to thinking what your eyes are to seeing. You cannot see without eyes, and you cannot think without the laws of logic. All thinking, all communication, and all science depend on them."[2]

It gets pretty hilarious once you remember that these atheistic, Darwin-loving materialists claim to be the world's beacons and champions of – you guessed it – *reasoning*. David Silverman, for instance (again, the former president of the American Atheists organization), once stated, "Reason is inherently atheistic."[3] Or just look at the *Reason* Rallies they organize, where they argue that any position other than theirs is not *reasonable*. Yet, they hold the philosophical position that reason *does not actually exist*! But not only does someone who argues in favor of materialism use the immaterial laws of logic to do so, they also use their *immaterial minds* (consciousness) by which their ability to use these tools of reasoning derives.

THE MIND-BRAIN RELATIONSHIP

With that in mind (pun intended), you intimately know that there is nothing we are more familiar with than our own consciousness. In fact, as you read these very words, you're having an immediate, direct, first-person, conscious experience. As we pay attention to our conscious states going on inside of us, we all experience the nature of our thoughts, perceptions, memories, sensations, desires, emotions, and beliefs as being immaterial. To believe otherwise would go directly against all common sense; yet, believing otherwise is exactly what materialists have historically done since the nineteenth century.

Their supposed solution to explain away immaterial consciousness is to claim that it is identical to the physical brain itself. In other words, you are nothing but a brain and central nervous system enclosed within your physical body. Lee Strobel states, "According to Darwinists, the physical world is all that there is. At some point, the human brain evolved, with its raw processing power increasing over the eons. When the brain reached a certain level of structure and complexity, people became "conscious" – that is, they suddenly developed subjectivity, feelings, hopes, a point of view, self-awareness, introspection, that "hidden voice of our private selves."[4]

So what is the answer? Are we strictly physical beings or are we more than that? Is our experience of consciousness just a byproduct of activity within the brain, or is it a distinct, immaterial entity that is separate from the brain? Well, at first glance, one may be quick to believe there is justifiable evidence suggesting the mind is produced by the brain itself. After all, what can be said to those who say this is evident because of the observations made in regards to impairment of mental functioning that takes place with patients dealing with brain injuries or dementia? Is not that proof the mind and the brain are one and the same?

Not at all! There is a great abundance of neurologists who, having a worldview referred to as "Dualism," conclude that the mind and the brain have an interconnected relationship and interact, yet are very distinct entities from one another: one being immaterial and the other being physical. In other words, the immaterial mind and physical brain work together but are not the same thing. As scientific studies show, your brain clearly is not the source of your mind but is simply *an instrument* that is used by your mind. This means, when a patient is dealing with a brain injury or dementia, the brain itself is what has been damaged and has a limited ability to access the undamaged mind. So, when we say that someone is "losing their mind," what we should really be saying is that someone is losing *access to* their mind. Referring to the mind as "the self," Craig explains,

> Several years ago I heard the Nobel Prize-winning neurologist Sir John Eccles lecture at The *World Congress of Philosophy* in *Düsseldorf*,

Germany. And Eccles had just written a book with Sir Karl Popper, one of the greatest of philosophers of science during the 20th century, [called] *The Self and Its Brain*. And the title is revealing. For Eccles and Popper, the self is not the same as the brain: the self . . . is a personal, immaterial, mental substance, and the brain is a material organ that sits in our cranium. And Eccles and Popper were defending what they called dualism interactionism: that there is an immaterial self which uses the brain as an instrument for thought. . . . And [they] compared the relationship of the self to the brain to that of a pianist to his piano. The piano is an instrument that the pianist uses to play music, and if the instrument is damaged (say out of tune, or the strings are broken), then clearly the pianist, though he has the ability to play good music, won't be able to produce music because the instrument that he uses to make music is damaged or incapacitated. And, similarly, Eccles said that the self and the brain are related in that way: the brain is an instrument that the self uses to think. And so it is not surprising that when the brain is damaged . . . that the self will not be able to use its instrument for [clear and proper] thinking.[5]

To use another analogy, think of this like you would a router and an Internet signal: when the router is damaged, then the Internet signal cannot get through to a computer, but just because the signal cannot get through does not mean the Internet signal ceases to exist. The router and the Internet signal are two separate things. A router is simply the instrument through which the Internet signal is transmitted to a computer. Or think of this like you would a TV: when you see a meteorologist on the screen, contrary to a child's imagination, you know that the meteorologist did not originate inside of it. Obviously, there was a message, created elsewhere, that the antenna had to receive so that the TV could process it. In the same way, when you hear the meteorologist speaking, though there is electrical activity that can be measured within the temporal lobe of your brain, does that activity mean *your brain* is producing the sound of that voice? Of course not. Similarly, when a study of the brain shows electrical activity related to any mental task, it only shows *correlation* and not causation. In the same way as these analogies work, the mind and brain are separate entities: the brain is not the source of the mind but is simply the instrument that the mind uses and, just because someone may have a brain injury, this does not mean their mind ceases to exist but, instead, inhibits the *access* to their mind.

So the fact that there are correlations between conscious states and the brain is not at all surprising. For the mind to use the brain as an instrument for thinking, one would certainly expect with this dualistic relationship for there to be correlations between conscious states and the brain. In fact, we can measure electrical activity in a person's brain and identify correlations between the activity within certain regions of the brain with the performing of certain mental tasks. However, when given a closer look, one comes to realize that while the brain is *involved* in our conscious states, that in no way means the brain *causes* our conscious states.

As renowned neuroscientist Maxwell Bennett and philosopher Peter Hacker write, just because we can find correlations between electrical activity in the brain and mental tasks, "That discovery cannot show that it is *the brain* that is conscious."[6] Bennett and Hacker continue, the only thing a neuroscientist can know about a person's brain while they are studying it on a monitor "is what goes on there *while he is thinking*; all functional magnetic resonance imaging (fMRI) scanners can show is which parts of his brain are metabolizing more oxygen than others when the patient in the scanner is thinking." Therefore, studies are entirely consistent with the view that conscious states do not originate inside of the brain itself but, instead, are received and processed by its regions.

Another reason as to why conscious states are not physical is because the properties of consciousness are not the same as the properties of the brain. As we discussed in our first example, a neuroscientist can measure electrical activity within the brain as having different sizes, shapes, and locations, but this is unique to the brain itself and not at all to conscious states. When you have a thought, a sensation, a desire, etc., those conscious states do not have any geometrical properties of size, shape, and location. Therefore, it would be ridiculous, for instance, if someone were to ask how much your thought weighs, what shape your sensation is, or where your desire is.

Another way in which the properties between consciousness and the brain differ is that activity within the brain can be publically known to neuroscientists whereas conscious states are private to the individual. Wallace writes:

> If I asked you to close your eyes and think of an imaginary car . . . the resulting vehicle would exist solely in your mind. If you are sufficiently creative, your imaginary vehicle would be like no other car on the planet, and only you would know precisely how it looks. Without referencing a physical car external to your body, you *imagined* the shape, color, and textures of the vehicle; it exists only in your *conscious thoughts*. This particular car is not the result of optical input from your eyes. Your brain is not referencing optical data from an object in the room. Neurophysiologists cannot open your physical brain and locate the car, its shape, or its properties. These characteristics cannot be accessed by surgeons sifting through . . . your brain, and even though neurologists may be able to pinpoint a location within the brain where neurological activity correlates with a thought or sensation, this . . . fails to identify one *as the other*.[7]

Furthermore, let us take rapid eye movement (REM) sleep, one of five distinct phases that your brain cycles through repeatedly throughout the night, as an example of how conscious states are private to the individual. How did we first come to discover that the "rapid, jerky, and binocularly symmetrical eye movements" of REM sleep is associated with deep dreaming?[8] The researchers had to wake up their patients and ask them! Because we have access to a person's brain states but do not have access to a person's conscious states, it would do no good whatsoever to refer to a brain monitor in hopes of getting that answer, let alone *what* a person is dreaming. We could witness REM sleep and correlate brain states, but we cannot know what is happening within the mind because, unlike brain states, it is private to the individual. Therefore, conscious states are not physical and are not one and the same with the brain.

CAUTION: EXTREME DESPERATION STRAIGHT AHEAD!

With those points in mind, you can see how conscious states and the brain cannot be the same thing. It is now of key importance to understand how that information flows into a turn of events that has begun occurring as of late.

As we stated at the onset of this discussion, materialists have historically believed consciousness exists and, since their worldview does not allow for immaterial entities, therefore, it must somehow be the product of the physical brain. But as Dr. Bruce Greyson, professor emeritus of psychiatry and neurobehavioral sciences at the University of Virginia summarizes, this nineteenth-century position of materialism, "fails to deal with . . . how an electrical impulse or a chemical trigger in the brain can produce a thought or a feeling or . . . anything that the mind does."[9]

Modern-day materialists grasp this fact and are frustratingly taking an entirely new position. As atheist and professor of philosophy at the University of California, Berkeley, John Searle (who has exposed a multitude of problems with materialism) observes, "Earlier materialists argued that there are not any such things as separate mental phenomena, because mental phenomena are *identical* with brain states. More recent materialists argue that there are not any such things as separate mental phenomena because they *are not identical* with brain states. I find the pattern very revealing, and what it reveals is an urge to get rid of mental phenomena at any cost."[10]

Staunch Darwinist and philosopher of science at Florida State University, Michael Ruse, adds to this modern-day belief: "Why should a bunch of atoms have thinking ability? Why should I, even as I write now, be able to reflect on what I am doing and why should you, even as you read now, be able to ponder my points, agreeing or disagreeing, with pleasure or pain, deciding to refute me or deciding that I am just not worth the effort? No one, certainly not the Darwinian as such, seems to have any answer to this."[11]

After all, since individual brain cells (neurons) do not have conscious ability, then the collection of a hundred, a thousand, or any amount of neurons also cannot give rise to consciousness. Atheistic philosopher and author Colin McGinn, who has taught at University College London, the University of Oxford, Rutgers University, and the University of Miami agrees and rules out a physical explanation for the origin of consciousness, asking, "How could the aggregation of millions of individually insentient neurons generate subjective awareness?"[12] Elsewhere, he continues: "How can mere matter originate consciousness . . . [and] convert the water of biological tissue into the wine of consciousness? Consciousness seems like a radical novelty in the universe, not prefigured by the after-effects of the Big Bang. So how did it contrive to spring into being from what preceded it?"[13] As Moreland adds to McGinn's point, it all boils down to the fact that,

You can't get something from nothing. It's as simple as that. . . . How, then, do you get something totally different – conscious, living, thinking, feeling, believing creatures – from materials that don't have that? That's getting something from nothing! And that's the main problem. If you apply a physical process to physical matter, you're going to get a different arrangement of physical materials. For example, if you apply the physical process of heating a bowl of water, you're going to get a new product – steam – which is just a more complicated form of water, but it's still physical. And if the history of the universe is just a story of physical processes being applied to physical materials, you'd end up with increasingly complicated arrangements of physical materials, but you're not going to get something that's . . . nonphysical. That's a jump of a totally different kind. . . . You're not going to have minds or consciousness.[14]

So in holding to their new belief, what exactly are materialists now trying to say? Well (extreme desperation straight ahead!), since they conclude the mind cannot be physical in nature, it must be just *an illusion*. In other words, now that we have made so many scientific advances since the 19th century, what modern-day materialists are doing is making a 180-degree change from their long-held belief and are now holding to a *new* belief that, because we know the mind is an entirely separate entity from the brain, the mind does not really even exist in the first place!

There is a pattern of belief here: first, atheistic materialists said the fine-tuning of the universe is an illusion, and now they say the mind is an illusion as well! Of course we, they all know their belief does not actually match with reality. After all, are not they *conscious* when they say and write that consciousness does not exist? As with our discussion about the laws of logic, this is yet another example of how one can point out that a materialist is a living contradiction by exposing their self-defeating beliefs: what does not exist in their worldview *must* exist for them to even argue that it does not exist!

This is where the discussion of our sixth and most lethal example as to why evolution cannot be the foundation for objective morality flows into why both historical and modern-day materialists have always attempted to, as Searle rightly stated, "Get rid of mental phenomena at any cost." If materialism were true, there would be two main consequences for humanity as a whole.

"CONSEQUENCES" OF MATERIALISM

The first of the two is that, since they are immaterial in nature, the worldview of materialism does not even allow for the possibility of gods, angels, souls, salvation, or forms of an afterlife. Of course, that belief may be all well and good for many materialists, so they, contrary to nearly every other person throughout the world, do not view it as a "consequence" per se. But what is *especially* appealing to the adherents of materialism is a second main "consequence." As we dig deeper and look at each layer of this worldview, we quickly see what follows from this: if consciousness is merely an illusion and does not really even exist in the first place, this would mean that we are entirely physical, material beings; if we are entirely physical, material beings, we are entirely made of physical matter; if we are entirely made of physical matter and we add that to the fact matter is entirely bound and controlled by the laws of chemistry and physics, then we also are entirely bound and controlled by the laws of chemistry and physics; and if we are entirely bound and controlled by the laws of chemistry and physics, this ultimately means that we can kiss goodbye what is called *free will* – the ability to make our own decisions.

Now, before we get into discussing free will specifically, you are probably (definitely) wanting more information on this whole us being "bound and controlled" stuff. After all, that sounds kind of odd and maybe even a little scary, right? Well, to gain a better grasp of what exactly that means, Moreland explains in a simple illustration that materialists view our lives as being bound and controlled by these laws just as a cloud is also bound to them: a cloud is "just a material object, and its movement is completely governed by the laws of air pressure, wind movement, and the like. So if I'm a material object, all of the things I do are fixed by my environment, my genetics, and so forth. . . . Whatever's going to happen is already rigged by my makeup and environment."[15] So what materialists believe is that, as Moreland continues, "We're just very complicated computers that behave according to the laws of nature and the programming we receive."[16]

Acting freely means that if you have a thought or perform an action, like thinking about classic hot rods or lifting your hands in the air while on a roller coaster, you ultimately had the power either to do those things or not to do those things. Acting *without* freedom, on the other hand, is the exact opposite. Just as a cloud has absolutely no control over its formation and movement because it is subject to the likes of air pressure and wind movement, a rock has no control over its rapid descent during a rock slide, and so on, we humans supposedly have no control over ourselves because we are subject to the random movement of particles of matter inside our brains. In other words, materialists believe we are just molecules in motion that merely *react* instead of reason. So, every time you have a thought or perform an action, according to this worldview, *you* did not actually do those things; without the ability to refrain, your brain forced you to do them. Therefore, materialism is the belief that, while we may *think* we have free will over our thoughts and actions, we actually do not and, therefore, both consciousness *and* free will are – yes, you guessed it – illusions.

While it is an expected response to think no one could ever hold such bizarre beliefs, there are prominently-known atheistic, Darwin-loving materialists who do believe them because their worldview leaves them with no other choice. Take what Richard Dawkins, for instance, wrote in his book *River Out of Eden: A Darwinian View of Life*: "DNA neither knows nor cares. DNA just is. And we dance to its music."[17] Dancing to the music of our DNA is another way of phrasing the belief that we have no free will because we are bound and controlled by the laws of nature. Elsewhere in a forum setting, Dawkins continues:

> I have a materialist view of the world. I think that things are determined in a rational way by antecedent events. And so that commits me to the view that when I think I have free will and I think that I'm exercising free choice I'm deluding myself, that my brain states are determined by physical events. And yet that seems to contradict, to go against, the very powerful subjective impression that we all have, that we do have free will.[18]

At this same forum with Dawkins, fellow materialist Lawrence Krauss gave his views. And in a quote that makes one think he should be a theoretical comic instead of a theoretical physicist, he (*so* eloquently!) stated,

> I also have to agree that I think that I don't I think there everything I know about the world tells me that there's no such thing as free will. I just think we act that, you know, but we act but the world behaves as if there's free will and so it doesn't make much difference. Just like, um, the particles in a in in a in the room don't we can discuss them statistically and they behave as if they can do things that they are not being forced to do.[19]

To finish the quote we covered in a previous chapter from William Provine: "Let me summarize my views on . . . modern evolutionary biology . . . and I must say that these are basically Darwin's views. There are no gods, no purposes, no goal-directed forces of any kind. There is no life after death. . . . *There is no ultimate foundation for ethics*, no ultimate meaning to life, *and no free will for humans*, either" [emphasis added].[20] He continues: "If you believe in evolution, you cannot hope for there being any free will. There's no hope whatsoever in there being any deep meaning in life."[21] Francis Crick writes in *The Astonishing Hypothesis*, "'You,' your joys and your sorrows, your memories and your ambitions, your sense of personal identity and free will, are in fact no more than the behavior of a vast assembly of nerve cells and their associated molecules."[22] Stephen Hawking and Leonard Mlodinow wrote in *The Grand Design*, "It is our physical brain, following the known laws of science, that determines our actions. . . . It is hard to imagine how free will can operate if our behavior is determined by physical law, so it seems that we are no more than biological machines and that free will is just an illusion."[23] According to Sam Harris in his aptly titled book, *Free Will*, "Free will is an illusion. Our wills are simply not of our own making. Thoughts and intentions emerge from background causes of which we are unaware and over which we exert no conscious control. We do not have the freedom we think we have."[24] Searle adds:

> Physical events can have only physical explanations, and consciousness is not physical, so consciousness plays no explanatory role whatsoever. If, for example, you think you ate because you were consciously hungry, or got married because you were consciously in love with your prospective spouse, or withdrew your hand from the flame because you consciously felt a pain, or spoke up at a meeting because you consciously disagreed with the main speaker, you are mistaken in every case. In each case the effect was a physical event

and therefore must have an entirely physical explanation.[25]

All of these and more well-known materialists agree with the belief that every thought we have and every action we perform is not our own doing but is merely the result of uncontrollable chemical and physical processes going on within our brains. Oddly enough, though, when they assert that we cannot trust *our* thoughts because the physical, unintelligent, blind, process of evolution has given us the illusions of consciousness and free will that are nothing more than uncontrollable, random, nonrational chemical secretions and electrical impulses in the brain, they are all saying we should trust *their* beliefs that materialism, evolution, and atheism as a whole are to be trusted! It is quite funny how that logic works!

After all, if everyone is bound by these laws, the materialist would only come to the conclusion that their beliefs are true simply because the laws have determined they would believe they were true! One ardent evolutionist who was honest enough to point out this poor logic was biochemist and geneticist J.B.S Haldane: "If my mental processes are determined wholly by the motions of atoms in my brain, I have no reason to suppose that my beliefs are true . . . and hence I have no reason for supposing my brain to be composed of atoms."[26] Darwin made a similar point that, if we are merely molecular machines controlled by the laws of chemistry and physics, how could we ever trust anything we believe: "With me the horrid doubt always arises whether the convictions of man's mind . . . are of any value or at all trustworthy."[27]

The materialist says we are all merely molecular machines; except for themselves, of course, because the worldview does not apply to them. So how is it exactly that the materialist has miraculously risen above these "illusions" of consciousness and free will to recognize that the rest of us are all being fooled? The answer is simple: they do not *really* believe what they claim they do.

Even the most hardcore materialist assumes their brains are rational and trustworthy and not systematically deceitful, and ultimately believes they are in full control of their beliefs. For instance, when Searle stated in his book that everything has an entirely physical explanation, if we were to take that statement to its logical ends, it would, in turn, mean that *his* own writings have an entirely physical explanation and cannot be trusted. But, obviously, Searle trusts that *he* has the mental freedom to think rationally and wants *his* readers to trust *his* thoughts! Or, imagine if Crick had replaced the words *you* and *your* with *me* and *my* in the quote from his book: "'*Me*,' *my* joys and *my* sorrows, *my* memories and *my* ambitions, *my* sense of personal identity and free will, are in fact no more than the behavior of a vast assembly of nerve cells and their associated molecules.'" Would it lead readers to trust a single word that *he* wrote in saying that *his* conclusions in *his* book are not due to the ability to reason and act freely but, instead, are due to mere reactions predetermined by the forced behavior of *his* nerve cells and associated molecules? Of course not.

Taking it one step further, not only do materialists simply exclude themselves from their own worldview, they even refer to themselves as "freethinkers" and form college clubs all across the country with that idea as the basis. Of course, the problem with that title is that *their worldview says freethinking does not even exist*! So, exactly like in our prior discussions about the laws of logic and consciousness, self-defeating beliefs once again expose the materialist as a living contradiction; what does not exist in their worldview *must* exist for them to even argue that it does not exist.

MATERIALISM IS UNLIVABLE

With that said, we put each use of the word "consequence" in quotation marks not only because materialists are perfectly content with their worldview not allowing for any gods, angels, souls, salvation, or forms of an afterlife to even be possible, but also because the second "consequence" that mankind has no free will is also incredibly appealing to them. If our universal sense of consciousness and free will are just illusions, as materialists say, we do not really have the personal freedom to think about or do anything on our own. Thus, we quickly see what conclusion would inevitably follow: if we do not have the freedom to make our own decisions, we *are not responsible* for our actions.

Ultimately, this worldview is so appealing to the materialist because it gives a supposed escape hatch from any *personal* responsibility. Having no consciousness and no free will does not even allow for actual *personal* desires. In fact, the very ideas of "I," and "you," and "we" are non-existent. Therefore, any action performed that would be viewed as wrong to others could easily be minimized and glossed over by the idea that it was not from our own desires but rather was entirely caused by the forced, predetermined activity within our bound, physical brains.

Moral responsibility presupposes that we first even have the freedom to choose. As Craig put it during a debate with Harris,

> "Ought" implies "can." A person is not morally responsible for an action which he is unable to avoid. For example, if somebody shoves you into another person, you're not responsible. . . . You had no choice. . . . If there is no free will, then no one is morally responsible for anything! In the end, Dr. Harris admits this, though it is tucked away in the endnotes of his volume. Moral responsibility, he says, and I quote, "is a social construct," not an objective reality: I quote: "In neuroscientific terms no person is more or less responsible than any other" for the actions they perform. . . . Therefore, on his view . . . right and wrong do not really exist."[28]

If materialism, and therefore the theory of evolution, were true, you guessed it: right and wrong would not really exist because morality would be just *another illusion* that can be added to the long list! Ruse, in his book *The Darwinian Paradigm*, writes, "The position of the modern evolutionist . . . is that . . . morality is just an aid to survival and reproduction . . . and any deeper meaning is illusory."[29] Further, states Ruse, along with Harvard University biologist Edward O. Wilson, "Morality, or more strictly our belief in morality . . . is merely an adaptation put in place to further our reproductive ends. . . . [Morality] as we understand it is an illusion fobbed off on us by our genes to get us to cooperate. . . . [Morality] is a shared illusion of the human race."[30]

Following the logic to its inevitable ends, think of what would happen if we were not responsible for our actions because morality is merely another illusion. You can see how it gets very, very dangerous because, if there is no free will and no morality, then this applies to all walks of people. After all, many people would find rape and murder to be fun. And if we all supposedly have no control over our own thoughts and actions, what is to stop them from saying, "My brain made me do it!" We might as well close down our courts and correctional facilities. Also, we should open up every jail cell because criminals are just "dancing to their DNA," right?

If one is to be a consistent materialist and truly live-out the worldview, anything goes. Thus, if materialism were true, Craig continues, "[It] becomes impossible to condemn war, oppression, or crime as evil. . . . [There] is no right and wrong; good and evil do not exist. That means that an atrocity like the Holocaust was really morally indifferent. You may think that it was wrong, but your opinion has no more validity than that of the Nazi war criminal who thought it was good."[31] Clearly, this worldview does not match reality and is not at all livable in the real world. Ravi Zacharias adds:

The next time you show up in science class with your homework unfinished, tell your teacher that Richard Dawkins said you could dance to your DNA. Actually, don't. Let's see how well Dawkins's theory works to explain the horrors of life. Could you tell a rape victim that her rapist merely danced to his DNA? Would it make sense to the victims of Auschwitz that their tormentors were fulfilling their genetic destiny? And would the loved ones of those cannibalized by Jeffrey Dahmer accept that he was merely drunk on his genetic juices?[32]

The fact that this worldview does not match reality and is not at all livable is evident when you realize that it even goes beyond the already scary beliefs of moral subjectivism and the social contract theory. You see, when one believes morality is subject to personal or majority-ruled opinions, those very beliefs are only opinions themselves and not necessarily the truth. But, with materialism, when one believes morality is subject to opinions, that belief is not even your own opinion because your brain forced you to believe it. In both cases, all actions are neither right nor wrong but, instead, are morally neutral and, therefore, morality is not objectively binding in any way.

It becomes *even more* evident this worldview does not match reality and is not livable once you see that materialists themselves continually contradict their own beliefs. Take Dawkins, for instance, who in a radio interview said, "I am a passionate anti-Darwinian when it comes to the way we should organize our lives and our morality. We want to avoid basing our society on Darwinian principles."[33] Well, if materialism were true, we would have no choice! After saying we are forced to dance to our DNA, here he is saying that we *should not* dance to our DNA. Elsewhere he states,

> I very much hope that we do not revert to the idea of survival of the fittest in planning our politics and our values and our way of life.

> I have often said that I am a passionate Darwinian when it comes to explaining why we exist. . . . But to live our lives in a Darwinian way, to make a society a Darwinian society, that would be a very unpleasant sort of society in which to live. . . . I feel that one of the reasons for learning about Darwinian evolution is as an object lesson in how not to set up our values and social lives.[34]

Known as "Darwin's Bulldog" for his advocacy of Darwin's theory of evolution, biologist Thomas Henry Huxley says of the supposed evolutionary instinct of survival of the fittest, "Let us understand, once for all, that the ethical progress of society depends . . . in combating it."[35] Combating it? Again, Huxley presents the same, contradictory problem as Dawkins: how can we possibly combat what our DNA is forcing us to do? States author Robert Morey,

> Materialists cannot logically believe in "love," yet they fall in love and marry. They cannot believe in "mind," yet they cannot avoid using "mind" terminology in their speech when referring to themselves or others. They believe that man is a random swarm of nonrational atoms no different than stones, yet they value people and relationships – they do not treat their children or mates as random atoms. What they say in the classroom is therefore contradicted by how they live in the home. They experience the mystery and beauty of this world and man while denying that such things exist. Materialism is not a faith to live by or die by. It is unlivable because it is merely a philosophy of negation, denying anything that is worth living or dying for.[36]

Turek adds to that line of thought: "Take a look at the people you love

MORALITY AND CONSCIOUSNESS (PART 2)

– your friends, your family, your children. Do you really think that they are nothing more than biological sacks of chemicals? If you're [a materialist], that's what you're saying. You're ignoring the fact that you and your loved ones are amazing multitalented creations, with unique minds, gifts, [and] personalities . . . that cannot be reduced to the periodic table."[37] Again, when taken to its logical, inevitable ends, materialism is entirely unlivable. Nevertheless, the adherents of materialism overlook all of the inevitable ends and simply find this second "consequence" of consciousness, free will, and morality all being illusions to be appealing strictly the comfortable, private level of supposedly doing away with moral accountability. Turek writes of this motivation:

> [The] late Julian Huxley, once a leader among Darwinists, admitted that sexual freedom is a popular motivation behind evolutionary dogma. When he was asked . . . "Why do people believe in evolution?" Huxley honestly answered, "The reason we accepted Darwinism even without proof, is because we did not want God to interfere with our sexual mores." . . . The motivation he observed to be prevalent among evolutionists was based on moral preferences, not scientific evidence. . . . Author and lecturer Ron Carlson has had Darwinists admit the same to him. On one such occasion, after lecturing at a major university on the problems with Darwinism . . . Carlson had dinner with a biology professor who had attended his presentation. "So what did you think of my lecture?" Carlson asked. "Well, Ron," began the professor, "what you say is true and makes a lot of sense. But I'm gonna continue to teach Darwinism anyway. . . . [It is] because Darwinism is morally comfortable. . . . [If] Darwinism is true – if there is no God and we all evolved from slimy green algae – then I can sleep with whomever I want. . . . In

Darwinism, there's no moral accountability."[38]

Though it is obvious that following scientific evidence wherever it leads cannot be the motivation behind atheistic, Darwin-loving materialists abiding by this worldview, this is also not to say there are only sexual motivations for doing so. Though, it is safe to say they do not want there to be a God by which they perceive *guilt* and, thus, their worldview attempts to entirely do away with both. After all, if free will and morality are illusions and, therefore, immoral behavior does not really exist, there is nothing for which we can be guilty.

At times, well-known and well-respected atheists candidly explain why it is that they do not believe in God. For instance, professor of philosophy at Pasadena City College, Edward Feser, in his book *The Last Superstition: A Refutation of the New Atheism*, gives further insight into such underlying motivations. Quoting Nagel, he states, "A desire to be free of traditional moral standards, and a fear of certain political and social consequences of the truth of religious belief, can also lead us to want to believe that we are just clever animals with no purpose to our lives other than the purposes we choose to give them, and that there is no cosmic judge who will punish us for disobeying an objective moral law."[39] As Russian novelist Fyodor Dostoyevsky succinctly observed in *The Brothers Karamazov*, "If there is no God, everything is permitted."[40]

With that said, one can expand from a religious standpoint as to why the belief of having no consciousness or free will is so appealing to materialists: if we do not have the freedom to make our own decisions, we are not responsible for our actions; if we are not responsible for our actions, there is no such thing as objective morality; if there is no such thing as objective morality, there is no such thing as sin; and if there is no such thing as sin, no need for salvation, no places called Heaven and Hell, and no God.

While materialists would love to live-out this worldview on a comfortable, private level, they know more-so than anyone that it cannot just stop there and must be applied to everyone. They also know that consciousness, free will, and morality are entirely real and that we are not just puppets whose strings are randomly jerked by our DNA. Needless to say, since the worldview of evolution does not even allow objective morality in the first place, this is clearly the most damning problem for it being the source for objective morality (on top of the already demonstrated fact that the theory is not scientifically credible).

GETTING TO THE SOURCE OF THE MATTER (AND NON-MATTER)

The eighteenth-century philosopher Immanuel Kant observed, "Two things fill the mind with ever new and increasing admiration and awe, the more often and steadily we reflect upon them: the starry heavens above me and the moral law within me. . . . I see them before me and connect them immediately with the consciousness of my existence."[41]

Kant is saying here that he, as we all do, intimately knows the objective moral law above the law is as real and wondrous as the night sky and cannot be dismissed as illusory. It also cannot be explained by appealing to personal or majority-ruled opinions, or to evolutionary development. It is abundantly clear, then, that the moral law transcends and precedes us, as it is completely independent of us. We do not invent or construct it any more than we invent or construct the laws of physics, the laws of chemistry, the laws of mathematics, and so on. Sir Isaac Newton did not invent gravity; even if humans were not on Earth, apples would still fall to the ground. No one invented the fact that two plus two equals four. In the same way, the moral law is not an invention – we *discover* it.

Seeing as how the social contract theory and the theory of evolution are both out of contention as the source of objective morality, what is the final candidate? In order for us to finally reach that point in our discussion, it is crucial to fully grasp the fact that there is much more to the universe than what we can use our five senses to interact with physically. Such examples that we have discussed include the laws of logic, the laws of physics, the laws of chemistry, consciousness, and free will. And there are further examples that we have not discussed, such as the laws of mathematics. So while we can observe the effects of, say, gravity on physical things, gravity itself is not physical. And while we can observe the neurological activity in your physical brain, say, while having a specific thought, nobody can open your brain and observe the geometrical properties of, say, the creative car you have uniquely imagined in your mind (hopefully it has Fleetwood Mac and Journey stickers on the rocket boosters).

If you are a materialist, this is where the worldview gets *really* embarrassing. We have seen that materialists claim to be the beacons of reason, yet claim that reasoning through the mind is an illusion. Further, materialists claim to be reasonable through their prideful use of science, when, in fact, their worldview does not even allow for the laws of physics, the laws of chemistry, and the laws of mathematics to exist. These laws are required to be precisely fine-tuned in order to even do science and for the universe itself to exist at all!

The moral law is yet another example that cannot be explained by physical molecules in motion. As we previously discussed in regards to conscious states, when you have a thought, a sensation, a desire, etc., it would be ridiculous if someone asked how much your thought weighs, what shape your sensation is, or where your desire is. In the same way, because moral standards are not made of molecules, it would be equally ridiculous if someone were to ask how much love weighs, what shape honesty is, or where the atom for hate is.

What does this all mean, then? How is it the case that materialism is entirely wrong; that there is so much about reality that we use continuously which cannot at all be explained within the limits of material terms? The answer is easy. The laws of nature that we have discussed are not only independent of us, says George F.R. Ellis, a mathematician and cosmologist at the University of Cape Town, "In some sense [the laws of nature] are not part of the Universe. They underlie the Universe because they control how matter behaves, but they are not themselves made of matter. Laws of physics are not made of lead or uranium or something."[42] The laws of nature are screaming out something we all innately know: not only is there a material realm, but there is a completely different, *immaterial realm* as well that is the home wherein these laws exist. With this second, immaterial realm in mind, then, it reveals the entirely reasonable existence of further immaterial entities that could exist within it – such as gods, angels, souls, salvation, and an afterlife.

PREMISE 3:
THEREFORE, THERE IS AN OBJECTIVE MORAL LAW GIVER

When we add the information about the objective, immaterial moral law to all we have discussed in previous chapters, it is reasonably evident about what – or might we say *Who* – is the true source of the moral law. Our distinct investigations from both science and morality now converge at one point, as the characteristics that are required of the Creator and Designer of the entire universe are also required of the objective, immaterial moral law Maker. Upon laying out these characteristics, we have seen that this God must have those which include being spaceless, timeless, immaterial, changeless, uncaused, powerful, intelligent, purposeful, and personal.

Our discussion on the moral law, then, adds to our knowledge on how

God must be from the immaterial realm, thus adding to our knowledge that God must be immaterial. We have already discussed that the Creator and Designer of the universe must be outside of space, time, and matter, thus being within this immaterial realm. We know that minds, because they are not physical in nature, are within the immaterial realm. We know that minds are necessary for making decisions. We have also already covered the fact that God must be personal in the sense of being able to make decisions. Adding to this, moral values and obligations do not reside in inanimate things and, therefore, only a personal being could be the ultimate source of moral values and duties that are commanded to us. Therefore, when all the facts are placed together, it makes total sense how God can be without a body and, instead, be an unembodied Mind.

Along with the fact that God must be immaterial, our discussion on the moral law also adds to our knowledge on how God cannot change. Just like the laws of logic and everything we know about the laws of nature, the moral law, by its very nature, is unchanging. Therefore, the moral law cannot be objective without an unchanging source by which we can measure all actions as either being objectively good or objectively bad. Clearly, because personal and majority-rules opinions change, and because the theory of macroevolution is a continually changing process as well, this is yet another reason why neither of these two candidates can be this unchanging source. Even devout atheists will admit to this fact. Philosopher and author Julian Baggini concedes, "If there is no single moral authority . . . moral claims are not true or false."[43] Dawkins writes, "It is pretty hard to defend absolutist [objective] morals on grounds other than religious ones."[44] Russ Shafer-Landau, professor of philosophy at the University of North Carolina and director of the Parr Center for Ethics states, "Some moral views are true, others false, and my thinking them so does not make them so. My society's endorsement of them does not prove their truth. Individuals, and whole societies, can be seriously mistaken when it comes to morality. The best explanation of this is that there are moral standards not of our own making."[45]

To better grasp this fact of the moral law requiring a source that is changeless, let us observe a situation that we have all likely experienced. Suppose you look down to check a text message while waiting in line at a red light. Next, once you look directly over at the car next to you, you quickly get an eerie feeling in the pit of your stomach: either *they* are slowly moving forward, or *you* are slowly moving backward and about to crash into someone! A billion things can run through your head. "Maybe the brakes have gone out!" At that point, the only thing you can do to have complete control of the situation is to hurry and look at a reference point that is not moving (unchanging), such as a road sign or the trunk of a tree, by which you can ultimately conclude who is moving.

In the same way, God is the only source that has the potential of being the changeless standard by which we can ultimately measure all actions. To have this standard means we can go beyond mere opinion from person to person, society to society, and era to era when we compare, say, the actions of Hitler and the actions of Mother Teresa. Because neither Hitler nor Mother Teresa can be the ultimate standard of the moral law, God can be the objective reference point, the changeless judge, that is entirely independent of opinion by which we have the validity to conclude who is the *better representation* of the moral law we all know. Thus, when atheists say they *want* atheism to be true so there is no moral accountability from such a changeless judge, it is merely a heart issue instead of an intellectual issue that keeps them from accepting the way reality actually is.

CROSSING OPINION

Our discussion on morality also adds another characteristic to the list: God must be all-loving. As Craig states in a debate with Harris at the University of Notre Dame,

> God is by definition the greatest conceivable being and, therefore, the highest Good. Indeed, He is not merely perfectly good; He is the locus and paradigm of moral value. God's own holy and loving nature provides the absolute standard against which all actions are measured. He is by nature loving, generous, faithful, kind, and so forth. Thus if God exists, objective moral values exist, wholly independent of human beings. . . . If God exists, then obviously objective moral values exist, independently of human opinion – they're grounded in the character of God – and there would be objective moral duties, if God exists, because our duties arise in response to the moral imperatives that God issues to us. . . . So once you understand the concept of God, you can see that asking, "Well, why is God good?" is sort of like asking, "Why are all bachelors unmarried?" It's the very concept of the greatest conceivable being, of being worthy of worship that entails the essential goodness of God.[46]

It is with this characteristic that we can narrow-down our already narrowed-down list of remaining world religions: Christianity, Judaism, and Islam. This is because, unlike the deities in Christianity and Judaism, the deity in Islam (Allah) is not characterized as all-loving. Therefore, because Allah is morally inadequate, he cannot be the greatest conceivable being who is the morally perfect lawmaker of the objective moral law above the law. In fact, there are ninety-nine names (also known as the ninety-nine attributes) which the Qur'an uses to describe various aspects of Allah's nature: for instance, the all hearing, the reckoner, the self exalted; but "love" or "loving" is not stated.

In the Qur'an it is emphasized, repeatedly, that Allah loves only himself and those *most* devout to him; as far as everyone else goes, states the Qur'an, Allah "is an enemy to unbelievers" and "loves not the unbelievers."[47,48] Thus, Allah can, by definition, change his mind from not loving someone, to loving someone, and vice-versa. Furthermore, Allah's love is extremely partial and must be earned by doing good works (after all, contrary to what is stated in the mainstream, "Islam" is the Arabic word for "submission"). In a debate at McGill University with president of the Islamic Information & Dawah Centre International in Toronto, Shabir Ally, Craig continues:

> So according to the Qur'an God's love is reserved for the God-fearing and the good-doers; but he has no love for sinners and unbelievers. Thus, in the Islamic conception of God, God is not all-loving. His love is partial and has to be earned. The Muslim God only loves those who first love Him. . . . What would you think of a parent who said to his children, "If you measure up to my standards and do as I tell you, then I will love you"? Some of you have had parents like that, and you know the emotional scars you bear as a result of the fact that they did not give you unconditional love. But as the greatest conceivable being, as the most perfect being, the source of all goodness and love, God's love must be unconditional, impartial, and universal.[49]

Of course, the "love" that Allah gives is not unchanging, unconditional, unselective, impartial, or universal. Thus, since Allah is characteristically defined as being morally inadequate, that allows for an even greater deity to be the morally perfect lawmaker by which the moral law would derive. So the religion of Islam is easily eliminated from the remaining list. Buddhism and Hinduism have already been eliminated in previous chapters, but it should be noted that we could also easily eliminate them again based on their beliefs when we take the existence of the moral law into account.

Buddhism does not teach discernment between good and evil. For example, as *The Teaching of Buddha* states, "People make a distinction between good and evil, but good and evil do not exist separately. Those who are following the path to enlightenment recognize no such duality, and it leads them to neither praise the good and condemn the evil, nor to despise the good and condone the evil."[50] Similarly, Hinduism teaches that everything is one and, therefore, no distinction between the two can be made. Further, Hinduism, going well beyond even the worldview of materialism, teaches that *everything* (e.g., Earth, mankind, animals, free will, moral values, and obligations) is merely illusory (referred to as Māyā, or "that which is not").

What, then, do the two remaining religions have to say about their deities being changeless? In regards to Judaism, the Tanakh says of YHWH in the book of Malachi, "For I am the LORD, I change not."[51] In regards to Christianity, the God of the Bible is described in multiple locations having this attribute of being changeless. For instance, this includes the verse from the book of Malachi in the Old Testament (a shared, sacred text between Judaism and Christianity), which we just discussed. In the New Testament, for instance, the book of Hebrews reads, "Jesus Christ is the same yesterday and today and forever."[52] And the book of James reads, "Every good and perfect gift is from above, coming down from the Father . . . who does not change."[53]

Finally, as with the characteristic of being all-loving, in regards to Judaism, we read in the book of Ezekiel, for instance, "Declares the Sovereign LORD, I take no pleasure in the death of the wicked, but rather that they turn from their ways and live. Turn! Turn from your evil ways!"[54] In the book of Deuteronomy, for instance: "For the LORD your God is God of gods and Lord of lords, the great God, mighty and awesome, who shows no partiality."[55] In regards to Christianity, once again we can include those two examples of verses from the Old Testament. In the New Testament, the book of Matthew reads, for instance: "I say to you, love your enemies and pray for those who persecute you."[56] And the book of John reads: "Let us love one another, for love comes from God . . . because God is love. This is how God showed his love among us: He sent his one and only Son into the world that we might live through him. This is love: not that we loved God, but that he loved us and sent his Son as an atoning sacrifice for our sins."[57] In quite a stark contrast, the God of the Bible sent His own Son to die an excruciating death for the people who Allah hates. Thus, it is understood by Jews and Christians alike that God's love is uniquely unchanging, unconditional, unselective, impartial, universal, and that He is the greatest conceivable being Who is the morally perfect Lawmaker of the objective moral law above the law.

RED HERRINGS AND RABBIT TRAILS

Now, it should be pointed out that there is a common misunderstanding among some atheists when they are presented with the conclusion that God is necessary for objective morality. Some of them have the wild idea that this conclusion is to attack their integrity by saying people who do not believe in God are not capable of living morally good lives. Take, for instance, the holiday ad campaign from the American Humanist Association in 2008 which was displayed in the New York Times and Washington Post and on over two hundred Washington DC Metro buses: "Why believe in a god? Just be good for goodness' sake."[58] Then there is their ad campaign the following year which was placed across transit systems in five major U.S. cities: "No God?...No Problem! Be good for goodness' sake."[59] Further, take these six quotes from six well-known atheists.

Dawkins has stated that "Many religious people find it hard to imagine how, without religion, one can be good, or would even want to be good."[60] Christopher Hitchens wrote, "Name one ethical statement made, or one ethical action performed, by a believer that could not have been uttered or done by a nonbeliever."[61] Daniel Dennett writes that he has "uncovered no evidence to support the claim that people . . . who do not believe in reward in heaven and/or punishment in hell are more likely to kill, rape, rob, or break their promises than people who do."[62] The actor Ricky Gervais wrote in an article for The Wall Street Journal, "'Do unto others...' is a good rule of thumb. I live by that. Forgiveness is probably the greatest virtue there is. But that's exactly what it is – a virtue. Not just a Christian virtue. No one owns being good. I'm good. I just don't believe I'll be rewarded for it in heaven.'"[63] Sam Harris stated in a debate-like discussion with Ben Shapiro, "How would you explain the moral character of my life? I mean I'm not raping and killing people. I live a life that you would recognize to be ethically well-structured."[64] And Penn Jillette stated in an interview,

> The question I get asked by religious people all the time is, without God, what's to stop me from raping all I want? And my answer is: I do rape all I want. And the amount I want is zero. And I do murder all I want, and the amount I want is zero. The fact that these people think that if they didn't have this person watching over them that they would go on killing, raping rampages is the most self-damning thing I can imagine. I don't want to do that.[65]

We referred to such quotes as a wild idea, because it is completely false! Of course, atheists can live morally good lives without a belief in God, and if a theist were ever to state otherwise then the theist is just flat-out wrong and clearly has not thought things through! That wild idea, in the vast majority of cases thought-up by *atheists themselves*, is just a red herring – something that distracts and takes the attention away from the real issue at hand.

The conclusion that God is necessary for objective morality has nothing whatsoever to do with whether a person is capable of living a morally good life without a *belief* in God; theists are not automatically murderers and rapists, just like those who profess to believe in God are not automatically saints. To think otherwise would be to confuse moral epistemology with moral ontology: it is an epistemological (moral knowledge) issue when discussing *that* we all know what is morally right and wrong, but the real issue at hand is an ontological (foundation of morality) issue – the fact that it would be impossible for objective morality *even to exist* in the first place without God. "Therefore," says Turek in a debate with writer and atheist Michael Shermer, "Epistemology and ontology is the difference between knowing and justifying morality: You can know what a book says while denying there's an author. But there would be no book to know unless there was an author. Likewise, atheists can know objective morality while denying God exists, but there would be no objective morality to know unless God exists."[66]

So how is it that God is the source for the moral law and, yet, believers and unbelievers alike all know and can abide by it? The Apostle Paul gives the answer: "Even Gentiles, who do not have God's written law, show that they know his law when they instinctively obey it, even without having heard it. They demonstrate that God's law is written in their hearts, for their own conscience and thoughts either accuse them or tell them they are doing right."[67] (*Gentile*, to be clear, is an ethnic name that refers to those who are non-Jews). Thus, as Paul explains, the answer is that *we are all born instilled with the moral law* – an immaterial conscience.

THE EUTHYPHRO DILEMMA

By going down that rabbit trail, we have cleared up any possible misunderstandings about whether or not those who do not believe in God can live morally good lives. But, in doing so, this brings us to yet another rabbit trail that atheists like to distract people in following – the Euthyphro dilemma.

If you have attended any philosophy class in college, you have surely heard of the Euthyphro dilemma. Inspired by Plato's dialogue, *Euthyphro*, in which Socrates and Euthyphro famously attempt to identify the ultimate source of holiness, this "dilemma" is a modernized argument from this traditional dialogue, formulated by twentieth-century atheists such as Bertrand Russell, which asks: "Is something good because God says it is good, or does God say something is good because it is good?"[68]

Atheistic professors and students bring up this so-called "dilemma" because they believe they have found the one way out of God being the ultimate, changeless source for the moral law. As was the case with the character Euthyphro, this modernized "dilemma" is now intended to be a two-fold problem for Christians that supposedly stumps and forces them between a rock and a hard place when trying to ground objective morality with God. But it is actually quite weak.

On one hand, states the first half of this "dilemma," we must obey what God establishes as being morally good and as being morally bad. Now, you may be thinking, "Well, of course. That is exactly what has been concluded in this chapter about God." But that is not at all the case. You see, if God simply establishes the moral rules of the universe as He sees fit, then He could just as well have arbitrarily declared immoral acts, such as murder and rape, as being morally good. In fact, in following that logic, God could make things up on the fly and suddenly declare at any time that these and other immoral acts are now morally good and we would then be commanded to obey those new rules. On the other hand, states the second half of this "dilemma," God looks in accordance to a standard that is independent of and even higher than Himself to establish whether something is morally good or morally bad. If that were the case and God was subservient in relation to another standard, it would imply that the buck does not stop with God because He is not actually the ultimate source of the moral law after all.

Atheist's claim, "How can God be the ultimate, changeless source for the moral law when He has to abide by one of these two options; either way, He cannot be this source." So what is the solution? Well, first of all, there is actually no "dilemma" – hence why we have been putting quotation marks around the word itself. Instead, atheists have done nothing but create a *false* "dilemma."

An actual dilemma presents two choices that are contradictory towards one another; between "A" or "non-A." For example, deciding whether or not to eat ice cream is a true dilemma: eat the ice cream and enjoy the flavor ("A"), or do not eat the ice cream and have a better chance of not gaining weight and rotting any teeth ("non-A"). In the case of concluding whether or not God is the source for the moral law, this "dilemma" does not even include all of the options.

The third (and correct) option is that the ultimate, changeless standard of the moral law is specifically God's very *character*; hence why Scriptures state that God *is* good, *is* rationality, *is* truth, *is* love, and so on. God is, thus, the paradigm of absolute moral perfection.

So, God does not and actually *cannot* arbitrarily declare immoral acts as being morally good. Says Craig, "'When the atheist demands, "If God were to command child abuse, would we be obligated to abuse our children?"' that is similar to beginning a question phrased like, '"If there were a square circle…." There is no answer because what it supposes is logically impossible.'"[69] In fact, arbitrarily declaring an act as morally good one day and immoral the next (a view known as known as ethical voluntarism) is actually the description given *of the god of Islam*. Writes ethicist Scott B. Rae: "[Muslims] believe that [Allah] cannot be accountable to anyone or anything. Because of this understanding of Allah, it is consistent for Muslims to hold that such a sovereign being can command whatever he desires, and that, in and of itself, makes it good. Critics of Islamic ethics insist that this makes Allah arbitrary and gives him freedom to be even capricious in his commands."[70] But, as for the God of the Christian Bible, Rae rightly notes: "Scripture portrays God as bound by his character."[71] Thus, God's commandments to us through the moral law above the law are the reflection of His unchanging character.

REVISITING OBLIGATION

We can clearly see that only God gives us an objective answer as to why we *ought* to do right unto others. It all goes back to what we discussed in our last science-based chapter; that mankind is created in God's image with inherent value and purpose.[72] In light of all of the new information that we have discussed since that chapter, let us expand further on exactly what it means to be made in God's image.

It also means that we are made in His likeness, in that we share some of His communicable attributes. For example, because God has a mind, has emotion, and has free will, mankind was created as also having those attributes. Further, because God *is* good, *is* rationality, *is* truth, *is* love, and so on, we as His image bearers can be (and *ought* to be) good, rational, truthful, and loving. But, needless to say, this does not mean we share God's incommunicable attributes, such as being omnipresent (present everywhere at the same time), omniscient (all-knowing), nor omnipotent (all-powerful). Finally, being made in His image means that mankind is distinct from and has superior worth compared to all else in the universe.

It is because mankind is created with immense value and immense purpose that God instills specifically into us His unchanging moral law, which communicates to us His desires on how we *ought* to act towards one another. We *ought* to value the lives of other individuals and love our neighbors as ourselves because, according to God, we are all equally finely-tuned creations that bear His image and can achieve our universally shared purpose of knowing Him and making Him known to the world in our vastly unique ways. President George W. Bush said it well in his speech during a memorial service for slain police officers in Dallas, Texas: "At our best, we honor the image of God we see in one another. We recognize that we are brothers and sisters, sharing the same brief moment on Earth and owing each other the loyalty of our shared humanity."[73]

It goes even further than this: adding to God granting mankind with value and purpose, He also grants mankind with rights – something that those who abide by worldviews that attempt to do away with God cannot at all justify. Therefore, ironically, when those who abide by such worldviews argue for human rights without any reference to God, they have actually eliminated the only possibility of having objective, unchanging human rights!

It is only with God that *all* humans – those in the womb all the way to the elderly – have equally been endowed with inalienable value, purpose, and rights, and are entirely justified in protesting against any acts of dehumanization, degradation, and devaluation. This is because our value, purpose, and rights are firmly established by God's objective, universal, transcendent, unchanging authority – that is higher than any individual, any government, or any form of earthly authority – and, therefore, can never, *ever* be taken away!

As Greg Koukl writes: "If I stood at an intersection and put my hand up, cars might stop voluntarily, but they'd have no [obligation] to respond. They could ignore me with no fear of punishment because I have no authority to direct traffic. If, on the other hand, a policeman replaced me, traffic would come to a halt. What is the difference between the policeman and me? My authority is not grounded."[74] Similarly, neither the social contract theory nor the theory of evolution has any authority. But God does. After all, He is the Creator and Designer of the entire universe and everything that is in it, and it is entirely appropriate for Him to be in this authoritative position – instilled by His unchanging moral law – that obligates each and every one of us – His creations that are most valuable above all else in His eyes – on how we *ought* to act towards one another.

REVISITING CONSCIOUSNESS

We have gone over the fact of why we all know and can abide by the moral law, that God's very character is the ultimate, unchanging source for the moral law, and that He also grounds moral obligation for mankind. And with that said, the next topic we have discussed but need to cover again, in light of our recently made conclusions about God, is the topic of consciousness.

We stated there is nothing we are more familiar with than our own consciousness, as it is a uniquely immediate, direct, first-person experience. As we pay attention to our conscious states going on inside of us, we all experience the nature of our thoughts, perceptions, memories, sensations, desires, emotions, and beliefs as being immaterial in nature. Of course, as we have discussed, scientific studies and our daily experiences consistently state consciousness is neither just a product of activity within the physical brain, nor merely an illusion, but is an entirely real, distinct, immaterial entity that is separate and takes place elsewhere from the brain itself. In other words, the brain is not conscious; the brain does not think, but *you* do.

So, then, how is that the case? And how is it that when we have thoughts, sensations, desires, etc., those conscious states do not have any geometrical properties of size, shape, and location? Also, how is it that we have access to a person's brain states but do not have access to a person's conscious states; that brain activity can be publically known to neuroscientists, whereas conscious states are completely inner and private to the individual?

It is absolutely unavoidable from what we have discussed that an immaterial realm coexists with the physical world around us and that, yet, they are distinct from one another. Christianity, then, having a core belief which holds to this dualistic view of reality, is right. Further, Christianity holds to the view that immaterial consciousness and the physical brain coexist and interact but, yet, are distinct entities. In other words, the mind and brain work together but are not the same thing; your brain is not the source of your consciousness, but is simply an instrument (like a computer's router or a TV's antenna) that is used by your mind (like an Internet signal or a TV signal). Thus, Scriptures agree that not only is the brain and mind different from each another, as we are beings who have both a physical body and immaterial consciousness, but our *self* is different from them both; we have brains and also immaterial thoughts, sensations, desires, etc., but *we* are not brains or conscious states.

Scripture makes sense of this, stating that our true *self* is a *soul*. This goes back to how mankind is made in the image of God. God is a spirit and, because we are His image bearers, therefore, we are also spirits.[75] Further, we have bodies, whereas God does not, but our bodies are merely temporal vessels for our soul (spirit) while on Earth; our bodies are "animated" (given life, enlivened) by our soul. Therefore, you are a *soul* that *has* a body and conscious states. Moreland explains well:

> There was a story on television about an epileptic who underwent an operation in which surgeons removed fifty-three percent of her brain. When she woke up, nobody said, "We have forty-seven percent of a person here." A *person* cannot be divided into pieces. . . .

I have no inclination to doubt that this very room is teeming with the presence of God, just because I can't see or touch or smell or hear him.... The existence of my soul gives me a new way to understand how God can be everywhere. That's because my soul occupies my body without being located in any one part of it. There's no place in my body where you can say, "Here I am." My soul is not in the left part of my brain, it's not in my nose, it's not in my lungs. My soul is fully present everywhere throughout my body. That's why if I lose part of my body, I don't lose part of my soul [emphasis added].[76]

Your hair may turn from brown to grey, but that does not affect *you*. In the same way, for those who have brain damage or dementia, they do not lose *themselves*. It is entirely reasonable, then, to firmly believe Scripture is right when it states that the existence of the immaterial, spiritual realm – everything that the atheist so desperately tries to avoid (e.g., salvation and an afterlife) – is real, and that we can be comforted that, while some of us will eventually lose part or nearly all of the access to our minds while temporarily here on Earth, we all will never, *ever* lose our souls.

A HISTORICAL INVESTIGATION OF THE RESURRECTION

(Part 1)

Now that we have completed our prior investigation into whether a supernatural being and the miraculous could be possible, the first and most apparent thing we must do is answer a preliminary question: is there even a scrap of historical evidence that Jesus actually lived on Earth? It is clear that the resurrection of Jesus is crucial in determining which religion, if any, is objectively true. However, that was ancient times; how can we know whether that event is one which actually matches reality or is merely a fairytale for grownups? After all, if there is nothing to backup the claim that Jesus lived as a human being roughly 2,000 years ago, what need would there be for us to take the Apostle Paul's advice and investigate a resurrection that never could have happened?

CROSSING OPINION

To answer our question at hand, let us look at examples of credible sources who are unbiased towards Christianity in any way, shape, or form. Agnostic professor, historian, and author who seems to always be on the New York Times bestseller list, Bart D. Ehrman, is a perfect example of such a source. In fact, in regards to Christianity, he describes himself in that way:

> The reality is that whatever else you may think about Jesus, he certainly did exist. . . . The view that Jesus existed is held by virtually every expert on the planet. . . . What I do hope is to convince genuine seekers who really want to know how we know that Jesus did exist, as virtually every scholar of antiquity, of biblical studies, of classics, and of Christian origins in this country and, in fact, the Western world agrees. Many of these scholars have no vested interest in the matter. As it turns out, I myself do not either. I am not a Christian, and I have no interest in promoting a Christian cause or a Christian agenda. I am an agnostic. . . . As a historian, I think evidence matters. And the past matters. And for anyone to whom both evidence and the past matter, a dispassionate consideration of the case makes it quite plain: Jesus did exist. . . . Jesus existed, and those vocal persons who deny it do so not because they have considered the evidence with the dispassionate eye of the historian, but because they have some other agenda that this denial serves.[1]

Even evolutionary biologist and arguably today's most universally well-known atheist Richard Dawkins succinctly affirms, "Jesus existed."[2] Of course, you will see many atheistic scholars in the university setting discussing without a second thought what Jesus and those around Him said and did, so it is obvious they certainly trust He existed. We could go on and on with such modern-day examples, but the point is that, whether they are believers in

A HISTORICAL INVESTIGATION OF THE RESURRECTION (PART I)

Christ or not, history is irrefutably settled in the minds of historical scholars that Jesus existed. In fact, to doubt His existence would be to espouse a modern myth and would place you into the infinitesimally small group of on the fringe Internet bloggers who, as Ehrman states, would even deny "the Holocaust, the landing on the moon, the assassination of presidents," and so on and so forth.[3]

As William Lane Craig writes, Jesus is not "A figure in a stained-glass window, but a real, flesh-and-blood person of history, just like Julius Caesar or Alexander the Great, whose life can be investigated by the standard methods of history."[4] What, then, exactly does the historical record have to say that informs historical scholars with facts about the life of Jesus, His supposed death by crucifixion, supposed resurrection from the grave, and supposed post-resurrection appearances?

THE HISTORICAL RECORD

Let us get one thing straight before we go any farther: historians do not have to view the New Testament as Scriptures inspired by God to conclude that it presents us with a treasure trove of information about Jesus. Therefore, when referring to the New Testament and the Bible as a whole to learn about ancient times, as professor, author and historical scholar Michael Licona states, historians are "simply accepting it for what it unquestionably is – a set of ancient documents that can be subjected to historical scrutiny like any other accounts from antiquity."[5] Licona continues: "In other words, regardless of my personal beliefs, I'm not giving the Bible a privileged position in my investigation. I'm applying the same historical standards to it that I would apply to Thucydides or Suetonius."[6] William Lane Craig adds:

> The writings contained in the New Testament can be scrutinized using the same historical criteria that we use in investigating other sources of ancient history like Thucydides' *Peloponnesian War* or the *Annals* of Tacitus. . . . The most important of these historical sources have been collected into the New Testament. References to Jesus outside the New Testament tend to *confirm* what we read in the gospels, but they don't really tell us anything *new*. Therefore, the focus of our investigation must be upon the documents found in the New Testament. Now I find that many laymen do not understand this procedure. They think that if you examine the New Testament writings themselves rather than look at sources outside the New Testament, then somehow you're reasoning in a circle, using the Bible to prove the Bible. If you even quote a passage out of the New Testament, they think you're somehow begging the question, presupposing that the New Testament is reliable. But that's not at all what historians are doing when they examine the New Testament. They're not treating the Bible as a holy, inspired book and trying to prove it's true by quoting it. Rather they're treating the New Testament just like any other collection of ancient documents and investigating whether these documents are historically reliable.[7]

As any serious and honest historical scholar would attest, the books of the New Testament have been found to be an overwhelmingly accurate and trustworthy collection of historical documents. Even the most adamant atheist believes many things in the Bible are historically true. Anytime the New Testament is mentioned within this chapter, it is not in a circular fashion. Instead, it is merely being used as the earliest, primary documents of ancient history that speak of Jesus' life, crucifixion, and possible resurrection that are used comparatively alongside ancient sources outside of the Bible to see what actually corresponds to reality.

Furthermore, regarding the outside sources, if Christianity is all just an elaborate lie it is safe to say there cannot possibly be such supporting material that corresponds with the New Testament. So let us see what the historical record has to offer and allow it to set the tone, serving as means to weigh the remainder of this chapter for any bias either for or against the New Testament.

JOSEPHUS

Our first outside, non-Christian source, Flavius Josephus (37 - 100 A.D.), was, as historical scholars declare, the greatest Jewish historian from the first century. Being a priest belonging to the party of the Pharisees and a historian for Emperor Domitian in Rome after being taken hostage by the Romans during the first Jewish-Roman War, it was there that he would author multiple works. In his now famous *Antiquities of the Jews*, in a passage coined the *Testimonium Flavianum*, Josephus states,

> At this time there was a wise man who was called Jesus. And his conduct was good, and he was known to be virtuous. And many people from among the Jews and the other nations became his disciples. Pilate condemned him to be crucified and to die. And those who had become his disciples did not abandon his discipleship. They reported that he had appeared to them three days after his crucifixion and that he was alive; accordingly, he was perhaps the Messiah concerning whom the prophets have recounted wonders.[8]

Here, Josephus refers to Pontius Pilate, an important figure in the New Testament, and confirms that Jesus was crucified between 26 and 36 A.D.

(since Pilate was the fifth prefect of the Roman province of Judaea from that 10-year timeframe). We have confirmation that Jesus gained many followers from many regions. Also, after Jesus had died, His followers would stand together and announce to the world that he was the risen Messiah.

Another passage in *Antiquities of the Jews* describes how the high priest, Ananus, jumped at the opportunity to do his own evil bidding after Governor Festus died in office in 62 A.D. during this three month period in which it took Albinus, the true successor to the position as governor, to reach Judea from Alexandria. Josephus writes: "Festus was now dead, and Albinus was but upon the road; so he [Ananus] assembled the Sanhedrin of judges, and brought before them the brother of Jesus, who was called Christ, whose name was James, and some others; and when he had formed an accusation against them as breakers of the law, he delivered them to be stoned."[9]

Josephus would go on to refer to Emperor Nero, Governor Festus, Ananus, the Sadducees, the Sanhedrin, King Agrippa II, Jesus' brother James, and John the Baptist – all of which were prominent figures in the New Testament. He would then confirm to us that Jesus was, in fact, called Christ (which also means "Anointed One" and "the Messiah"), and had a brother named James who, along with "others," was the victim of ruthless martyrdom. Being "breakers of the law" corroborates with the New Testament that James converted to Christianity and that he and many other early Christians would not stop proclaiming that Christ was the risen Messiah.

TACITUS

Publius (Gaius) Cornelius Tacitus (56 - 120 A.D.), similar to Josephus being acclaimed as the greatest Jewish historian from the first century, is attested by scholars as the greatest *Roman* historian from the First Century. On top of also being a senator to the Roman Empire under Emperor Vespasian and the proconsul of Asia, Tacitus also authored many works; one of which is relevant to our discussion. In *The Annals*, Tacitus describes how Emperor Nero diverted suspicion away from himself for setting The Great Fire of Rome (64 A.D.) by both placing the blame on and immensely persecuting Christians:

> Consequently, to get rid of the report, Nero fastened the guilt and inflicted the most exquisite tortures on a class hated for their abominations, called Christians by the populace. Christus, from whom the name had its origin, suffered the extreme penalty [i.e., crucifixion] during the reign of Tiberius at the hands of one of our procurators, Pontius Pilate, and a most mischievous superstition, thus checked for the moment, again broke out not only in Judaea, the first source of the evil, but even in Rome. . . . An arrest was first made of all who pleaded guilty [of being Christians]; then, upon their information, an immense multitude was convicted, not so much of the crime of firing the city, as of hatred against mankind. Mockery of every sort was added to their deaths. Covered with the skins of beasts, they were torn by dogs and perished, or were nailed to crosses, or were doomed to the flames and burnt, to serve as a nightly illumination, when daylight had expired. . . . Even for criminals who deserved extreme and exemplary punishment, there arose a feeling of compassion.[10]

To fully understand this passage, it is necessary to give some background in regards to the Roman view of religion at this time in history. In the eyes of the Romans, religion was a means that formed a bond of social unity among the entire Empire. As long as the Roman gods and the emperor were shown respect and were worshipped, well-being would be sustained and the ancient religious beliefs of inhabitants that the Empire had conquered would remain legal. This is where hatred towards the Christians would come in to play. Christianity was new, therefore prone to distrust, and was deemed a superstition. The Christian form of worship would become significantly misunderstood, as they would go on to be falsely accused of being disloyal citizens and, because Romans did not understand what Jesus meant when saying believers were to eat bread and drink of the vine as symbols of His flesh and blood in order to remember His eventual sacrifice on the cross, even cannibals.

All in all, Christian beliefs and customs were not in line with those of the Empire. And out of fear that the Roman gods would become angry and cause unrest, the Roman authorities had to deal with this immense amount of Christians. No, they were not told to sit in a corner and think about what they have done; they were tortured and murdered in the most humiliating and gruesome ways imaginable. As Tacitus states, they were covered and sewn into animal skins to then be fed alive to hungry dogs, crucified, and impaled onto stakes and set on fire in order to serve as human candle lights for the Roman passerby. From the testimony of other sources, we also know that Christians were beaten and stoned to death, disemboweled, and beheaded. Yet, even with the shared belief that Christians should be punished, the forms of persecution caused sympathy to be felt by the typical Roman onlooker.

Tacitus confirms that Jesus was crucified during the reign of Pilate (between 26 and 36 A.D.) and Emperor Tiberius (between 14 and 37 A.D.). We also have confirmation that Christians received their name from Christ (Christus in Latin), the Christian movement originated in Judea, that many Christians were willing to and did lose their lives through martyrdom for not denouncing their firm beliefs, and that something significant must have happened in regards to Jesus in order for them to stand firm and to go through such hell on earth for Him.

Not only is Tacitus a non-Christian source like Josephus but he is our first example of an actively *anti-Christian* source. And what is most noteworthy about Tacitus mentioning Jesus and His followers is the very fact of, well, *Tacitus mentioning Jesus and His followers*! Though there are much more, one can rightly confirm from this account alone that Jesus lived and His followers did what the New Testament says they did. Further, with Tacitus being such an enemy of the whole Christian movement, that only adds fuel to the fact that the reach of the movement was growing more and more successful having reached a hostile Rome in such a short amount of time.

PLINY THE YOUNGER

Gaius Caecilius Secundus (61 - 113 A.D.), later Gaius Plinius Caecilius Secundus (after being adopted by his uncle) and best known as Pliny the Younger, was not only a man of many names but also of many titles. On top of being a Roman senator, lawyer, and Governor of the Roman province of Bithynia-Pontus (present-day Turkey), he was also the author of a now famous collection of historical letters, the *Epistulae*. In book 10, letter 96, in an exchange with Emperor Trajan, he, as an apparent enemy of Christianity, would seek advice on how to handle the interrogation and persecution of Christians he arrested:

> I have asked them if they are Christians, and if they admit it, I repeat the question a second and third time, with a warning of the punishment awaiting them. If they persist, I order them to be led away for execution; for, whatever the nature of their admission, I am convinced that their stubbornness and unshakable obstinacy ought not to go unpunished. Now that I have begun to deal with

this problem, as so often happens, the charges are becoming more widespread and increasing in variety. . . . They also declared that the sum total of their guilt . . . amounted to no more than this: they had met regularly before dawn on a fixed day to chant verses alternately amongst themselves in honor of Christ as if to a god, and also to bind themselves by oath, not for any criminal purpose, but to abstain from theft, robbery, and adultery. . . . This made me decide it was all the more necessary to extract the truth by torture from two slave-women, whom they called deaconesses. . . . I have therefore postponed any further examination and hastened to consult you. The question seems to me worthy of your consideration, especially in view of the number of persons endangered; for a great many individuals of every age and class, both men and women, are being brought to trial, and this is likely to continue. It is not only the towns, but villages and rural districts too.[11]

Pliny gives us even more insight into how the Roman view of religion conflicted much with that of Christianity. After having looked into the matter he confirms that Christians are ethical people, did not partake in rumored activities (such as cannibalism), and that their illegality came only from their refusal to worship as the Romans wished. He confirms the early church contained deacons and deaconesses and consisted of every class of people (including Roman citizens), there was a significant population of Christians in Bithynia-Pontus, and the early church's belief in Christ's deity. Then, in a reply from Emperor Trajan, it is confirmed that all Christians had to do to be pardoned from persecution was to renounce Christ and offer prayers to the Roman gods – something they would not do.

SUETONIUS

Gaius Suetonius Tranquillus (69 - after 122 A.D.) was a Roman court official, chief secretary to Emperor Hadrian, and author. In his most famous work, *Lives of the Twelve Caesars* (a collection of biographies about Julius Caesar and Rome's first eleven emperors), Suetonius writes in the biography of Emperor Claudius: "As the Jews were making constant disturbances at the instigation of Christ, he [Claudius] expelled them from Rome."[12]

This "instigation" is referring to conflict among the Jewish people themselves after many converted Jews were preaching in Rome about the risen Jesus. From this short account, we learn a lot of information about Christianity that supports the New Testament text. Here we have confirmation that the reach of Christianity was so successful that by year 49 A.D. (a mere sixteen years after Jesus' crucifixion) not only was the population of Christians large enough to be identified as such, but there were enough Christians in Rome to justify all Jews being expelled from the region (as the Apostle Paul states in Acts 18:2).

Further, we find information about the persecution of Christians in the biography of Nero. Suetonius writes: "Punishment by Nero was inflicted on the Christians, a class of men given to a new and mischievous superstition."[13] Here we have additional confirmation that Christians were persecuted under Roman rule (Nero being emperor at the time that the historical fact of the Apostle Paul and other apostles being brutally murdered for their preaching the Gospel occurred).

CELSUS

Celsus was a Greek philosopher and opponent to Christianity. Ridiculing Christians for worshipping Jesus, he wrote (circa 178 A.D.),

Now, if the Christians worshiped only one God they might have reason on their side. But as a matter of fact they worship a man who appeared only recently. They do not consider what they are doing a breach of monotheism; rather, they think it perfectly consistent to worship the great God and to worship his servant as God. And their worship of this Jesus is the more outrageous because they refuse to listen to any talk about God, the father of all, unless it includes some reference to Jesus: Tell them that Jesus, the author of the Christian insurrection, was not his son, and they will not listen to you. And when they call him Son of God, they are not really paying homage to God, rather, they are attempting to exalt Jesus to the heights.[14]

Celsus, through his clear misunderstanding of Christian teachings, first confirms first that the early Christians were monotheists and rejected polytheism. Second, though the Holy Spirit is not mentioned, this was due to their doctrine of the Trinity (God the Father, Son, and Holy Spirit are one) which in turn, as did Pliny, also confirms the early church's belief in the deity of Christ. And third, as with Pliny, he confirms the early church's strong, unshakable belief in Christ's deity.

LUCIAN

Lucian of Samosata (circa 125 – after 180 A.D.) was a Roman rhetorician, pamphleteer, and satirist. He wrote,

> The Christians, you know, worship a man to this day – the distinguished personage who introduced their novel rites, and was crucified on that account. . . . You see, these misguided creatures

start with the general conviction that they are immortal for all time, which explains the contempt of death and voluntary self-devotion which are so common among them; and then it was impressed on them by their original law giver that they are all brothers, from the moment that they are converted, and deny the gods of Greece, and worship the crucified sage, and live after his laws.[15]

Lucian is yet another example of a hostile source. His words align with that of the New Testament regarding the crucifixion and deity of Christ, everlasting life through salvation, and the early church's firm conviction to live their lives – even to martyrdom – according to the teachings of Christ and not any other gods.

THE TALMUD

The Jewish Talmud is a collection of teachings central to Rabbinic Judaism. And in them, they report, "'On the eve of the Passover, *Yeshua* was hanged. For forty days before the execution took place, a herald went forth and cried, "He is going forth to be stoned because he has practiced sorcery and enticed Israel to apostasy. Anyone who can say anything in his favor, let him come forward and plead on his behalf. But since nothing was brought forward in his favor he was hanged on the eve of the Passover."'[16]

We learn several facts from this passage. First of all, *Yeshua*, of course, is translated as *Jesus* in Greek, while being hung on a tree is an alternative reference to crucifixion. A fascinating reference is when The Talmud states Jesus practices sorcery. A source in opposition to Christianity would not have admitted to Jesus performing miracles, so to say Jesus practiced sorcery is confirmation that something unusual (perhaps miracles?) was happening through the works of Jesus.

CROSSING OPINION

THALLUS, AFRICANUS, AND PHLEGON

Our final examples give historical evidence about a specific event from two places within the New Testament. In the book of Luke, we read, "'By this time it was about noon, and darkness fell across the whole land until three o'clock. The light from the sun was gone. And suddenly, the curtain in the sanctuary of the Temple was torn down the middle. Then Jesus shouted: "'Father, I entrust my spirit into your hands!' And with those words he breathed his last."[17] Then in the book of Matthew we read, "At that moment the curtain in the sanctuary of the Temple was torn in two, from top to bottom. The earth shook, rocks split apart..."[18]

Writing about Jesus' crucifixion and the darkness that occurred upon Jesus' death, quoting the Roman historian Thallus from the third book of his three-volume work of the Mediterranean world (circa 52 A.D.), the historical scholar Julius Africanus states, "On the whole world there pressed a most fearful darkness; and the rocks were rent by an earthquake, and many places in Judea and other districts were thrown down."[19]

Thallus would go on to try and explain away this event as "an eclipse of the sun." The funny thing is that this "explanation" is entirely impossible seeing as how Jesus was crucified during the Jewish Passover. Of course, Passover always falls at the time of a full moon, and an eclipse of the Sun cannot happen during a full moon but, instead, only during a new moon. Other historians describe this event, some attempting to use this "explanation" as well, and they all coincide with the year that Jesus was crucified. What we learn from this passage is that Jesus lived, He was crucified, and that an earthquake and "fearful" darkness occurred at the time of the crucifixion.

To add, the Greek historian, Phelgon, wrote his account (circa 137 A.D.) about the crucifixion of Jesus that was followed by darkness. He reported that in the fourth year of the 202nd Olympiad (33 A.D.) there was "the greatest eclipse of the sun" and "it became night in the sixth hour of the day [i.e., noon] so that stars even appeared in the heavens. There was a great earthquake in Bithynia, and many things were overturned in Nicaea."[20]

CONSTRUCTING A LIST

As historian Paul Maier writes, "Many facts from antiquity rest on just one ancient source, while two or three sources in agreement generally render the fact unimpeachable."[21] This is but a handful of examples among the abundance of Roman, Greek, and Jewish outside sources which we could discuss. In total, there are 43 sources with surviving works that speak of Jesus within 150 years of His life, making Him (a carpenter from the remote province of Galilee, whose public ministry lasted a mere three years) the most affirmed person *in all of ancient history*.[22] This number is even more amazing when, for instance, compared to the 10 sources with surviving works for Tiberius Caesar, who had been in politics since the age of seventeen and, among other positions, reigned as emperor over the entire Roman Empire for 22 years!

What is most noteworthy about these historical accounts is that they *never* argue against the historicity of Jesus or the sudden rise of the early church. Instead, the facts they present are entirely consistent with and do not contradict the New Testament. If Christianity was all just an elaborate lie, how could *non-Christian and hostile* sources corroborate with the New Testament text, which was all written much sooner than any of the outside sources, on all of these points? In fact, if we did not have the New Testament to go by and used only the information about Jesus and the early church that we learn about from these outside sources, we would be able to construct a considerably long list of points:

1. Jesus was born, supposedly to a virgin, and had an earthly father who was a carpenter.
2. Jesus was a wise, Jewish teacher.
3. He lived a moral life.
4. Performed wonders such as healings and exorcisms (though often attributed this to sorcery from Satan, note the fact they were not denying that Jesus was actually performing them.)
5. Had at least one brother named James.
6. Had many disciples.
7. Led many of the Jews away from their traditional beliefs.
8. Was said to be able to predict the future accurately.
9. Was rejected and despised by the Jewish leaders.
10. Was severely beaten and forced to wear a crown of thorns.
11. Was sentenced to crucifixion under the governorship of Pontius Pilate.
12. His crucifixion was during the reign of Tiberius Caesar.
13. Was crucified on the eve of the Jewish Passover holiday.
14. A darkness from noon to three in the afternoon occurred at His crucifixion.
15. Great earthquakes occurred at His crucifixion.
16. Was buried in a tomb and the tomb was later found to be empty.
17. Was said to have been seen alive by many after rising from the grave three days later.
18. Was said to be the expected Messiah.
19. His brother was the leader of the church in Jerusalem and died as a Christian martyr.
20. His disciples ranged from many backgrounds and from many regions.
21. His disciples met on Sunday, worshipped, and partook in new rituals such as Communion.
22. Communion would cause a rumor to spread that Christians were, among other things, cannibals.

23. Many of His disciples were willing to be persecuted and die for their new, firm beliefs.
24. Many of His disciples were persecuted and martyred by the Jews.
25. Many of His disciples successfully and rapidly spread the News of Jesus' resurrection well beyond Jerusalem.
26. Many of His disciples were persecuted and martyred by the Romans.
27. Many of His disciples would not deny Jesus as God.
28. Many of His disciples would not worship the Greco-Roman gods or the Roman emperors.
29. Some of His disciples were able to perform miracles such as healings (as with Jesus, they often attributed this power as sorcery from Satan. Again, they did not deny the miracles).
30. After what all that Christians would go through, they would be persistent and their number would only grow in size.

Says Craig Blomberg, New Testament scholar and Distinguished Professor of the New Testament at Denver Seminary, "When you stop to think that ancient historians for the most part dealt only with political rulers, emperors, kings, military battles, official religious people, and major philosophical movements, it is remarkable how much we can learn about Jesus and His followers even though they fit none of those categories at the time these historians were writing."[23] It is quite extraordinary knowing that these outside sources listed are historians and writers who were not sympathetic to the Christian cause whatsoever. Taking that in mind, when enemies and opponents reference the same people, places, and events, historians take those facts as being historically certain. Once such facts are listed, it is clear that the life of Jesus and the sudden rise of Christianity are historical facts as the New Testament claim. To state otherwise would mean succumbing to the intellectually irresponsible realm of blind faith.

THE MINIMAL FACTS

When it comes to Jesus' resurrection, there are facts that *many* credible historians would agree are historically true, facts that *most* credible historians would agree are historically true, and then there are facts that *all* credible historians would agree are historically true. Historian, New Testament scholar, and philosopher Gary Habermas, "has compiled a list of more than 2,200 sources in French, German, and English in which experts have written on the resurrection from 1975 to the present" and has "identified . . . facts that are strongly evidenced and which are regarded as historical by the large majority of scholars" states Licona.[24] Coined "the minimal facts," scholars from all walks agree on *at least* these twelve facts as historical bedrock:

1. "Jesus died by Roman crucifixion.
2. He was buried, most likely in a private tomb.
3. Soon afterward, the disciples were discouraged, bereaved, and despondent, having lost hope.
4. Jesus' tomb was found empty very soon after His interment.
5. The disciples had experiences that they believed were actual appearances of the risen Jesus.
6. Due to these experiences, the disciples' lives were thoroughly transformed, even being willing to die for this belief.
7. The proclamation of the resurrection took place very early, at the beginning of church history.
8. The disciples' public testimony and preaching of the resurrection took place in the city of Jerusalem, where Jesus had been crucified and buried shortly before.
9. The Gospel message centered on the death and resurrection of Jesus.
10. Sunday was the primary day for gathering and worshipping.

11. James, the brother of Jesus and a former skeptic, was converted when, he believed, he saw the risen Jesus.
12. Just a few years later, Saul of Tarsus (Paul) became a Christian believer due to an experience that he believed was an appearance of the risen Jesus."[25]

These "minimal facts" add yet another layer to the historical record serving as a method to weigh for any bias for or against the New Testament. Let us delve deeper into just five of them (and, in doing so, briefly touch on all of them) to aid in a further discussion later on in the chapter. Our first point of focus is the indisputable fact of Jesus' death by crucifixion.

JESUS' CRUCIFIXION

We have seen from outside sources – without even opening the Bible – that the crucifixion of Christ is a historically certain event; Josephus, Tacitus, Lucian, and the Jewish Talmud among others all corroborate with the New Testament that Jesus died by crucifixion. Further, modern-day leading atheistic and agnostic scholars will agree that His death by crucifixion is, without a doubt, historically certain. Licona states,

> Even an extreme liberal like Crossan says: "That he was crucified is as sure as anything historical ever can be." Skeptic James Tabor says, "we need have no doubt that given Jesus' execution by Roman crucifixion he was truly *dead*." Both Gerd Lüdemann, who's an atheistic New Testament critic, and Bart Ehrman, who's an agnostic, call the crucifixion an indisputable fact. . . . Jesus was crucified and died as a result. The scholarly consensus . . . is

absolutely overwhelming. To deny it would . . . get you laughed out of the academic world."[26]

Historians obviously put significant weight on historical reports that are presented from eyewitness, early, corroborated, and enemy accounts, and the case is especially so when reports fit the category of more than one of those avenues. But there is one more avenue that historians put significant weight on: when reports are from *embarrassing* accounts.

The "cover-up test" is a critical method that historians and judges both use on a daily basis to test whether a source is being reliable or not. Author and professor Lee Strobel considers this is such an important method because, "When people testify about events they saw, they will often try to protect themselves or others by conveniently forgetting to mention details that are embarrassing or hard to explain. As a result, this raises uncertainty about the veracity of their entire testimony."[27] Therefore, if someone were to include such details in their testimony, this would give good reason for others to believe that it is authentic. With that said, it is a natural next step to examine Jesus' original twelve disciples to see if their reports fit into the avenue of embarrassing accounts.

In examining their reports, it does not take long at all to come across a handful of embarrassing examples. These examples include a numbskull misunderstanding on the disciples' behalf about bread; their continual misunderstanding and total lack of concern of Jesus' well-being, to the extent of cutting Him off while talking just to find out which of them was His favorite disciple; Jesus once referring to Peter as Satan; Jesus being livid with them for rebuking children who were seeking blessings and possible healings from Him; Jesus criticizing two disciples for seeking their own prideful motives of heart; Jesus' own siblings thinking He was "out of his mind"; Jesus being accused as a demon-possessed deceiver; Jesus twice escaping being stoned to death by a group of His deserted followers; and Jesus a prostitute permission to wash His feet with expensive perfume and her hair.[28]

Another instance occurred during the time at the Garden of Gethsemane before Jesus was forcibly captured and put on trial. Knowing that death on the cross was coming after His trial, we read that Jesus was in deep spiritual and physical agony; so much so He began to pray even more fervently and began to sweat drops of blood. This is a rare medical condition known as *Hematohidrosis*, or *Hematidrosis*, in which the blood vessels that surround the sweat glands rupture due to experiencing severe emotional and physical stress and anguish.[29] In agony and having not slept a wink Himself, not once but three times the disciples fell asleep as they were supposed to be on watch. On top of this, one of the disciples, Judas Iscariot, betrays and helps with His arrest, all of the disciples but Peter deserted Him and fled in fear, then Peter even denied knowing Jesus three times.[30] John was the only original disciple not hiding in fear of the authorities, and Jesus' female disciples (including His mother) stayed with Him until He took His very last breath.[31] And, speaking of His female disciples, it was they who were the first to discover Jesus' tomb empty (a topic which we will discuss in more detail).[32]

We give such examples first to now discuss one especially embarrassing point for our purpose of providing an overview of the "minimal fact" that Jesus died by crucifixion. The point is really quite simple: what was so embarrassing to the disciples (and any followers of Jesus for that matter) and the overall startup of Christianity in regards to Jesus dying by crucifixion was, well, *Jesus dying by crucifixion*.

Dating back to 722 B.C., the Jewish people had been continually conquered by empires and dynasties alike. Needless to say, they were fed up with constant oppression. They were eagerly awaiting a conquering, political and military-minded Messiah who would once and for all defeat and free them from their oppressors. By the time Jesus comes onto the scene and begins His public ministry in A.D. 30, the Jews had been under Roman rule for nearly a century. They were not at all looking for a Messiah like Jesus, but as He gained many followers they were enthusiastically hoping that He was the One to establish a Jewish-ruled kingdom. So when He was taken captive, tortured, and killed, you can understand how that caused many issues for His followers starting a religion based on Him being the Messiah.

It is not just *that* He died but *how* He died; the Jewish people traditionally held the view that anyone who was crucified was guilty of a capital offense and under a curse from God. A *dead Messiah*, let alone a *crucified Messiah*, was an oxymoron; as self-contradictory as a circular triangle or a tall, short person. So, for those who were not present to witness Jesus' ministry, once they heard Jesus was crucified, they would have automatically assumed He was nothing more than a shameful, humiliated criminal (that would be even worse than trying to explain the vehicle you are selling is amazing, and a Hyundai; no one would take you seriously!).

If Jesus' death by crucifixion was just a made-up story, it makes absolutely zero sense to include the embarrassing details of Jesus being killed in the New Testament writings. It would only have made presenting the testimony that He was the long-awaited, immortal, triumphant Messiah downright impossible to believe. In fact, the Apostle Paul would later touch on this difficulty: "We preach Christ crucified, a stumbling block to the Jews and foolishness to the Gentiles."[33] As for the details relating to the disciples, it would have been much easier and much more productive to have just left these and other details about Jesus out of the writings. The only logical reason why such details were included in the Gospel accounts is that the writers were simply presenting the facts, regardless of the inevitable implications. That is exactly what *had* to be done, or else everyone locally would have known otherwise that they were lying!

With every point we have discussed thus far, the writers of the New

Testament knew that everyone who witnessed Jesus' ministry knew the truth and that they could only verbally present the message of His life, death, and resurrection to the world if what they stated was the truth. Upon being written down in the form of the Gospel accounts, the locals would have also known whether or not what was written down was entirely factual.

JESUS' TOMB

The next "minimal fact" that occurred after Jesus' crucifixion was His burial. Not only was proper, honorable burial the Roman law to respect traditional customs from regions they ruled, Jewish law strictly commanded it: "If someone has committed a crime worthy of death and is executed and hung on a tree, the body must not remain hanging from the tree overnight. You must bury the body that same day, for anyone who is hung is cursed in the sight of God. In this way, you will prevent the defilement of the land the LORD your God is giving you as your special possession."[34] In all four Gospels, it is specifically stated that Jesus' body was immediately requested from Pilate by Joseph of Arimathea, and that He was placed personally by Joseph and aided by Nicodemus in Joseph's own private tomb.[35] Craig writes, "'Most New Testament critics concur that Jesus was buried by Joseph of Arimathea in a tomb. According to the late John A. T. Robinson of Cambridge University, the burial of Jesus in the tomb is "one of the earliest and best-attested facts about Jesus."'"[36]

Clearly, the crucifixion was a complete disaster to the faith of the disciples and followers who were so confident that Jesus was the Messiah. Just when they had finally grown to get comfortable with the fact and became vulnerable with trust, He was murdered; His cold body lying in a tomb. His death on the cross was proof that He was not the Messiah. Three days pass with discouragement and all hope lost:

> But very early on Sunday morning the women went to the tomb, taking the spices they had prepared. They found that the stone had been rolled away from the entrance. So they went in, but they did not find the body of the Lord Jesus. As they stood there puzzled, two men suddenly appeared to them, clothed in dazzling robes. The women were terrified and bowed with their faces to the ground. Then the men asked, "Why are you looking among the dead for someone who is alive? He is not here! He is risen from the dead! Remember what he told you back in Galilee, that the Son of Man must be betrayed into the hands of sinful men and be crucified, and that he would rise again on the third day." Then they remembered that he had said this. So they rushed back from the tomb to tell his eleven disciples – and everyone else – what had happened. It was Mary Magdalene, Joanna, Mary the mother of James, and several other women who told the apostles what had happened. But the story sounded like nonsense to the men, so they did not believe it.[37]

As the disciples and all of the Jewish people firmly believed, the Messiah was not supposed to die; Jesus was not the real deal. Jesus had died in a humiliating way, was rotting in a tomb, and now they are supposed to believe that He has miraculously risen from the dead? This story that "sounded like nonsense" was not going to change a single mind, especially because it came from the testimony of women.

The disciples were quick to dismiss what these women said, but that was expected within their culture. In those ancient times, Jewish and Roman women were not the most sought-after sources for reliable information. First, women were not regarded as credible witnesses. Even their testimony during legal trials was not welcome as valid. Second, women occupied a low rung on the Jewish social ladder. So, compared to men, women had considerably lower status and were viewed as second-class citizens. For example, the Jewish Talmud says, "Sooner let the words of the Law be burnt than delivered to women," and that, "Any evidence which a woman [gives] is not valid (to offer), also they are not valid to offer. This is equivalent to saying that one who is Rabbinically accounted a robber is qualified to give the same evidence as a woman."[38][39] And Josephus writes, "But let not the testimony of women be admitted, on account of the levity and boldness of their sex, nor let servants be admitted to give testimony on account of the ignobility of their soul; since it is probable that they may not speak truth, either out of hope of gain, or fear of punishment."[40]

It would have been *highly* embarrassing for the disciples to detail *in all four* Gospel accounts that women were the discoverers of and primary witnesses to the empty tomb. It was then that Peter and "the beloved disciple" reached the tomb, looked in, and *still* "did not understand that Jesus had to rise from the dead."[41] If the disciples were merely making up an elaborate story, their including the story that women were the ones who found the tomb empty would have been a completely unnecessary thing to do. This is especially true seeing as how the text states Mary Magdalene, "the woman from whom Jesus had cast out seven demons," was the very first person to see the resurrected Jesus![42] The disciples *never* would have harmed their own credibility by saying they received testimony first from women (including one who had previously been possessed!) and that they themselves still did not understand Jesus' words that he would be killed. No, they would have made themselves out to be the brave ones who discovered the empty tomb and who valiantly comforted the women who were in hiding and trembling with fear!

On top of this, it was Joseph of Arimathea and Nicodemus who was responsible for the burial that Jesus received. Both were members of the Sanhedrin, the Jewish high court that condemned Jesus and was the masterminds behind His murder. Given the titles of Joseph and Nicodemus, for the disciples to state it was these two men and not themselves who properly buried Jesus would be an incredibly embarrassing and hard to explain detail that was completely unnecessary to include if it were not true. As we saw with the crucifixion, the only logical reason the disciples would have included all of these details, regardless of the credibility implications caused by them or regardless of how embarrassing the details were, is the fact that it was the truth and everyone locally would have picked up on blatant lies.

And there is more. Among other reasons, there are two additional reasons that historians believe there is strong evidence that what the Gospel accounts state about the empty tomb is the truth – the first being what is referred to by historians as "enemy attestation."

What we mean by enemy attestation, or enemy testimony, in this regard is that it was not just the testimony of women stating Jesus' tomb was found empty; as we read in the book of Matthew, the Jewish leaders (whom the disciples ran and hid from out of fear for their own lives) *themselves* agreed and even came up with a devised reason for why it was empty:

> There was a violent earthquake, for an angel of the Lord came down from heaven and, going to the tomb, rolled back the stone and sat on it. His appearance was like lightning, and his clothes were white as snow. The guards were so afraid of him that they shook and became like dead men. . . . [The] guards came into the city and reported to the chief priests everything that had happened. After the priests had assembled with the elders and agreed on a plan, they gave the soldiers a large sum of money and told them, "Say this, 'His disciples came during the night and stole Him while we were sleeping.' If this reaches the governor's ears, we will deal with him

and keep you out of trouble." So they took the money and did as they were instructed. And this story has been spread among Jewish people to this day.[43]

This is evidence from a hostile source – evidence that was not at all in the favor of the Jewish leaders or Roman authorities – that the tomb was, in fact, empty. Now, you may be thinking to yourself (or screaming out loud) "that is strictly relying on the text of the New Testament, though. We do not have any other sources that corroborate that information." But *we do* have other sources. Not only is this account reported in the book of Matthew, but also by Justin Martyr (100-165 A.D.) and Tertullian (160-225 A.D.) who corroborate not only that Jewish leaders sent representatives throughout the Mediterranean world to state Jesus' tomb was empty because His disciples stole His corpse, but also that the rumor was still being spread well into the second and third century![44][45] Additionally, we have *every single person in Jerusalem* as sources! Why? Well, this flows into our second point which leads historians to believe even further that what the Gospel accounts state about the empty tomb is the truth: the locality of the tomb.

Just like *everyone* knew the location of where Jesus was publically crucified, *everyone* knew the location of where Jesus was publically buried. *Everyone* also knew the story that was spread by the Jewish leaders. And *everyone* could go see for themselves whether or not the tomb really was vacant.

Craig writes, "'Taken together these . . . lines of evidence constitute a powerful case that Jesus' tomb was indeed found empty on the first day of the week by a group of his women followers. . . . According to D.H. Van Daalen, "It is extremely difficult to object to the empty tomb on historical grounds; those who deny it do so on the basis of theological or philosophical assumptions."'[46] Such lines of evidence led classical scholar Michael Grant to conclude that historians "cannot justifiably deny the empty tomb" because "the evidence is firm . . . to necessitate the conclusion that the tomb was indeed found empty."[47] And historical scholar and specialist in the resurrection Jacob Kremer agrees: "By far most . . . hold firmly to the reliability of the biblical statements concerning the empty tomb."[48]

JESUS' APPEARANCES

Jerusalem would be *the very place* on Earth where a lie about Jesus would have been squashed in a heartbeat. So with such a story being spread across the entire Mediterranean world, how did Christianity ever gain any traction? Furthermore, the disciples deserted Jesus, went into hiding, became discouraged, lost all hope after His crucifixion, and thought the message from women that He was resurrected from the grave was nonsense. But in just a few days, and mere months later for thousands and thousands more in Jerusalem, however, they would suddenly abandon their most treasured traditional beliefs and practices in Judaism and confidently begin to preach that He was the Messiah after all.

As Emory University New Testament scholar Luke Timothy Johnson writes, "Some sort of powerful, transformative experience is required to generate the sort of movement earliest Christianity was."[49] *Something happened.* Something happened that changed the world forever by completely reversing the verdict about Jesus the "dead criminal." But what exactly was *it* that was so powerful to have immediately blossomed into the origin of Christianity in Jerusalem and the rapid growth throughout and beyond the entire Roman Empire?

Jesus would confirm His resurrection and His identity as the Son of God by appearing alive and well to multitudes of groups and individuals. The texts state He appeared over a period of 40 days, to individuals and groups ranging from one person to more than 500 people, on at least twelve different occasions, at different times, in different places, and under different circumstances![50] Lüdemann, again an atheist, also admits to this minimal fact stating it is "historically certain that Peter and the disciples had experiences after Jesus' death in which Jesus appeared to them as the risen Christ."[51] Licona states of Habermas' overview of scholarly sources on the resurrection: "Perhaps no fact was more widely recognized than that the early Christian believers had real experiences that they thought were appearances of the risen Jesus."[52] Licona continues,

> As Paula Fredriksen of Boston University put it – and, again, she's . . . a very liberal scholar – "I know in their own terms what they saw was the raised Jesus. That's what they say and then all the historic evidence we have afterwards attests to their conviction that that's what they saw. I'm not saying that they really did see the raised Jesus. I wasn't there. I don't know what they saw. *But I do know that as a historian that they must have seen something.*" In fact, Fredriksen says elsewhere that 'the disciples' conviction that they had seen the risen Christ . . . is [part of] historical bedrock, facts known past doubting.

The early Christians had absolutely nothing to gain in this world, such as prestige or wealth. Nevertheless, they were imprisoned, beaten, tortured in every possible way, and murdered. Every conceivable method was used to try and make them stop talking about Christ as the risen Messiah. Yet, to the point that Christianity was the primary faith over the entire Roman Empire by year 313 A.D., they would continue to spread the Gospel message without recanting their firm convictions.

After all, writes Paul E. Little, "Men will die for what they *believe* to be true, though it may actually be false. They do not, however, die for what they *know* is a lie."⁵⁴ This commitment is vastly different than, say, terrorists dying for what they *think* is the truth, as the early Christians were in the position to *know* whether or not Jesus really rose from the grave. And as Nicholas Thomas (N.T.) Wright, a leading British New Testament scholar, states, "That is why, as a historian, I cannot explain the rise of early Christianity unless Jesus rose again."⁵⁵

If their mission was all just an elaborate lie and Jesus had not actually made public appearances after supposedly resurrecting from the grave, someone among these new followers would have given in and announced the lie to the world. They could have easily saved themselves and the lives of countless others by simply confessing. In the face of certain persecution and death, such conditions did nothing to weaken the faith of the early church. Instead, they were emboldened even more-so to stay committed to what they knew was true, their number would increase even higher, and the Gospel message would spread even farther.

Then when the New Testament was compiled and these works – meant for *public* reading – were observed, anyone could easily have picked up on exaggerations or outright lies. For instance, the book of Acts describes the Apostle Paul spreading the message across the entire Mediterranean world. If Paul really had not done the detailed events, such as perform miracles, or make multiple journeys to specified towns to check on and encourage churches that actually existed, there were plenty who would have known the texts were fabricated. Another example is that a large number of new followers in the early church were Jewish priests who, prior to the resurrection, were likely hostile towards the belief that Jesus was claiming to be the Son of God.⁵⁶ So were there really a large number of converted priests? Again, plenty of people would have known this answer (especially the priests themselves!). By mentioning such events in their works, which was completely unnecessary to do, the New Testament writers were giving their enemies and the public altogether *numerous* chances to expose Christianity as a lie.

When mentioning the 500 witnesses (which could be a much higher number if it did not include women and children) who supposedly saw Jesus at once, why would Paul then state about them to his audience in the city of Corinth, "most of whom are still alive, though some have died," if he did not have firsthand knowledge of contact with these witnesses and knew his statement could certainly be backed up? New Testament scholar of Cambridge University, C.H. Dodd, observes, "'There can hardly be any purpose in mentioning the fact that most of the 500 are still alive, unless Paul is saying, in effect, 'The witnesses are there to be questioned.'"[57] Paul never could have said that Jesus appeared to at least 500 witnesses on one occasion, and others, so close to the event had it not truly happened. He never could have challenged anyone to reach out and question these so-called witnesses if no witnesses actually existed.

Not only did the writers of the New Testament speak of events about everyday townspeople and even chief priests, but they also included powerful government leaders as well. One example is when Paul boldly presents his testimony of conversion to King Herod Agrippa II and Governor Festus in Rome:

> As he was making his defense this way, Festus exclaimed in a loud voice, "You are out of your mind, Paul. Too much study is driving you mad!" But Paul replied, "I am not out of my mind, most noble Festus, but I am speaking words of truth and god judgment. For the king knows about these things. For I am convinced that none of these escapes his notice, since this was not done in a corner. King Agrippa, do you believe the prophets? I know you do." Then Agrippa said to Paul, "Are you going to persuade me to become a Christian so easily?"[58]

Do you think that such powerful leaders would have allowed their names to be used if they were portrayed untruthfully in any way, or if the events outright did not happen? By mentioning specific names in their works – which was also completely unnecessary to do – the New Testament writers were, again, giving their enemies and the countless public chances to expose Christianity as an elaborate lie. As Blomberg says of the early church, "We have a picture of what was initially a very vulnerable and fragile movement that was being subjected to persecution. If critics could have attacked it on the basis that it was full of falsehoods or distortions, they would have. But that's exactly what we don't see."[59]

Adding to this is the fact that what the Gospel accounts state about the resurrection and post-resurrection appearances was proclaimed very early-on after these said events. Reading the likes of atheistic Internet blogs or Dan Brown's 2003 novel, *The Da Vinci Code* (which has sold more than 80 million copies and popularized Gnosticism), for instance, you will surely come across claims that the proclamation of Christ's resurrection and post-resurrection appearances began roughly 300 years after Jesus' crucifixion, during the reign of Emperor Constantine. The idea behind such claims is that this length of time allowed the elaborate lie of the resurrection and these appearances and Christianity as a whole to prosper because, by then, nobody was around to state facts to the contrary. These claims are blatantly false and incredibly easy to disprove.

Especially due to early surviving manuscripts and the fact they were quoted from numerous times by first-century writers, even the most ardent atheistic scholars will admit that the Gospel accounts and all of the New Testament books were finished very close to the event of Jesus' crucifixion and supposed resurrection. The apostle Paul authors the earliest of these New Testament books, and they present ample reliable evidence that a large number of Christian churches had been established throughout the Roman

A HISTORICAL INVESTIGATION OF THE RESURRECTION (PART 1)

Empire within a just few decades of the supposed resurrection. Tacitus, Pliny, Suetonius, and the Roman authorities would not have taken notice at all of the early Christians had their number not been significant. Upon specifically digging to see when the message of Jesus' resurrection and post-resurrection appearances were first being proclaimed, we can get even closer to the time of those said events.

In the book of First Corinthians, Paul lists a creedal summary of early Christian beliefs that he received, three years after his own conversion to Christianity, while having spent two weeks visiting Peter and James (the half-brother of Jesus) in Jerusalem.[60] He writes, "I passed on to you what was most important and what had also been passed on to me. Christ died for our sins, just as the Scriptures said. He was buried, and he was raised from the dead on the third day, just as the Scriptures said. He was seen by Peter and then by the Twelve. After that, he was seen by more than 500 of his followers at one time. . . . Then he was seen by James."[61] Even the most ardent atheistic scholars will admit this creed is dated extremely early. Let us trace it back just like they do.

What year do historical scholars believe Paul first went to the city of Corinth? 51 A.D. And what year do they believe Paul received this creedal message that he presented to the people of Corinth? 35 A.D. This would place the receiving of this creed five years after Jesus' crucifixion and supposed resurrection. Of course, Peter and James already knew this creed. Citing Lüdemann yet again, "The formation of the appearance traditions mentioned in [1 Corinthians 15:3-8] falls into the time between 30 and 33 C.E."[62] And, of course, the beliefs as stated in the creed were being preached verbally prior to taking creedal form. So the origin of this message goes back even closer to Jesus' crucifixion and supposed resurrection. Licona states, "As one expert said, 'This is the sort of data that historians of antiquity drool over.'"[63]

By tracing back the timeline, we have confidently come extremely close –

potentially within days – of these events. This becomes even more impressive once you compare this timeframe with the timeframes from other ancient writings. Let us take Alexander the Great for example. Do you think that we can know a considerable amount of data about Alexander the Great? You might say, "Yes, of course, we do. Despite his short life of only 33 years, he was born in 356 B.C., was the King of Macedonia, conquered the great Persian Empire, by age thirty conquered the known world and created one of the largest empires of all time, and died in Babylon in 323 B.C." All of that information is firmly believed to be historically accurate by historical scholars. But where did we get such accurate information? Well, the earliest and best sources are the surviving accounts from Greek historian Arrian of Nicomedia and Greek biographer Plutarch of Chaeronea in 120 A.D., *443 years* after the death of Alexander the Great! Yet classical historians still consider them to be trustworthy.

Licona similarly adds to this line of thought: "As for Caesar Augustus, who is generally regarded as Rome's greatest emperor, there are five chief sources used by historians to write a history of his adulthood: a very brief inscription, a source written between fifty and a hundred years after his death, and three sources written between a hundred and two hundred years after he died."[64] It is clear, then, that we can be confident the preaching of Christ's death, burial, resurrection, and post-resurrection appearances has been central to Christianity from the very time the events occurred.

SAUL/PAUL

It should be noted that, before he was referred to as Paul (meaning "little one"), he was referred to by his Hebrew name, Saul (meaning "great one") of Tarsus. Saul was a devout Jewish rabbi, respected Pharisee, and a mass persecutor who was instrumental behind many evil deeds (including executions) towards the early church. In his mind, they were all following a false Messiah. This by-the-book Jew and Pharisee viewed them all as heretics and, as the early church would disperse well beyond Jerusalem and spread the Gospel message into many distant regions, he made it his mission to hunt down as many as he could and bring them in to be tried, imprisoned, tortured and even murdered.[65] From his viewpoint we read,

> I myself was convinced that I ought to do many things in opposing the name of Jesus of Nazareth. And I did so in Jerusalem. I not only locked up many of the believers in prison after receiving authority from the chief priests, but when they were put to death I cast my vote against them. In all the synagogues I often tried to make them blaspheme by punishing them. Being exceedingly mad against them, I persecuted them even to foreign cities.[66]

You could not find anyone more ruthless than Saul; the terminator before Arnold Schwarzenegger. But take notice that the words used within that viewpoint were written in past tense. Roughly two years after Jesus' half-brother James was the last witness during the forty day period, it was then that Saul would have his life-changing experience as a witness to what he was convinced was the resurrected Jesus:

> Now Saul, still breathing threats and murder against the disciples of the Lord, went to the high priest and requested letters from him to the synagogues in Damascus, so that if he found any who belonged to the Way, whether men or women, he could bring them as prisoners to Jerusalem. As he traveled and was nearing Damascus, a light from heaven suddenly flashed around him. He fell to the ground and heard a voice saying to him, "Saul, Saul, why are you persecuting

me?" And he asked, "Who are you, Lord?" And the Lord said, "I am Jesus, whom you are persecuting."⁶⁷

This was the end of Saul's old ways. Taking the name Paul, he would go on to live the remainder of his life as a dedicated apostle of Jesus and leader of the early church. And as Paul formed numerous churches during his multiple, distant journeys, he would go through seemingly never-ending persecution along the way:

> Five different times the Jewish leaders gave me thirty-nine lashes. Three times I was beaten with rods. Once I received a stoning [and was thought dead]. Three times I was shipwrecked. Once I spent a whole night and a day adrift at sea. I have been constantly on the move. I have been in danger from rivers, in danger from bandits, in danger from my fellow Jews, in danger from Gentiles, in danger in the city, in danger in the country, in danger at sea, and in danger from false believers. I have worked hard and long, enduring many sleepless nights. I have been hungry and thirsty and have often gone without food. I have shivered in the cold, without enough clothing to keep me warm. Besides everything else, I face the daily the anxious concern for all the churches.⁶⁸

The last time we hear from Paul, the early church – now referred to as "Christians" – have long reached Rome.⁶⁹ And it is there where Paul is imprisoned for being a determined Christian and awaiting his trial before Emperor Nero. We then learn from the historian Eusebius, "'It is related that in his [Nero's] time Paul was beheaded in Rome itself and that Peter was likewise crucified, and the title of "Peter and Paul," which is still given to the cemeteries there, confirms the story.'"⁷⁰

So why is the conversion of Saul/Paul among the minimal facts? Why is it that historical scholars are virtually unanimous in their conclusions that Saul of Tarsus was an enemy of the early church but was soon thereafter wholly transformed into a dedicated defender of the Christian faith after he firmly believed he was a witness to a post-resurrection appearance by Jesus?

As Saul, he was definitely someone whom the early church feared and hated the most, and he was definitely among those who hated the early church the most. He was highly educated and would not fall for something that was not true, and his conversion to Christianity was the equivalent to if Adolf Hitler had become a Jewish priest! It is possible that Paul gave up the use of his Hebrew name, Saul, due to its regal connotation ("great one") because he desired to become smaller to present Christ as greater. And that he did, to the death. *Something* happened that transformed his life from being a ruthless murderer to an apostle who, outside of Jesus, is the most important figure in all of Christianity, having "crisscrossed the Mediterranean on three occasions walking some 10,000 miles on foot and many more by sea" preaching the Gospel message.[71] *Something* happened that made him announce to the world embarrassing details, such as his admission of being wrong in regards to Jesus not being the Messiah, and being shipwrecked without food and clothing. He was set with a comfortable life; he did not have to give up his high, respected status, abandon his long-held Jewish faith and traditions, and suffer and die for the Christian movement he had so vehemently persecuted. He had nothing whatsoever to gain in this world by living out an elaborate lie. *Something* happened. And this *something*, as Paul himself boldly proclaims, was him being a personal witness to the bodily appearance of the risen Christ on the road to Damascus.

These points are well documented by sources in addition to Paul himself – Luke, Polycarp, Clement of Rome, Origen, Dionysius of Corinth, and Tertullian. Further, Tertullian even states that the beheading of Paul was in the historical archives of the Roman Empire: "That Paul is beheaded has been written in their own blood. And if a heretic wishes his confidence to rest upon a public record, *the archives of the empire will speak*, as would the stones of Jerusalem."[72] Therefore, we have multiple, early, and primary testimony of this minimal fact.

JAMES

If you could name two people in the entire world at that time who were the least likely candidates to convert to Christianity, one of them would be Saul. He was martyred after becoming the most influential follower of Jesus ever to live. As for the other candidate, that would be James the half-brother of Jesus.

We read in the book of Matthew that Jesus had blood-related half-siblings: Four brothers (James, Joseph, Simon, and Judas), and a number of sisters (there are no details on an exact number nor names).[73] They thought Jesus was "out of his mind" and not even one of them believed He was the long-awaited Messiah during His public ministry.

This was a highly embarrassing detail to be included and reasonably leads one to believe it is a true account. After all, such details would only have further made preaching Jesus' message more difficult to explain; after all, who would believe in a "dead criminal" that did not even have the backing of His own siblings? Additionally, there is the embarrassing detail at the cross when Jesus entrusted the care of His mother to his disciple John instead of the natural choice of any of His brothers. Jesus had stated, "Anyone who does God's will is my brother and sister."[74] Had James been a believer, he would have received the nod before John.

James was a devout Jew and spent much time in study and in prayer; so much so that historian Hegesippus wrote of James: "And he frequently entered the temple alone and was frequently found situated upon his knees asking forgiveness for the people, so that his knees became hard after the manner of a camel, on account of always bending down upon a knee while worshipping God and asking forgiveness for the people."[75] Therefore James would have been fully aware that someone who was crucified was accursed by God. Jesus' crucifixion would have solidified the long-held conclusions that James had about Jesus not being the Messiah all the more. So what comes next for James is nothing short of a miracle.

We read in the book of Acts that Jesus' brothers soon became emboldened leaders within the church.[76] Of course, the apostle Paul discusses how he visited with James and Peter for two weeks in Jerusalem. In fact, James may have been directly involved in passing along this creed to Paul and, therefore personally authenticating his name being used within it. Years later when Paul revisited Jerusalem, he says that "James, Peter, and John," were known as the three "pillars of the church."[77] Finally, according to Josephus, Hegesippus, Clement of Alexandria, and Eusebius, James was stoned to death by the Sanhedrin, under the rule of the high priest Ananus in 62 A.D., after he had become the leader of the church in Jerusalem.[78] Thus, as with the life and conversion of the apostle Paul, we have multiple, early, and primary testimony of this minimal fact.

This conversion to Christianity is the equivalent of *you* quickly changing your mind and concluding that a family member of yours – who you have lived with your entire life under the same roof – is God, and believing that conclusion so strongly *you* would die for it. That is exactly what happened to James. It would have taken a whole lot for James to be convinced that Jesus was the Son of God and not merely his older half-brother. *Something* significant had to of happened to convince this skeptic. That *something*, as with the apostle Paul and all of those who first began the early church, had to be what the creedal summary in First Corinthians stated: James was the personal witness to what he was certain was a bodily appearance by the risen Christ.

A HISTORICAL INVESTIGATION OF THE RESURRECTION

(Part 2)

Virtually every scholar who has intensely studied the subject agrees on at least these twelve minimal facts. Of course, the evidence may be ignored, but it cannot be denied. Now, what we must seek is the best overarching explanation for all of these facts.

Regardless of their religious beliefs, scholars agree to all of these minimal facts. However, there is a minuscule number on the fringe who, though they agree to the minimal facts, will differ on specifically *why* Jesus' tomb was found empty. This is generally due to their philosophical and theological presumptions that miracles cannot happen. For instance, writes author and philosopher Paul Copan, when John Dominic Crossan was asked in a debate with William Lane Craig if there was any evidence that could ever convince him Jesus rose from the grave due to God's intervention, or if his preconceived ideas about miracles would always skew his historical judgment, Crossan responded it is, "a theological presupposition . . . that God does not operate that way."[1] In other words, for those such as Crossan, it is not that the evidence for a resurrection event is not strong; instead, it is their unwavering, metaphysical bias towards miracles that has abruptly ruled miracles out of consideration from the very beginning.

Due to such philosophical and theological presuppositions, these individuals have proposed so-called "alternative naturalistic explanations" to appeal to a natural cause and try to bypass this supernatural event. Thus, their attitude can be summed up as so: "These events definitely happened. But since I have a bias against miracles, there is *surely* another explanation other than intervention from God." With a popular heyday in the 1800s during the reign of German liberalism, the same old handful of formulated theories that have attempted, again and again, to account for the minimal facts continue to pop up after a hiatus. For us today, this would be the equivalent of their supposedly being sightings of Bigfoot or Loch Ness, only to see the same old blurry pictures; a celebrity who has to do something controversial every now and then just to gain the spotlight again for a week; or the fanny pack trying to come back in style under new names (e.g., a hip pouch, a pocket belt, or the best name yet: a zippered waist organizer).

It is entirely understandable that such theories exist; after all, people do not typically rise from the grave! By definition, supernatural goes above and beyond nature. Of course, when it comes to claims of miracles, the historian first has to seek-out all possible natural explanations first before looking at an event from a miraculous standpoint. However, the ironic thing about these naturalistic theories is that, once you look into them see how logically and historically incoherent they are, you realize that it is far more difficult to believe them than a supernatural miracle.

In fact, from the moment of their conception, by the likes of Friedrich

Schleiermacher, Heinrich Paulus, Theodor Keim, and David Strauss, they were criticized to the point of giving "death-blows" by *fellow, fringed skeptics*![2] "The result," writes Gary Habermas, "was that, shortly after the turn of the century, none of these theses was left standing."[3] Raymond E. Brown wrote from his vantage point in the 1960s: "No longer respectable are the crude theories . . . popular in the past century . . . . Serious scholars pay little attention to these fictional reconstructions."[4] Craig writes of this time period: "It is also instructive to note that twentieth century critics usually rejected these theories wholesale. . . . The naturalistic attempts to disprove the resurrection were . . . dismissed in their entirety by recent critical scholars."[5] And speaking of the present time, Craig adds that they "have been almost universally rejected by contemporary scholarship. None of these naturalistic hypotheses succeeds in meeting the conditions."[6]

Therefore, it seems that Christians are entirely justified in concluding that God raised Jesus from the grave. To be entirely objective in our investigation and arrive at the most plausible explanation, though, let us discuss the three theories that have ever been deemed "popular" and then briefly touch on others afterward. (And do bear with the fact that there will be times of repeating information from theory to theory).

THE CONSPIRACY THEORY

As we discussed in the previous chapter, the Jewish chief priests proposed a version of this theory: the disciples stealing Jesus' corpse and then lying about His subsequent, postmortem appearances to fabricate the resurrection story. Of course, we would not be discussing the theory here if there were not many significant problems with it. As Craig writes, "Today . . . this explanation has been completely given up by modern scholarship. . . . No scholar would defend the conspiracy hypothesis today. The only place you read about such things is in the popular, sensationalist press of Internet fantasies."[7] Before we begin taking a brief look into examples of critical problems this theory definitely has in regards to the topic of *whether* anyone could have stolen His body and fabricated the resurrection and surrounding events, we first need to discuss if there were any motives for *why* anyone would steal His body.

Though the Jewish chief priests claimed the disciples stole Jesus' body, it has since been proposed that either the Jewish leaders or Roman authorities themselves stole it, then the disciples discovered the empty tomb and jumped to the conclusion Jesus had been resurrected. Is there any possible truth behind these claims; any possible motivation behind either the Jewish or Roman authorities doing such a thing? Starting with the Jewish leaders, the answer is an emphatic *no*.

Jesus' public ministry was causing unrest among the Jewish leaders because He, a blasphemer in their eyes for claiming to be one with God the Father and was gaining thousands of followers, was breaking the monotony of their long-held status and place in the religious society they dominated.[8] When Jesus claimed to be the Messiah it ultimately meant His authority would outweigh their manmade authority. As author Eric Metaxas writes, Jesus "had been a troublemaker of the first order, had thrown sand in the gears of the well-oiled political order of which they were an integral part. But as Jesus became more prominent and daring and troublesome, they saw that the only way to deal with him was by having him executed."[9] Thus, it was purely hypocrisy, pride, and arrogance that made them demand Jesus' execution.

Not only did they want to put an end to the unrest Jesus' ministry was causing, but they also wanted to prove that Jesus was not the Messiah. So you can understand that they were not taking any chances and administered every precaution to make sure He "stayed dead." In other words, the only potential risk of having Him executed would be for someone to come along, steal His body, show off the empty tomb, claim that He had miraculously accomplished that feat, and then accuse them of murdering the true Messiah. Furthermore, they not only would have been very concerned with getting rid of Jesus, but after His death, they wanted His followers out of the picture as well. This is clear since it was they who hired Saul of Tarsus to persecute them.

There was absolutely no reason at all for the Jewish leaders to steal Jesus' body and allow the public to have the slightest idea that He rose from the grave. They were literally the *last* group of people on Earth who would have done such a thing. But for argument's sake, let us assume that they did. Would they not eventually speak up and display the body in order to silence any stories saying He had been resurrected? But that is exactly what they did not do and, instead, quickly spread the story that the disciples had stolen it in order to fabricate Jesus rising from the grave.

As for the Roman authorities, did they differ from the Jewish leaders and have a motivation for stealing the body? Again, the answer is *no*. There were political reasons that they wanted Jesus dead, as there was a constant, unstable situation on the verge of bursting between them and the Jewish people, and they simply did not want any more trouble. Even the idea of Jesus being the risen Messiah could have led to them having a sense of empowerment and causing an uprising against Rome itself far worse than what would have ever occurred had He not been executed in the first place.

As with the Jewish leaders, there was no reason for the Roman authorities to steal Jesus' body and allow the public to think for even a second that He had rose from the grave. But, again, for argument's sake, let us assume that they did steal it. Like the Jewish leaders, they, too, would have spoken up and displayed it to stop any stories saying He had been resurrected. Instead, they took the highest precautions to prevent it from being stolen.

Having safely eliminated these two groups of candidates, this leaves us with the theory that perhaps the disciples stole His body. This theory has a number of critical problems, and it is of the utmost importance that we take time in order to look into all of them since, after all, this was the only "alternative explanation" proposed by people (i.e., the Jewish leaders) who were actually there. In doing so, we must start by briefly doing an overview of Jesus' tomb itself to better grasp what all we are going to investigate.

When we say that the Jewish religious leaders and the Roman authorities took precautionary measures to prevent Jesus' body from being stolen, we mean it. Jesus' tomb was hewn out of solid rock, and a massive disk-shaped stone weighing 3,000 to 4,000 pounds was rolled against the entrance to close it. Further describing the attributes of the tomb,

> Each tomb had a groove, or trough, cut into the rock in front of it to act as a track for moving the stone. The trough was deepest immediately in front of the entrance, and angled upward. The disk-shaped stone was placed in the higher part of the groove, and a block was placed beneath it to keep it from rolling. When the block was removed, the stone would roll down and lodge itself in front of the opening. Clearly when the body of Jesus was sealed into such a tomb, getting it out would take extraordinary effort.[10]

In every instance, the Roman authorities would take extreme, precautionary measures to ensure that no one tampered with burial stones. A cord would be stretched across the stone, with each end sealed either by clay or wax connecting it to the tomb and then stamped with the Roman imperial mark of the governor. This seal, an authentication that the tomb was occupied, represented the full power and authority of Rome. The guard knew that if this seal was broken, providing evidence that there was an attempt to move the stone, they would be killed for allowing it to be tampered with to any extent. And, speaking of "the guard," this does not mean there was a single guard but, rather, sixteen meticulously disciplined and confidently armed soldiers. Josh and Sean McDowell continue:

> Supercilious pictures of the tomb of Christ show one or two guards standing around with wooden spears and miniskirts. That's really laughable and could not be further from the truth. . . . Normally a unit charged with guarding an area would work in this way: 4 men were placed immediately in front of what they were to protect. The other 12 would sleep in a semi-circle in front of them with their heads pointing in. To steal what these guards were protecting, thieves would first have to walk over the guards who were asleep. Every four hours, another unit of four guards was awakened, and those who had been awake took their turn at sleep. They would rotate this way around the clock. . . . Guards in ancient times always slept in shifts, so it would have been virtually impossible for a raiding party to have stepped over all their sleeping faces without waking them. . . . Dr. George Currie, who carefully studied the military discipline of the Romans, reports that the death penalty was required for various duty failures such as desertion, losing or disposing of one's [weapons], betraying plans to an enemy, refusing to protect an officer and leaving the night watch. To the above, one can add "falling asleep." If it was not apparent which soldier had failed in duty, then lots were drawn to see who would be punished with death for the guard unit is failure.[11]

The public saw Jesus die on the cross, knew exactly where He was buried and that the tomb was abundantly secure, and there is not a single instance that reports even the slightest doubt that the tomb was not empty. As Dr. Wilbur Smith writes,

> No man has written, pro or con, on the subject of Christ's resurrection, without finding himself compelled . . . of Joseph's empty tomb. That the tomb was empty on Sunday morning is recognized by everyone, no matter how radical a critic he may be; however [anti-supernatural] in all his personal convictions, he never dares to say that the body was still resting in the tomb, however he might attempt to explain the fact that the tomb must have been empty.[12]

And this includes the conspiracy theory. Taking into consideration all of these security precautions that the Jewish religious leaders and the Roman authorities made, you can quickly start picking up on critical problems the conspiracy theory cannot overcome.

First of all, looking back at the story the Jewish leaders conspired, we read in Matthew 28: "You are to say, 'His disciples came during the night and stole Him away while we were asleep.'" Do you see the contradiction in the story? How could the guards know exactly who stole the body if they were fast asleep? Their story refutes itself. Nobody would have believed the disciples could have done that. Also, no guard would ever admit to falling asleep on the job (again, an offense punishable by death). The Jewish leaders bribed the Roman guard with a large sum of money to keep their story straight and to spread the lie of the disciples stealing Jesus' body. This, ironically, made them great evangelists for Christianity!

Second, the disciples, like the Jewish leaders and Roman authorities, had no motivation to steal Jesus' body. To them, He was nothing more than a dead disappointment. As we previously discussed, in the eyes of the first-century Jew, it was believed that being killed on a cross meant the person was under a curse from God. A *dead* Messiah, let alone a *crucified* Messiah, was as much an oxymoron as a married bachelor or a jumbo shrimp. Just as any first-century

Jew would have thought, Jesus was dead and was obviously not sent to lead them. It was game over. So why in the world would they go to such great lengths to try stealing the body of whom they identified as merely that of a man? The idea would not have even entered their minds.

Third, to think that this small group of scaredy cat disciples who denied even knowing Jesus before His arrest and then ran into hiding would even attempt to steal His corpse is preposterous! Are we to be so naïve to believe that they snuck by these sixteen, eagle-eyed, heavily-armed, "sleeping" soldiers, broke the Roman seal, and removed the two-ton stone unseen and unheard? Better yet, are we to believe they even attempted, let alone successfully fought off, the soldiers?

Fourth, for argument's sake, if we were to grant this impossible scenario, are we to believe that the disciples would go through imprisonment, torture, and martyrdom for what they knew was a lie? If the disciples were guilty of stealing the body and creating an elaborate hoax, why did they suddenly become fearless proclaimers of the Gospel message? As Dr. John Lennox writes, if the Jewish leaders and the Roman authorities "had the slightest evidence that the tomb was empty because the disciples had removed the body, then they had the authority and the forces to hunt down the disciples, arrest them, and charge them with tomb-robbing, which at the time was a very serious offence."[13] Yet, right in their faces, they proclaimed the message in the very city where He had been crucified and buried. Neither the Jewish leaders nor the Roman authorities had Jesus' body, so an exhaustive search would have been made to recover it. If quarterback Tom Brady's stolen jersey from Super Bowl LI garnered so much attention, you could imagine how crazy these leaders and authorities would have been to try and recover Jesus' body to silence everyone! But there was never a report of them even searching for it.

So are we to believe that when the non-Christian, hostile sources we discussed in the previous chapter wrote about the years of imprisonment, gruesome torture, and martyrdom of the Apostle Paul, James, and countless others, that these Christians put themselves through all of that by living-out what they knew was a lie? Further, if this was all a conspiracy, why did the early Christians not take the Gospel message elsewhere, not only where it was safer but also away from *the very place in the entire* world where everybody knew what was true and what was not? After all, it does not take long for a conspiracy to fold. Metaxas writes,

> Wouldn't one or more of them have told the truth *eventually*? Can we really believe that in all the years that followed, through all the horrific persecutions, not one of them would have changed his story? It is also a well-established fact that the more people involved in a conspiracy the harder it is to keep it quiet. If this were a conspiracy, it would have involved scores of people. But human beings crack under torture and under threat and death and, as the years pass, under the weight of their own consciences. So how could it be that these many disciples and the other devout followers of Jesus could have all continued to lie along the same lines for years and years? .. Can we really imagine that not one of them would have recanted, would have spilled the proverbial beans to save his own skin?[14]

A convicted accomplice to the Watergate scandal of U.S. President Richard Nixon, Charles "Chuck" Colson, elaborated this very point in an American Family Radio commentary. Being a prime example of someone who needed to keep a secret, Colson stated to his listeners,

> Watergate involved a conspiracy to cover-up, perpetuated by the closest aides to the President of the United States – the most powerful

men in America, who were intensely loyal to their president. But one of them, John Dean, turned state's evidence, that is, testified against Nixon, as he put it, "to save his own skin" – and he did so only two weeks after informing the president about what was really going on – two weeks! The real cover-up, the lie, could only be held together for two weeks, and then everybody else jumped ship in order to save themselves. Now, the fact is that all that those around the President were facing was embarrassment, maybe prison. Nobody's life was at stake. But what about the disciples? Twelve powerless men, peasants really, were facing not just embarrassment or political disgrace, but beatings, stonings, execution. Every single one of the disciples insisted, to their dying breaths, that they had physically seen Jesus bodily raised from the dead. Do you not think that one of those apostles would have cracked before being beheaded or stoned? That one of them would have made a deal with the authorities? None did. You see, men will give their lives for something they believe to be true; they will never give their lives for something they know to be false.[15]

Political scandals throughout time or in everyday instances where someone thinks they are going to be in trouble, someone *will* quickly come forward to tell-all. And like Colson rightly says, that is just for avoiding embarrassment and possible jail time. The early church, on the other hand, knew their public proclamation of Jesus being the risen Messiah automatically put a target on their heads that they could not escape. Even with the inevitable threat of death facing them, the early church did not recant. This speaks volumes the early church was not living out an elaborate hoax but was united and going to their deaths boldly proclaiming far and wide what they wholeheartedly knew was true and worth dying for; after all, *that* is the only possible response after seeing someone miraculously rise from the grave and ascend to Heaven. As mathematician, physicist, and philosopher Blaise Pascal summarized well, "I believe those witnesses who get their throats cut."

Fifth, with all of this talk about security precautions because an empty tomb would potentially cause unrest, would an empty tomb have *actually* caused such a thing? The Jewish leaders and Roman authorities were paranoid and cautious, but by no means would an empty tomb convince anyone. Michael Licona states,

> It's like with David Koresh in the 1990s. He predicted that when he died he would rise from the dead three years later. Well, he did not. But let us suppose three years after the date of his death at Waco, some Branch Davidians said, "Hey, Koresh is back to life again." You go and check for his remains at the coroner's office and they're missing. Would you . . . abandon your faith and become a Branch Davidian because of that? Of course not. You'd say, "C'mon, the remains were moved, stolen, or misplaced."[16]

It was not the empty tomb that convinced *anyone* of Jesus being the risen Messiah, including the women who first discovered the tomb empty and concluded someone stole His body, the disciples who were unfazed by the report of the empty tomb, or Jesus' own half-brother James. This is especially true seeing as how a resurrected Messiah was the last thing that would have been in their minds. Instead, Christianity was built on what was genuinely believed to be Jesus' bodily appearances from the grave to hundreds and hundreds of people over multiple occasions. It only makes sense that the first-century Christians came to firmly trust in Jesus because He proved Himself worthy of their belief, not because they were blindly committing themselves to something irrational. If there were only an empty tomb but no appearances, nobody would have believed in a resurrection and, therefore, Christianity never would have quickly blossomed like it did. The conspiracy theory *does not even try* to account for these numerous appearances.

Sixth, something much more significant than the disciples supposedly stealing Jesus' body must have happened to cause the reaction given by the Roman guard that was never denied by the Jewish leaders. Not only do we have the reaction from the guard to inform us that a significant event took place, but we also have the reaction from the Jewish leaders themselves. As you can recall, a large sum of money was given for the guard to lie. The money, though, was not the most important aspect of the bribe, but was the lie itself: "You are to say, 'His disciples came during the night and stole Him away while we were asleep.'" Logically, the opposite of what the leaders were saying was the truth: the guard *was* doing their job to the tee, but now was being bribed to lie and say they were foolishly and lazily asleep on the job. Of course, the guard was comforted that things would be smoothed over with the Roman authorities. But what exactly was in it for the Jewish leaders anyway? Why would they form a council to come up with an elaborate lie and to present a hefty bribe for the *Roman* guard if there was not something in it for them?

The only reasonable answer is that they wanted to keep quiet the fact that a significant event happened at the tomb. But what event could possibly have brought about such a worried and hurried response? Well, the Bible gives us some insight into what may have happened. Not only does it tells us that the giant stone at the entrance of the tomb was moved, but that it was moved to an eye-opening position. The disciple Mark uses the Greek preposition *"ana"* and verb *"kulio"*, making *"anakulio"*, indicating about the stone that it seemed to have been rolled up an incline. Luke uses *"apokulio"*, meaning that it was separated from the tomb, up an incline, to a great distance away. And John uses *"airokulio"*, stating that the stone seemed to have been picked up and carried up an incline. Dr. Bill White, who was formerly in charge of the Garden Tomb in Jerusalem, states,

> If the stone were simply rolled to one side of the tomb, as would be necessary to enter it, then they might be justified in accusing the men of sleeping at their posts, and in punishing them severely.... There was some undeniable evidence which made it impossible for the chief [authorities] to bring any charge against the guard. The Jewish authorities must have visited the scene, examined the stone, and recognized its position as making it humanly impossible for their men to have permitted its removal. No twist of human ingenuity could provide an adequate answer or a scapegoat and so they were forced to bribe the guard and seek to hush things.[17]

Each of the critical problems show how the conspiracy theory does not hold any water, and that fact is highlighted even more-so once they are combined as such. This, then, leads us to the next "alternative" theory.

THE HALLUCINATION THEORY

As we have seen in the previous chapter when discussing the "minimal fact" of Jesus' post-mortem appearances, not even the most ardent atheistic historian will doubt these appearances. Gerd Lüdemann, for instance, stated it is historically certain that many people experienced appearances of Jesus as the risen Christ. And Paula Fredriksen stated that it is part of historical bedrock that the early church had seen post-mortem appearances of Jesus. There are a small handful of atheistic scholars, though, who have posited what is called the hallucination theory, not only because they do not believe in miracles but also because they see the critical holes in the conspiracy theory.

Based on the proposal from David Strauss' 1835 book, *The Life of Jesus Critically Examined*, atheist, historian, and philosopher Richard Carrier sums up this theory which is attempted to try and explain away the hand of God being behind the physical appearances: "The first Christians experienced hallucinations of the risen Christ."[18] As with the conspiracy theory, this theory also has zero credibility in modern academia.

First, there is the very nature of hallucinations. A hallucination is a false perception of someone or something that is not really there. Though it is rare, they can happen to a person experiencing specific psychological conditions, such as the intense mental and physical deprivation of military training or while being under the influence of certain types of drugs. But they could *never* occur like is being claimed with this theory. Supposedly, as the theory wants us to believe, the eyewitnesses to Jesus' post-mortem appearances genuinely believed they had seen Jesus physically risen from the grave only because they were experiencing a *shared* hallucination. This becomes an even *more* far-fetched theory when we consider the appearances were to individuals and groups as large as 500-plus, none of which who were ever expecting a resurrection event, male and female, friend and foe, of different ages, of various personalities, in various mindsets, in various places indoors and out, and at various times over a period of forty days.

According to clinical psychologist, author of over 170 articles and over 50 books, and former president of a national association of psychologists, Gary Collins, "Hallucinations are individual occurrences. By their very nature, only one person can see a given hallucination at a time. They certainly are not something which can be seen by a group of people. Neither is it possible that one person could somehow induce a hallucination in somebody else. Since a hallucination exists only in the subjective, personal sense, it is obvious that others cannot witness it."[19] Licona adds to this point: "Hallucinations are not contagious. They're personal. They're like dreams. I could not wake up my wife in the middle of the night and say, 'Honey, I'm dreaming of being in Hawaii. Quick, go back to sleep, join me in my dream, and we'll have a free vacation.' You cannot do that. Scientists will tell you that hallucinations are the same way."[20] So, like a dream, if even two people cannot share a hallucination at the same time, or one initiate a hallucination into the other, how on Earth could more than 500 experience the same one at the same time? Two people, let alone 500-plus having a shared hallucination, would completely contradict the psychological facts about the nature of hallucinations and, ironically, would be *an even greater miracle* than the event of Jesus being resurrected from the grave by the hand of God!

Second, the hallucination theory does not at all explain the sudden rise of the early church. Regardless of whether or not shared hallucinations like this theory claims really can occur, individual hallucinations very rarely convince a person long-term that someone or something they saw was actually real; either because they figured it out on their own once they regained their normal frame of mind or because others informed them that what they saw was not real. It would be considerably rare for even one person to be convinced of their hallucination being real.

In Jewish culture, or in any culture for that matter, one did not believe in resurrections from the grave. So even if any eyewitnesses believed long-term that they really had seen a physical appearance of Jesus, they would never have concluded He was resurrected, but that He was appearing to them as a Heavenly vision that only would have provided further confirmation of His death. This is exactly how anyone anywhere would act today; if you were to be, say, grieving over the death of a loved one to the point that you thought you saw an appearance of them, the most that you would ever conclude is simply that their spirit was visiting you because they knew you needed comfort in knowing they are doing all right.

Also, hallucinations never would have drastically changed the lives of even a small handful of these eyewitnesses. None of them would have given up everything to proclaim the Gospel message while being jailed and tortured and martyred for it if they had even the tiniest idea the appearances may have been mere hallucinations. They would have to be completely certain what they had seen was actually real. One reason they were certain is that hundreds and hundreds of people confirmed them. They were also certain because they claimed not only to be able to see Jesus but that they could physically touch Him, walk with Him, talk with Him, and eat with Him on multiple occasions and in multiple locations.

Third, the hallucination theory only attempts to explain the post-mortem appearances and does not *even try* to account for the empty tomb. Even if 500-plus people, the original disciples, James, and Paul all merely saw hallucinations of Him, His body would still have been in the tomb all safe and secure! If all of the appearances can be explained away by mere mass hallucinations, why did not the Jewish leaders or Roman authorities simply take a short walk to get Jesus' body to prove He was still dead? You cannot build a church on a dead Messiah, and that would definitely have calmed down any person or groups of people from thinking He actually rose from the grave. Of course, His body could not be paraded around because of the fact that the tomb was empty. If people experienced hallucinations, yet the tomb was still occupied, nobody would have concluded Jesus was resurrected; likewise, if there was only an empty tomb but no experiences of appearances, nobody would have concluded Jesus was resurrected.

Fourth, the hallucination theory cannot account for Jesus' appearance to Saul on the road to Damascus. Saul had an extreme hate for Jesus and His followers and was definitely the last person who would have experienced a hallucination out of grief of Jesus' death or expectation of His return. Further, Saul was an educated and proud man and would not have changed his life to the point of death for an event he had even the tiniest idea could have been a mere hallucination.

As with the conspiracy theory, each of these problems show how this theory does not hold any water. This leads us to the next "alternative" theory.

THE SWOON THEORY

This theory would have us believe that, after being tortured and crucified, Jesus did not really die but only fainted, "swooned," into an unconscious state, was mistakenly buried alive, and later escaped and tricked the public that He was the risen Messiah. Finally, after he tricked the public, he did not recover but soon thereafter died due to his numerous, gruesome injuries. As with the conspiracy theory and the hallucination theory, there are critical problems with this theory as well.

First, Jesus' death crushed His family and any hopes His followers had that He was the Messiah. Are we to think that those present would not have double and then triple-checked for the most obvious signs of life? For any parents out there, you know that time and time again, ever since they were newborns, you have gone into your children's bedrooms while they were sleeping to make sure they were still breathing. Being overprotective is a parent's job! You can imagine that Jesus' mother, Mary, would have been desperately watching for any signs of life left in her Son. And do you not think that the professionally trained Roman centurion and other soldiers observing Him at the cross would have known whether or not He was dead? Crime scene investigator J. Warner Wallace writes,

> It has . . . been my experience that three conditions become apparent in the bodies of dead people: temperature loss, rigidity,

and lividity. Dead people lose warmth until they eventually reach the temperature of their environment. They begin to feel "cold to the touch" (this is often reported by those who find them). In addition, chemical reactions begin to take place in the muscles after death occurs, resulting in stiffening and rigidity known as "rigor mortis." Dead people become rigid, retaining the shape they were in when they died. Finally, when the heart stops beating, blood begins to pool in the body, responding to the force of gravity. As a result, purple discoloration begins to become apparent in those areas of the body that are closest to the ground. In essence, dead bodies look, feel, and respond differently from living, breathing humans.[21]

The Roman centurion and other soldiers would have been more than qualified to make a conclusive determination on whether or not Jesus was dead. After all, they were professionals in Roman crucifixion, crucifying thousands and thousands of people per year in the first century alone. Yet those who hold to this theory must believe they were too incompetent to make this determination. Incompetency gets even more difficult to believe when you realize the penalty for allowing someone to survive crucifixion was death (with the possibility of being crucified themselves). They would never have allowed for a living person to be removed from a cross.

When they came to Jesus and could clearly tell that He was already dead, one of the soldiers pierced His side with a spear ensuring His death. According to John in his Gospel account, "Immediately blood and water came out" from His side."[22] Medical examiner Dr. Alexander Metherell explains why this occurred:

> Even before He died . . . the hypovolemic shock would have caused a sustained rapid heart rate that would have contributed to heart

failure, resulting in the collection of fluid in the membrane around the heart, called a pericardial effusion, as well as around the lungs, which is called a pleural effusion. The spear apparently went through the right lung and into the heart, so when the spear was pulled out, some fluid – the pericardial effusion and the pleural effusion – came out. This would have the appearance of a clear fluid, like water, followed by a large volume of blood, as the eyewitness John described in his gospel. John probably had no idea why he saw both blood and a clear fluid come out – certainly that's not what an untrained person like him would have anticipated. Yet John's description is consistent with what modern medicine would expect to have happened.[23]

In these ancient times, the eyewitnesses to this phenomenon would not have had even the slightest idea what this signified; they were simply reporting what they saw. Due to modern-day medical science, we know that after someone had died the blood inside their body clots and separates from the watery serum. From our standpoint today we know that by the time He was impaled by a spear while on the cross Jesus had already been dead for some time. Modern-day medical studies observing crucifixion have further shown how death by crucifixion has a 100% death rate. Additionally, even the non-Christian, enemy attested sources we listed in the previous chapter affirmed Jesus' death on the cross and never once proposed that He survived or even could potentially have survived being crucified.

Second, the swoon theory fails to take into consideration that it was customary to encase and wrap a dead body in roughly one hundred pounds of spices and linen cloths before being placed in a tomb. This theory would have us believe Jesus not only survived His injuries and crucifixion, but that He also managed to somehow not suffocate the entire time, gain consciousness, and unravel Himself from this encasement. To fully grasp this point, let us observe what occurred just prior to the crucifixion. Further, not only does this theory want us to believe that Jesus survived crucifixion (which lasted for *hours*), and His side, lung, and heart being impaled by a Roman spear, but also that He survived those horrible things after having been beaten to a pulp.

So to what extent of hell did Jesus go through before being crucified? While the Jews administered scourging for certain offenses, these were incredibly mild in comparison to the ruthless scourging by the Romans. The Jews stopped at thirty-nine lashes in order not to go over their maximum limit of forty; however Roman law had no such limit. Roman scourging was not intended to kill, as it was desired for victims to barely stay alive to suffer from the crucifixion which always followed. However, it was definitely brutal enough to be fatal and actually did lead to death in many cases. The instrument used to deliver this form of punishment was called a flagrum; a whip with several braided leather strands, each roughly three feet in length, with metal balls, sharp pieces of bone, rock, and long hooks tied into them at increments throughout, made to lacerate, break open, and rip skin, internal muscles, and organs to shreds.

The ancient historian Eusebius gives a personal account of the wicked torture of scourging: "The bystanders were struck with amazement when they saw them lacerated with scourges even to the innermost veins and arteries, so that the hidden inward parts of the body, both their bowels and their members, were exposed to view."[24] The victim of Roman scourging would have been so weak from blood loss and internal damage that they would die more quickly, of course, than if they had not been scourged. In fact, had someone been only scourged and *not* crucified afterward, they would most likely die from massive blood loss as a result.

Dr. Brad Harrub, who holds a doctorate in neurobiology and anatomy at the Health Sciences Center of the College of Medicine at the University of

Tennessee, and Dr. Bert Thompson, who holds a doctorate in microbiology at Texas A&M University, where he was professor in the Department of Anatomy and Public Health and Director of the College's Cooperative Education Program in Biomedical Science, give their take on the hell of Roman scourging. In *An Examination of the Medical Evidence for the Physical Death of Christ*, Harrub and Thompson write,

> Initial anterior blows undoubtedly would have opened the skin and underlying subcutaneous tissue of His chest. Subsequent blows would have tattered the underlying pectoralis major and pectoralis minor muscles, as well as the medial aspects of the serratus anterior muscle. Once these layers were ravaged, repetitive blows could fracture intercoastal ribs and shred the three layers of intercoastal muscles, causing superficial and cutaneous vessels of the chest to be lacerated. . . . Edwards and his colleagues described Christ's scourging in the following manner: Then, as the flogging continued, the lacerations would tear into the underlying skeletal muscles and produce quivering ribbons of bleeding flesh. Pain and blood loss generally set the stage for circulatory shock. . . . During scourging, the victim would experience an oozing of blood from cutaneous capillaries and veins until the wounds went deep enough to cause arterial blood tospurt out rhythmically with each successive heartbeat. In many cases, scourging was itself fatal. Blows to Christ's back would have started in a similar fashion, with skin being torn with the initial strikes. Subsequent blows then would have resulted in the laceration of the superficial back muscles (i.e., trapezius and latissimus dorsi). Continued beatings would begin to flay into the deep erector spinae muscles (iliocostalis, longissimus, and spinalis) that are innervated by dorsal rami from the spinal cord. The

perforation of these muscles would have sent excruciating pain to the spinal cord and then directly to the brain. No doubt in many victims the spinous processes that extend out in a posterior fashion from each vertebrae would have splintered as a result of the harsh blows. . . . During the scourging, it would be commonplace for the lacerated skin and bloodied, underlying muscle tissue to take on the appearance (in a quite literal fashion) of shredded meat. . . . The blood loss suffered by Christ during His scourging would have been substantial, and would have resulted in a lowered blood pressure and reduced flow of blood throughout His body. If this condition persisted, hypovolemic shock would have set in (characterized by reduced blood flow to cells and tissues), which then would lead to irreversible cell and organ damage, and eventually death. . . . Yet, sadly, the worst was still to come.[25]

After having been scourged, it was customary for the victim to carry their own cross to the site of their execution. Whether He carried the patibulum of the cross (weighing roughly 125 pounds) or the entire cross (roughly 300 pounds), He would have to walk a distance of 650 yards, along the Via Dolorosa ("Way of Sorrow") to a place outside of Jerusalem called Golgotha ("Place of the Skull"). Once on the cross, the pain was so agonizing that the word "excruciating" (which literally translates to "out of the cross") had to be invented to better describe the intense torment. Jesus being on the cross, with nails the size of railroad spikes through His wrists and overlapping ankles, Harrub and Thompson continue:

It would not be uncommon by this time for insects to burrow into open wounds or orifices (such as the nose, mouth, ears, and eyes) of a crucified victim; additionally birds of prey frequently were known to feed off the tattered wounds. . . . Even though blood poured from His lacerated back, one major pathophysiological impairment Jesus faced during crucifixion was normal respiration (i.e., breathing). Maximum inhalation would have been possible only when the body weight was supported by the nailed wrists of the outstretched arms. When Christ first was lifted onto the splinter-covered surface of the cross, His arms and body were stretched out in the form of a "Y." A momentary "T" position would be required to allow proper support for inhalation. Thus, in order to breathe He was required to lift His body using His nailed wrists for leverage. Exhalation would be impossible in this position, and the immense pain placed on the wrists quickly would become too great; therefore, Christ would have to slump back into a "Y" position to exhale. Jesus would be forced to continue alternating between the "Y" and "T" positions with every breath, trying all the while not to reopen the wounds He had received from the scourging. Fatigued muscles eventually would begin to spasm, and Christ would become exhausted from these repeated tasks, slumping permanently into the shape of a "Y." In this position, chest and respiratory muscles soon would become paralyzed from the increased strain and pain. Without strength for breath, Christ's body would begin to suffer from asphyxia. . . . As exposed nerves exploded into unbearable pain with each movement . . . His internal organs began failing due to a lack of sufficient oxygen... While death on the cross may have been caused by any number of factors, and likely would have varied with each individual case, the two seemingly most prominent causes of death probably were hypovolemic shock and exhaustion asphyxia. Others have proposed dehydration, cardiac arrhythmia, and congestive heart failure   with the rapid accumulation of pericardial and pleural effusions as possible contributing factors. . . . It is with medical . . . certainty that we know Christ died upon the cross at Calvary.

Third, the swoon theory does not make sense of the rise of the early church. It would have been impossible for Jesus to survive the scourging, crucifixion, and encasement of spices and linen cloths. But this theory would have us believe He not only defeated death, but also single-handedly rolled the two-ton stone up a hill, defeated the sixteen heavily armed soldiers, and then appeared to the public as the risen Messiah and Lord of life three days later. If Jesus did all of those things, that would be an even greater miracle than the resurrection event itself! Further, if He had made it to the public eye, He would have been on the verge of death. By no means would His unrecoverable condition convince anyone whatsoever that He was the Messiah.

While the swoon theory was popular at its conception in the early nineteenth century, that changed once Strauss, a fringe atheist himself, delivered fatal criticism to this theory in regards to the rise of the early church in his 1865 book, *A New Life of Jesus*. Strauss wrote, for instance,

> It is impossible that a being who has been stolen half-dead out of the sepulcher, who crept about weak and ill, wanting medical treatment; who required bandaging, strengthening and indulgence, and who still at least yielded to his sufferings, could have given to the disciples the impression that he was a Conqueror over death and the grave, the Prince of Life, an impression which lay at the bottom of their future ministry. Such a resuscitation could only have weakened the impression which He had made upon them in life and in death . . . [and] could by no possibility have changed their sorrow into enthusiasm, have elevated their reverence into worship.[26]

This scene of a critically wounded, soon-to-be dead-Jesus, leaving a blood-soaked trail behind as He crawled or limped profusely, looking like "death warmed over," as Ehrman puts it, and begging for medical attention, would only have confirmed that He was not the long-awaited Messiah.[27] Not only would the early church have never formed from this scene, nobody especially ever would have been tortured, imprisoned, and martyred for it.

Fourth, the swoon theory does not explain the appearance to and conversion of James, Jesus' half-brother. James was already incredibly skeptical of Jesus, and a near lifeless appearance would not have changed things but would only have confirmed the suspicions he had all along that Jesus simply had lost His mind. And fifth, the swoon theory does not explain the appearance to and conversion of Saul. In fact, the theory does not even attempt to explain it.

As we have seen in the previous chapter when discussing Jesus' death by Roman crucifixion, the vast majority of even the most ardent, atheistic historians on the fringe will not doubt this fact. For instance, Crossan said this fact of Jesus' death by crucifixion under Pontius Pilate is as sure as anything historical can be, James Tabor agreed there is no doubt that Jesus died on the cross, and both Lüdemann and Ehrman concluded that, despite theories of deception such as the swoon theory, His death by crucifixion is an indisputable fact. As with the other theories, these critical problems are just the tip of the iceberg when it comes to all that we could point out about the swoon theory. But, clearly, as with the other theories, you can see that it does not at all explain what happened. Habermas writes: "By the turn of the [twentieth] century, it was declared to be only a curiosity of the past."[28]

Like a broken record, as with the conspiracy theory and the hallucination theory, each of these problems by themselves show how this theory does not hold any water. Yet again, this fact is highlighted even more-so once you combine them all. This, then, leads us to the best explanation.

A HISTORICAL INVESTIGATION OF THE RESURRECTION (PART 2)

THE BEST EXPLANATION

Like the common infomercial says: "wait, there is more!" Other, though far less popular, theories have been proposed to try and explain away God raising Jesus from the grave.

The wrong tomb theory states that everybody went to the wrong tomb, which so happens to be empty itself, and then they all assumed He had been resurrected. The twin theory would have us believe that Jesus had an unknown, identical twin brother, they were separated at birth, and this brother came back to where Jesus lived just in time to see that Jesus was being crucified, stole Jesus' body out of the tomb, and then tricked everyone into thinking that he, the impersonator, was the risen Messiah. A.N. Wilson, even suggests this "twin" could have been James himself (such a scenario sounds reminiscent to a specific scene from the movie Mrs. Doubtfire, with James being Robin Williams' character running back and forth changing his clothing and putting on a mask pretending to be two people at once!).[29]

Other theories include Jesus spiritually ascending to Heaven and using mental telepathy to transmit visions of Himself to the public, dogs digging into the tomb and eating His body, His body spontaneously evaporating, and His body being stolen by aliens from outer space. Seeing that these theories are based merely on witless conjecture, and seeing the extravagant, desperate lengths to which atheism must go, it makes you wonder what theories were so hilariously bad that these beat them to the public eye. Ironically, these "alternative" explanations to try and explain away the resurrection event have only strengthened the faith of those who trust Jesus is the risen Christ.

With that said, by going through each of these supposed alternative theories, we did what any good historian would do in the given situation: before concluding the minimal facts were due to a miracle, looking first for natural explanations that may make sense of the facts. After having gone through these theories and seen that not only do they break all principals one should follow in an honest historical investigation, go against all common sense and historical facts, and they have been universally rejected by modern-day scholarship, it is both logically and historically reasonable to conclude the best explanation is exactly what the New Testament says happened.

The reason for rejecting all alternative theories is not due to preconceived bias but, instead, is because they are easily refuted by the facts and collapse by their own weight. On this note, says Norman Geisler and Frank Turek,

> It is one thing to concoct an alternative theory to the Resurrection, but it is another thing to actually find first-century evidence for it. . . . For example, if someone were to claim that all of the video footage from the Holocaust concentration camps was staged and manufactured by Jews . . . would you believe that theory? Of course not, because it flies in the face of all the . . . evidence. To be taken seriously, those who offer such a theory must present credible, independent eyewitness reports and other corroborating evidence to counter the numerous reports that say the Holocaust was real and . . . carried out by the Nazis. But no such counterevidence exists. . . . This is the case with the Resurrection. While skeptics have formulated numerous alternative theories . . . there is no evidence from any first-century source supporting any of them.[30]

Anyone wishing to refute Christianity must first refute the case for the resurrection. Of course, no "alternative" explanation even comes close. Therefore Christians today can have well-reasoned confidence, as did the early church, that their faith is not blind and is not based on myth or legend but on the solid historical fact of the risen Christ. This is, for instance, the exact conclusion that Sir Lionel Alfred Luckhoo came to when he examined the facts.

A HISTORICAL INVESTIGATION OF THE RESURRECTION (PART 2)

If you go to the Guinness Book of World Records, and you look up who was the most successful lawyer who ever lived . . . Sir Lionel Luckhoo, as a defense attorney, won two hundred and forty five murder trials in a row. . . . this guy was the most successful lawyer who ever lived! I used to think the reason I admired this guy is how smart must he be! How savvy must he be! . . . This guy must be able to take what looks like on the surface to be an air-tight case against his client and find all the loopholes, all the shortcomings, all the problems in that case. More than anybody, Luckhoo must understand what constitutes reliable and persuasive evidence. And all that was true of Sir Lionel Luckhoo, who was knighted twice by Queen Elizabeth, and who was a member of the highest court of his land. Wouldn't it be interesting if the most successful lawyer who ever lived took this monumental legal knowledge and his savviness and his street smarts and he applied the legal test of evidence to the historical record for Jesus Christ and came to a conclusion. You know what? He did it. He was an atheist. But he spent several years of his life doing that very thing, and I will recite to you . . . the conclusion of Luckhoo after investigating from a legal perspective the resurrection of Jesus Christ. "I say unequivocally that the evidence for the resurrection of Jesus Christ is so overwhelming that it compels acceptance by proof which leaves absolutely no room for doubt." This from the most successful lawyer who ever lived. And based on the evidence, Luckhoo gave his life to Jesus Christ.[31]

You may be asking, "So what? How does the resurrection relate to me? What is the significance?" Craig states that, if true,

> The resurrection is tremendously existentially significant because it

means that Jesus holds the key that unlocks the door to eternal life. The threat of death and of non-being at the end of our days . . . puts a question mark behind everything in life. . . . The resurrection of Jesus provides an answer to [these questions], because it says that death is not the end. That through faith in Christ, we can have eternal life with Him. . . . And that means that the things we do now in this life are filled with an eternal significance. Every day you wake up, you know that the things [you] do today matter for eternity, because the grave is not the end.[32]

Death is either a period or a comma. In Christianity, it is merely a comma. This is the message of the resurrection.

CROSSING OPINION

Keep in mind what the major religions of the world teach about Jesus. Islam, for instance, teaches "they did not kill him, they did not crucify him."[33] Obviously they do not believe Jesus was resurrected from the grave. In fact, only Christianity and Judaism even teach He was crucified, with Christianity alone teaching He was resurrected. Since only Christianity is aligned with all of these historically accepted facts, it seems, then, that we can eliminate every other religion from the list we compiled in chapter one of the religions referred to as the greatest, most well-known, and by which all minor religions derive. After all, everything points to the fact that Jesus defeated death and, if so, His resurrection would set Him apart from all other religious figures such as Muhammad, Buddha, Confucius, and so forth, whose bodies have long rotted away.

We have now came full-circle to see which side of the coin Christianity is on in regards to the Apostle Paul's ultimatum we discussed in our first chapter: "If Christ has not been raised, your faith is useless." After every avenue of investigation we have discussed, it seems entirely reasonable to conclude that the resurrection event was a true, historical event. It verified Jesus' identity as the Messiah and Son of God, and it verified the truth to all that He taught. Further, as Jesus constantly taught from and honored the Old Testament as having divine authority, stated that all He taught was of divine authority, and taught that all of the soon-to-come New Testament would have divine authority, we are also given ample reason to conclude that what the entire text of the Bible teaches is true.[34] It seems, then, we have good reason to trust specifically what the Bible teaches about all aspects of reality.

With that said, we have one essential question remaining that we need to answer: what happens to us after we die? We have already seen how, as we concluded in a previous chapter about the existence of the immaterial, spiritual realm, it is entirely reasonable to believe the Bible is right when it states that our souls live on after our physical deaths. But then what happens? How can we have knowledge of something so mysterious? Well, what better authority to find the answer to this last essential question than Jesus, Who defeated death itself and Who's name literally translates to "salvation."

SALVATION

Recalling the discussion of our ultimate purpose in life, "To know God and make Him known" clearly comes in a specific order of two steps. Now comes the time we dig deeper into this first step, not only in learning *how to accomplish* our ultimate purpose in life but it just so happens that the step is key to answering the question of what happens to us after we die.

You always hear it said, "You might as well have fun with your money because you cannot take it with you!" Take it with you where exactly; to the grave itself? According to Scripture, there exist real places called Heaven and Hell, and our souls will be sent to one of those two places for all eternity. So, for our soul's sake, what exactly determines which place we will end up upon death? Well, the answer all starts with the context of mankind's predicament from the very beginning of life being placed on Earth.

At that time, God made Adam and Eve to be in close alliance in His presence forever. There was one simple rule: they, created in a state of innocence, were forbidden to eat from one mere tree that would cause them to lose their immortality. This "tree of the knowledge of good and evil" was there for the sole purpose of giving them the freedom to either obey or disobey Him.[1] Eventually, Eve was tempted by God's enemy, Satan ("the serpent"), with the idea that God was lying to them and that to eat from the tree would not bring death but, instead, would make them gods.[2] This attempt to destroy the sacred connection with God worked; both Adam and Eve ate from the tree and, in doing so, not only lost their innocence but cursed mankind and the entire Earth with the consequences of death, sickness, toil and hardship, pain, conflict, evil, and suffering.[3]

Could God have created Adam and Eve both with no freedom to make choices? Absolutely. But God granted them both, as He does each and every one of us, with the freedom to choose between right and wrong. Ever since that point in time, humanity has attempted to remove the stain of sin by doing "good" deeds. In fact, many of us today, if given the question of whether or not we think we will go to a place like Heaven when we die, would say something on the lines of, "Of course. I am a good person. Just look at people of history like Hitler, or just turn on the news and see what the members of ISIS do every single day. See, I am not like them and God will be able to see that."

This is a reminder of a game show that aired from 2008 to 2009 called On the U.S. game show "Moment of Truth," where contestants are to answer increasingly personal and embarrassing questions to win money, one particular contestant was a standout.[4] After having truthfully answered questions such as whether she (a hair salon assistant) had ever told a client their hair looked good when it actually did not, if she would give food to a stray animal before giving food to a homeless person, if she had ever been fired from a job due to stealing money, and even admitting that she was in love with someone else on her wedding day and has cheated on her husband, the last, all-or-nothing question came: "Are you a good person?" She answered "yes," the lie detector test clearly showed she was lying, and she lost all of the money (and probably her marriage).

We may laugh at this: "Obviously she was not a good person!" But think about why such a seemingly easy question was the final question: we can say all day long that we are good people, to the point of betting a truckload of money on it, but we are not. You may not *think* that you are as bad as other people, but in reality, you are. Let us take a quick test to see exactly why.

The entire message of the Bible can be summed up in one word: reconciliation. We have paradise lost in Genesis, paradise regained in Revelation, and everything in between is the story of reconciliation between *you* and God. His first coming to Earth and defeating the grave has provided a way for rebellious mankind to have a personal relationship with Him; salvation comes through trusting in Him as the one and only Savior. But, with this Gospel message, we cannot fully understand what we are saved *to* unless we also understand what we are saved *from*.

Have you ever told a lie? We all have. Have you ever stolen anything? Come on; you just said you were a liar! Have you ever committed adultery? Scripture says if you even look lustfully at another person then you have already committed adultery with that person in your heart. Have you ever used God's name in vain? Again, we all have. Have you ever murdered someone? Scripture says if you hate another person then you are a murderer at heart. Thus, you are a liar, a thief, an adulterer at heart, a blasphemer, and a murderer at heart, and that is only five of the Ten Commandments. So even if you were to miraculously sin a mere five times a day, in a lifetime you are well on your way to 200,000 sins and you will have to answer for *every single one of them* on Judgment Day – when Scripture says each of us will have to give an account of ourselves to God.

This goes to show how high of a holy standard God has. Isaiah 64:6, for instance, says that "all our righteous acts are like filthy rags" to God, and by no means can we impress and buy our way to Heaven. No matter what "good" deeds we may do, they are the equivalent of trying to scrub clean a dirt floor. We *need* a Savior.

"But God will forgive me, right?" Let us try that line of thought in an analogy of a courtroom. Imagine that someone is in the presence of a judge and says, "I know I keep breaking the law, more-so than I can comprehend, but cannot you let it all slide?" Only a corrupt judge would take that argument. A just judge, on the other hand, would say justice demands that you pay for your crimes. Similarly, because you have sinned (rebelled) against God, more-so than you can comprehend, a debt is there which has separated you from God, and somebody has to pay that debt.

To use an analogy inspired from author Ray Comfort of awareness vs. conviction, let us look for a moment at civil law. Imagine if someone said to you, "I have some good news. Someone has just paid a $25,000 speeding fine on your behalf!" You would probably respond with some sharp skepticism in your voice: "What are you talking about? That is not good news, because I do not have a $25,000 speeding fine!" Your reaction would be quite understandable. After all, if you do not know that you have broken the law in the first place, the good news of someone paying a fine for you will not be good news at all. In fact, it would be foolishness to you. But more than that, it would be offensive to you, because it is insinuated that you have broken the law when you do not believe that you have. However, if someone were to put it this way, it would make more sense: "Today, a law enforcement officer clocked you traveling at fifty-five miles an hour in an area designated for a blind children's convention. There were ten clear warning signs indicating that the maximum speed was fifteen miles an hour, but you must have ignored them and went through at fifty-five miles an hour. What you did was extremely dangerous. The penalty is a $25,000 fine or imprisonment." As you begin to see the seriousness of what you have done, not just the awareness that speeding is bad, but the conviction that you are guilty of it, they explain: "The law was about to take its course when someone you do not even know stepped in and paid the fine for you." *That* is good news!

SALVATION

Scripture states that we can never do enough ourselves to earn going to Heaven. Romans 3:23, for instance, says, "For all have sinned and fall short of the glory of God." The first half of Romans 6:23 says, "For the wages of sin is death…" So how can anyone get to Heaven with a standard like *that*? Well, *that* is the whole point! God does not view our lives in reference to any other person – other than Jesus. The second half of that verse gives us this answer: "…but the gift of God is eternal life through Jesus Christ our Lord."

Jesus willingly came to Earth, willingly became fully God and fully man amongst us – with hunger and thirst pains, experiences of working long days in the heat, temptations, emotions of awe, fear, love, and so on. He willingly lived a perfect life that only He could. And even though He had the power to remove Himself from the situation, it was when He was brutally tortured to the point He was unrecognizable and murdered at the cross that He suffered the punishment we each deserve as He presented Himself as the perfect sacrifice for the sin debt of all. Even though Jesus never committed a single sin, at that moment, God poured out His wrath on Him like He was the worst sinner of all. When He hung on the cross, it was like He walked up to God and said, "Here is the payment in full. Me. Punish Me instead." And just before He breathed His last breath on that cross, He said, "It is finished." It *is* finished, and our crimes are *forever* erased if only we repent of our sins and trust in Jesus as the one and only Savior.

Three days later He rose from the dead, verifying that He is the Son of God and that, like a check being cleared, the sacrifice had been made. Similar to how those who lived before Christ's time on Earth were saved by trusting in the promise that God the Father would send a Savior someday, we can now be saved by trusting that the Savior has come, lived, died, and was resurrected as the payment for each and every one of our past and future sins so that we can be forgiven. One can imagine that He thought of everyone's face and their fate every second of those long, agonizing hours to and on the cross;

the only relief being that He knew He was freeing us from what we deserved. As the book of Isaiah states: "He was pierced for our transgressions, he was crushed for our iniquities; the punishment that brought us peace was on him, and by his wounds we are healed."[5] Speaking of those wounds, Jesus carried the wounds from the nails and spear with Him into Heaven. As the only man-made things in Heaven, they are a lasting memorial of His becoming man, God in the flesh, for us to see for all eternity: "'And one shall say unto him "what are these wounds in thine hands?" And he shall answer "those with which I was wounded in the house of my friends."'"[6] When we enter into Heaven, we will see those wounds showing that, as promised, Jesus saves.

The world offers promise full of emptiness, but Jesus' tomb offers emptiness full of promise; what happened to Christ can happen for us; death is not the end if we trust in Him to eternally save us. From the Greek word for "good news," that is the Gospel message – and oh what good news it is.

BELIEVE + RECEIVE = BECOME

Now that we have gone through all avenues of investigation, you hopefully may be thinking to yourself, "I believe this is all true. I genuinely believe that Jesus died for me so that my sins can be forgiven and I can enter into Heaven upon death." That is a truly, truly fantastic step. And you have got one more step to go.

John 3:16 states that, "For God so loved the world that He sent His only begotten Son, that whoever believeth in Him shall not perish but have everlasting life." This is without a doubt the most famous verse, the most life-changing verse and, yet, one of the most misunderstood verses in the whole entire Bible. The word "believe" here does not mean to simply believe. James 1:20 says even Satan's demons believe in God! If we were to read this verse in the original language in which it was originally composed – Greek – the word for "believe" would be "*pisteuō*," which means to have an assurance of, to put one's trust in, and to be persuaded. In fact, every single time you see the words "believe" or "faith" in reference to the existence of God, His saving grace, His promises, and so on, it comes from this either "*pisteuō*" or "pistis" in the Greek, both having the same meaning. After all, you cannot put your faith in a God who you believe is not there! So with both of these statements in mind, believing that Jesus is the Son of God is not the whole equation of salvation. Award-winning legal editor of *The Chicago Tribune*, Lee Strobel, after having interviewed respected scholars from around the country as an atheist searching for answers to questions about belief in Jesus, said well:

> I thought, "I've been spending two years checking into this stuff. I need to reach a verdict." So I went alone in my room and I took a yellow legal pad. And I just began to summarize all of the evidence I'd encountered during this investigation. And I wrote page after page after page after page after page. And, finally, I put my pen down and . . . in light of this avalanche of evidence that points so powerfully toward the truth of Christianity, I realized it would take more faith for me to maintain my atheism than to become a Christian. . . . I pictured it like a river with a strong current. And I felt like the only way in light of the evidence that I could maintain my atheism would be like swimming upstream against the torrent of evidence flowing in the opposite direction. I could not do that; I was trained in journalism and law to respond to truth. And so I concluded on that day, based on the historical data that Jesus not only claimed to be the Son of God, He backed it up by returning from the dead. And then I was stuck. . . . It was kind of anticlimactic. . . . And then I remembered a Christian friend who pointed out a verse to me earlier. So I got a

Bible and I looked it up: John 1:12. It says, "But as many as received Him, to them He gave the right to become children of God, even to those who believe in His name." So I said, "Oh I get it now; there's a formula in that verse of what it means to become a child of God: believe plus receive equals become. So I had the belief part down . . . but I realized that wasn't enough; I had to receive this free gift of forgiveness and eternal life that Jesus purchased when He died on the cross as my substitute to pay for all of my sins."[7]

We do not have to work up towards God, because He has come to us. God has done His part by extending His grace to everyone, and our part is to accept His sacrifice as full payment for our sins and, therefore, accept and trust Him as our Savior. This leads to us having free will, being in the driver's seat of either accepting Jesus' sacrifice as full payment of our sins and asking for forgiveness, or not accepting it and not asking for forgiveness.

It is one thing to believe *that* Jesus rose from the grave, and another thing to trust *in* Him as your needed Savior. In order to take a step from belief *that* to trust *in*, you must move from an examination of *Jesus* to an examination of *yourself*. Maybe that is where you are at this exact moment. As you examine the evidence, ask yourself one question: "Am I rejecting this because there is not enough evidence, or am I rejecting this because I do not want there to be enough evidence?" The question for you personally is not just whether the claims of Jesus are true, but how you are going to respond. Take this personal account from an atheist-turned-Christian, Marilyn Adamson:

> I concluded that the evidence for God was so strong that it made more sense to believe in God than to believe He wasn't there. Then I had to act on that conclusion. I knew that just intellectually concluding God existed, was way too light. It would be like deciding

airplanes exist. Faith in an airplane means nothing. However . . . you have to decide to act and actually get on the plane. I needed to make the decision to actually talk to God. I needed to ask Him to come into my life.[8]

This is what Scripture calls repentance: the changing of your mind from the rejection of Christ to a trust in Christ, and confessing that you are a sinner that, like everyone, needs His forgiveness. Thus, to receive salvation means to humbly ask for forgiveness. No matter what you have done in the past or are doing in the present, no matter how bankrupt and valueless you feel your life is, God loves us all and promises that His salvation is for *everyone*. In fact, those who were considered to be the low-life's and outcasts – tax collectors, those with disease and sickness, beggars, foreigners, prostitutes – were the very ones who Jesus spent the most time with, ministered to, and encouraged to help others see that He was the Son of God. The book of Romans, for instance, speaks of this promise: "'If you confess with your mouth, "Jesus is Lord," and believe in your heart that God raised Him from the dead, you will be saved. . . . Whoever calls upon the name of the Lord shall be saved.'"[9] And Jesus states, "The one who comes to Me, I will by no means cast out."[10]

Now, as words alone cannot save you, a "sinner's prayer" only represents that you have an understanding about your need for salvation and is a declaration that you are relying on Jesus Christ as your Savior. With that in mind, if you trust that Jesus died for your sins, to receive His salvation, in your own private, humble time in prayer, either in your thoughts or out loud, express your repentance of sin as well as your newfound trust in Him as your Savior in a prayer such as the one below.

I did not understand why I needed salvation. But now I see and admit that, like everyone, I am a sinner. I see that I cannot save myself. And I now put my trust in and receive salvation from You, my Lord and Savior Who died and defeated death to wash away my sins. I ask You to forgive me, and I thank You for forgiving me of my sins. Scripture says that now Your Spirit will live inside of me and, from this day forward, help me to slowly but surely do away with my sinful ways. Take a chisel to my life and change me for the better so that others can see a difference in me and that I can see the importance of leading others to you. In Jesus' name, Amen.

ETERNALLY SAVED

Whether you have been saved, have just become saved, or are genuinely thinking about becoming saved, once you receive Jesus' salvation, it is in that very moment of receiving salvation that your sins are wiped clean, your name is written in His book of life, you can have a personal relationship and prayer life with God, and Heaven becomes your home after death. And on top of the already good news of the Gospel itself is the good news Scripture is abundantly clear that we can never lose our salvation (though, as stated in Romans 6:1-2 and 1 John 3:6, for instance, this does not give us a license to deliberately sin). If we could lose our salvation from sin, we would all be doomed.

Because Jesus Christ so thoroughly obliterated our deserved punishment for sins, we have the eternal assurance that God will never refer to our sins again after we are saved. In fact, you can see in numerous verses that forgiveness is a completed act. For instance, in Hebrews 9:28 we read that, "Christ, having been offered *once* to bear sins of many, will appear a second time *without reference to sin*." We read in Romans 8:38-39, "For I am convinced that neither death nor life, neither angels nor principalities, neither the present nor the future, nor any powers, neither height nor depth, nor anything else in all creation, will be able to separate us from the love of God that is in Christ Jesus our Lord." 1 John 5:13-14 states, "I write these things to you who believe in the name of the Son of God so that you may *know* that you have eternal life." In John 10:28-29, Jesus states, "I give them eternal life, and they will never perish. No one can snatch them out of My hand. My Father who has given them to Me is greater than all. No one can snatch them out of My Father's hand." And signifying having finished His mission to rescue us, we read in Hebrews 10:12-18, "But when Christ had offered for *all time* a *single* sacrifice for sins, He sat down at the right hand of God. . . . For by that *one* offering he forever made perfect those who are being made holy. . . . And when sins have been forgiven, there is no need to offer any more sacrifices."

Psalm 103:12 states that when we are saved God removes our sins "as far from us as the east is from the west." In other words, our sins and their deserved punishment are as far away from us as possible and cannot affect us anymore. Therefore, as our eternal assurance is not a result of us maintaining our salvation (whew!). Author, Andrew Farley gives an illustration of this truth:

> Let's say you are a married man. Imagine if every night before you went to sleep, you leaned over to your wife and asked her to marry you. It's just something that would make you feel better – asking her again and again. It's your way of confirming that you're married. . . . This ritual is a bit strange, is not it? Your wife would never let you get away with something so ridiculous. . . . Repeating a question like that over and over might even be insulting. If I were to try this with my wife, she would ask me to reconsider my thought processes: "Don't you remember the ceremony? The vows? The witnesses? . . . It's now a past event. We live in a constant state of being married. There's no need to ask me over and over if I'll marry you." It's the same way with our forgiven state. . . . Have you thought

about how many times the epistles urge us to keep asking God for forgiveness? The answer is *zero* times. . . . They were fully aware of their forgiveness as an accomplished fact.[11]

When God places our name at salvation into His book, we can never be removed. Truly, thus goes the saying that God's pencil has no eraser.

"IT'S DANGEROUS TO GO ALONE! TAKE THIS"

Contrast eternal salvation of Christianity with what is taught in all other religions, and you will quickly see that Christianity is entirely unique. Not only is it unique among all world religions in that we can have the assurance of salvation, but it is also unique in that – and this goes hand-in-hand with the assurance of salvation – we do not have to try to do good works to desperately try and work our way to God.

Scripture states in Ephesians 2:8-9, "For by grace you have been saved through faith. And this is not your own doing; it is the gift of God, not a result of works, so that no one may boast." Now, contrast that with, say, Islam for example.

As we have recently discussed, the word for "Islam" is the Arabic word for "submission." And as we discussed in our first chapter, in order to be saved, Muslims believe they (and only they, as Muslims do not believe anyone else can be saved) must diligently do works in hopes that their good deeds outweigh their bad deeds.[12] Yet, at the same time, the Qur'an also teaches that even if their good deeds outweigh their bad deeds, that may or may not affect Allah's decision to save them; Allah gives zero promises and can simply act arbitrarily.

Therefore, as many Muslims would admit, they are deeply troubled

SALVATION

inside. One reason is that they hold to the belief illness and poverty are signs that Allah hates them and is pouring out his wrath on their sins. Primarily, they are troubled because their religion does not offer an assurance of where their souls and the souls of their loved ones will go upon death; even Muhammad himself was unsure, and he was who wrote the Qur'an![13] This is not good news.

Or take Mormonism as another example (which, contrary to what you may think, because it denies the essential doctrines, is not Christian). Mormons believe there are many works that must be done obediently as prerequisites in order to obtain salvation.[14] States Brigham Young University (BYU, a Mormon-based university) professor Daniel Ludlow, "Men can no more be saved without obedience than they can be healed without faith. All things operate by law; blessings result from obedience to law and are withheld when there is no obedience."[15]

The book of Mormon also states that "If ye shall deny yourselves of all ungodliness, and love God with all your might, mind and strength, then is his grace sufficient for you."[16] Did you catch that: "*all* ungodliness"? Now that is a tall order; *an impossible order*! Doing well towards others is a great thing, but what the teachings of this particular religion mean is that a person can and must do away with not most but *all* ungodliness. And in further teachings by leaders of the Mormon church, they confirm that Mormonism is the belief that, to be saved, we cannot ever sin again and, if we do, we lose salvation; for example, "We also have to forsake the sin and never to repeat it not even in our minds, in order to remain forgiven we must never commit the sin again."[17] This is not good news, either.

It is not wise to go into death with our subjective opinions about what may or may not happen to our souls. And there are *a lot* of opinions out there. For instance, going back to a study we referenced in our first chapter, according to a recent U.S. Religious Landscape Survey by the Pew Research

Center, 65% (down from 70% in their prior study) of those affiliated with a religion hold the view that, "Many religions can lead to eternal life."[18] The study also shows that only 30% hold to the view that beliefs matter when it comes to eternal life, whereas many others hold to the view that works and "being a good, moral person" (e.g., Catholics at 61% and 29%) are the keys to eternal life. And, elsewhere, Pew also reports only 48% of all individuals even believe in Heaven and only 36% even believe in Hell.[19]

In contrast to all the subjective opinions of the world, Christ says that all works in an attempt to be saved (e.g., baptism, knocking on doors for a number of years, praying five times a day in a certain direction, adhering to a strict diet and wardrobe, etc.) are not necessary and will not "work." Succinctly, He states that "I am the way and the truth and the life. No one comes to the Father except through me."[20] Because He Has proved to be the Son of God and says that only taking His eternal salvation to the grave will suffice, it would be wise to trust Him.

With that said, because God came down to *us*, Christianity is not a religion (a religion being, by definition, man trying to reach God). Because they do not like church, or "churchy" people, many have decided that they do not want religion. Well, guess what? Religion is not what anyone has ever needed! "Getting religion" has never got anyone into Heaven, and pious living has not got anybody closer to God. It was religious people who killed Jesus. In fact, they tried to ten times before they tortured and murdered Him. It was religious people who stoned and beheaded Christians. You say you do not like religion? Well, God does not like religion either. The living God who created the universe is not sitting up in Heaven hoping you find religion; He is waiting for you to find Him! Therefore, seeing as how Christianity is not a religion at all but is a relationship, we can reasonably cross the bottomless, empty, feelings-based chasm of opinion and plant our feet firmly on the solid ground of truth.

SALVATION

WHAT WILL HEAVEN BE LIKE?

I'm just a poor wayfaring stranger
Traveling through this world below
There is no sickness, no toil, nor danger
In that bright land to which I go

I'm going there to see my father
And all my loved ones who've gone on
I'm just going over Jordan
I'm just going over home

I know dark clouds will gather 'round me
I know my way is hard and steep
But beauteous fields arise before me
Where God's redeemed, their vigils keep

I'm going there to see my mother
She said she'd meet me when I come
I'm just going over Jordan
I'm just going over home[21]

Is there any truth to the lines of this well-known folk and bluegrass song, with its protagonist contemplating on better times with their family in Heaven? Or what about other songs that have also been written about death and the mystery behind it, such as Eric Clapton's "Tears in Heaven," where he asks the question such as if he will get to hold hands again with his late four-year-old son. Will there really be an end to all pain and suffering, and will we truly be with and know our loved ones again?

The primary reason that most people would prefer to postpone death is the fact that the afterlife is the utmost mysterious. It is simply hard not to be scared to die; after all, the afterlife is always described as being somewhere for *eternity*. Add to that the misconceptions, and it is easy to see why we are so reserved about the topic of Heaven.

In starting this discussion on what Heaven will be like, the first important point to make is that the Bible is clear that we are more familiar with Heaven than we think. In fact, Heaven is many times referred to as the "New Earth."[22] Author Randy Alcorn adds to this line of thought:

> In order to get a picture of Heaven . . . you do not need to look up at the clouds; you simply need to look around you and imagine what all this would be like without sin and death and suffering and corruption. . . . So look out a window. Talk a walk. Talk with your friend. Use your God-given skills to paint or draw or build a shed or write a book. But imagine it – all of it – in its original condition. The happy dog with the wagging tail, not the snarling beast, beaten and starved. The flowers unwilted, the grass undying, the blue sky without pollution. People smiling and joyful, not angry, depressed, and empty.[23]

Because "no longer will there be any curse," Heaven will be like Earth but perfected.[24] Alcorn continues:

> I heard a pastor say on the radio, "There's nothing in our present experience that can suggest to us what Heaven is like." But if the eternal Heaven will be a New Earth, doesn't that suggest that the current Earth must be bursting with clues about what Heaven will be like? Scripture gives us images full of hints and implications about

Heaven. Put them together, and these jigsaw pieces form a beautiful picture. For example, we're told that Heaven is a city (Hebrews 11:10; 13:14). When we hear the word *city*, we shouldn't scratch our heads and think, "I wonder what that means?" We understand cities. Cities have buildings, culture, art, music, athletics, good and services, events of all kinds. And, of course, cities have *people* engaged in activities, gatherings, conversations, and work. Heaven is also described as a country (Hebrews 11:16). . . . (These familiar features are specifically mentioned in Revelation 21-22.) We're told we'll have resurrection bodies (1 Corinthians 15:40-44). When God speaks of us having these bodies, do we shrug our shoulders and say, "I cannot imagine what a new body would be like"? No, of course we can imagine it. We know what a body is – we've had one all our lives! Some of the best portrayals I've seen of the eternal Heaven are in children's books. Why? Because they depict earthly scenes, with animals and people playing, and joyful activities. The books for adults, on the other hand, often try to be philosophical, profound, ethereal, and otherworldly. But this kind of Heaven is precisely what the Bible *does not* portray as the place where we'll live forever.[25]

What, then, about the question of whether we will recognize our loved ones in Heaven? Many places in Scripture give answers to this question. One example is when King David's infant son dies, David states that he "will go to him" in Heaven.[26] Another example is that Abraham, Lazarus, and the rich man were all recognizable after death.[27] We also see that Moses and Elijah appeared and spoke with Jesus in front of Peter, John, and James.[28] Paul states clearly that it will be our own bodies that will be raised and glorified in Heaven.[29] And, most obvious, on all occasions, everyone recognized Jesus as He conversed and ate with many in His glorified body after His resurrection.

We can take immense comfort in Paul confidently saying that it will be "far better" than being on this cursed Earth, and the Psalms stating that one day there is better than a thousand elsewhere (days including seeing your children being born, seeing them walk for the first time, falling in love with your spouse, and so on).[30][31] Imagine how great it will be to live in the direct presence of Christ and God the Father: "God's dwelling place is now among the people, and he will dwell with them. They will be his people, and God himself will be with them and be their God. He will wipe every tear from their eyes. There will be no more death or mourning or crying or pain, for the old order of things has passed away!"[32] A place where we will be freed from the fear of personal and physical harm to our loved ones and us, the burden of financial pressures, depression, anxiety attacks, addictions, insecurities, disabilities, and sickness; that is the Biblical promise of Heaven.

No, Heaven will not be a never-ending worship service. No, Heaven will not be an empty expanse of white, where all we do is fly around together with angel wings and play harps like in a toilet paper commercial. And, no, we will not be like robots stripped of our free will or our unique past, memories, appearance, interests, and personality. In fact, anything about Heaven that has ever caused you dread, to be depressed, to be weighted down with fear, or hesitancy in your walk with God is always due to a misconception that could not be farther from the truth.

THERE IS SUCH A PLACE CALLED HELL

With all of this talk about being saved and going to Heaven, from where exactly are we being saved? What is the consequence in the afterlife of not asking God for forgiveness? Well, you will not hear it from prosperity preachers on TV, but there is a very real place called Hell. We know this because Jesus and the Bible as a whole speak of both Heaven and Hell.

Many probably view Hell as a fun place that beats a supposed boring Heaven, having beers with friends and sinning to their heart's content. Scripture, though, describes Hell as being a place of unimaginable torment where the inhabitants are "punished with eternal destruction, forever separated from the Lord."[33] Just as the rich man is portrayed alone in Hell in the Gospel of Luke, each person is confined solitarily absent from their loved ones, away from others entirely, and away from God. And being away from God means being away from everything that is good (e.g., love, relationships, peace, joy, laughter, affection).[34] The keyword is *eternal*; physical and mental torment, suffering with no help coming – ever.

Now, we do not cover that fact in order to scare anyone into Heaven; it is to give the facts as Jesus plainly states. While there are those who say they do not want to be with God for all eternity, even they would say they do not want Hell. Nobody especially wants Hell for their loved ones. Therefore, we have to take this reality seriously and lead others to God and away from that awful place! Let us, then, look at two true, contrasting stories by author and pastor Craig Groeschel as to how we normally fail when telling others about Hell and how we should change our strategy.

> Years ago I received a call from a church member explaining that her dad, Frank, was close to death. His concerned daughter asked if I'd visit him in the hospital to explain the gospel so her dad would have a final chance to know Christ before he died. . . . Walking down the long, sterile hallway, I glanced in each room and wondered about the patients. Some would recover and go back to their lives, while others would never leave this building. . . . When he heard me enter the room, Frank stirred and seemed glad for a visitor, even if the visitor was a pastor. Not wanting to come across like a typical fire and

brimstone preacher, I kept the conversation light. The whole time we talked, I looked for the opportune moment to shift the conversation toward spiritual issues. We talked about his favorite football team. Frank loved the Redskins and hated the Cowboys ever since Tom Landry left. (No apparent opportunity for a spiritual segue.) He told me about his grandson . . . we chatted about the unseasonably hot weather. . . . The perfect moment to transition the conversation to a spiritual issue never came. I decided not to force it. I told myself that I'd developed a better relationship with him and would return the next day to try and talk to him about Christ and eternity. . . . When I turned the corner to enter his room, I could not see Frank because the room was packed with people. Instantly I realized what had just happened. Moments before I arrived, Frank had died, and all of his family had gathered to say goodbye. Standing outside the room, I could barely breathe. Frank's body may still have been warm, but my heart felt suddenly cold with disappointment in myself.

Many people can understand my hesitancy in sharing with Frank. People who are pushy about their beliefs are not well-respected. The book *The Day America Told the Truth* tells how Americans ranked different professions according to their degree of integrity and honesty. Televangelists, known mostly for asking for money, ranked below lawyers, politicians, car salesmen, and even prostitutes. Out of seventy-three professions, only organized crime members and drug dealers scored lower than televangelists. . . . Why are so many of us . . . slow to share our faith? There are many possible answers, among them the strong desire not to be pushy or disliked. Also, many don't feel they know enough. And the list could go on and on, But I believe one of the main reasons people don't share their faith in Christ is that they don't really believe in hell. Many of us are out of touch with the genuine urgency. As a pastor, I'm often confronted by death. One thing I've observed is that when someone dies, that person's loved ones want to believe their relative went to "a better place." We'll say things like, "She wasn't a religious person, but deep down, she had a good heart," or, "He wasn't a saint, but he did some good things." When it comes to death and eternity, it's human nature to hope for the best and avoid contemplating the worst. . . . But [opinion doesn't] determine reality.[35]

Because tomorrow is never a guarantee, obviously this was not the way we are to approach telling others about the afterlife. Thus, there is a much better way of approaching such an important topic.

I once visited a man named Mark in the hospital. Like Frank, Mark was not a believer in Christ, and he did not have much time to live. At the tender age of forty-two, this husband and father of two had an advanced brain tumor. When I walked in, Mark recognized me. He was obviously in pain, and he did not look thrilled at my visit. "My wife sent you, did not she, preacher? . . . "I guess you came to 'save' me from hell," Mark said, obviously positioning himself for a verbal conflict. "Mark, that's exactly why I'm here," I said. . . . "Your wife loves you more than you know, and frankly, she's concerned for you spiritually. She's tried to talk to you about Christ, but you always shut her down. She thought you might be willing to talk to me." Mark wasn't rude, but he was firm. "I don't have long to live. I don't want to waste a minute of what's left of my life talking about religion." He grimaced in pain. "If you don't mind, please shut the door on the way out so I can rest in peace." Not wanting to be pushy,

I politely excused myself. As I walked down the hospital hallway, my mind flashed back to Frank.

Overwhelmed with a sudden spiritual courage, I turned. I charged back into his room, and with tears in my eyes I blurted out, "You know what, Mark? That's exactly what your family wants from you. They want you to rest in peace – eternally." Mark did not speak. For several awkward moments, we simply stared at each other. I did not know what else to say. . . . His face slightly softened and he said, "Well?" Seeing a crack in the door, I tried to open it and show him God's good news. I began explaining to him how God sent His son Jesus as a sacrifice for our sins. Soon I realized I had not taken a breath, so I paused and asked hopefully, "Mark, would you like to trust Jesus with your eternity?" Mark did not speak. He nodded his head gently, affirmatively. We prayed together. . . . Two days later I went back. Mark's wife was sitting by the side of the bed, holding her husband's hand. Although she was about to lose her husband, she beamed with assurance that she and her husband would be reunited in heaven. Through closer to death than ever, Mark's eyes looked more alive than a healthy man's. "Preacher," he said, affectionately this time, "God has forgiven me of all my sins." Mark pushed his next words out slowly: "I'm going to see my family again in heaven one day. . . . You'll never know what a difference you've made in my life."[36]

A MATTER OF THE HEART

It is incredibly sad how we will focus so much energy, say, arguing (USING ALL CAPITAL LETTERS!) in the comment section of a political-based post on social media, all because someone else does not believe exactly like we do.

Heaven and Hell are where we will spend (and here are some capital letters that actually matter) ETERNITY, yet we focus so little on something that will last so long. Whether it is in Heaven or in Hell, forever is a long, long time.

This urgency to accept Christ is a reminder of a particular scene in the children's movie *Madagascar: Escape 2 Africa*. The watering hole for all of the animals has just dried up, and they are digging a well to see if they can find a source of groundwater. "Any water?" asks one character, to the reply from another in a disappointed tone of voice, "No, just more diamonds and gold."[37] Of course, that quote is meant to make the viewer chuckle, but it rings with truth. Dying of thirst, and with no water in sight, what would be the most precious thing for one to obtain: a big plate of nachos, the Mona Lisa, a neon green Lamborghini, *two* big plates of nachos? When we wake up to reality and see that we, without salvation, are walking dead people, we see that doing anything else other than accepting Christ as our Lord and Savior would be like finding diamonds and gold (something we would otherwise have been excited about and thought was highly important to stockpile) when all we desperately need to live is water.

Yet, we do not take eternity seriously. We have seen that only 48% of people in the U.S. believe in Heaven and only 36% believe in Hell. We have seen that atheists clearly do not believe in God, the afterlife, the immaterial, and so on. Popular books claim to be the supposed ultimate guides to what happens after we die. And it is commonly seen that popular figures such as the Dalai Lama will say on TV that Heaven and Hell does not exist, and Joel Osteen who, in his sermons streamed on TV and online around the world, refuses to preach about the existence of Hell. Alcorn adds:

> The sense that we will live forever *somewhere* has shaped every civilization in human history. Australian aborigines pictured Heaven as a distant island beyond the western horizon. The early Finns

thought it was an island in the faraway east. Mexicans, Peruvians, and Polynesians believed that they went to the sun or the moon after death. Native Americans believed that in the afterlife their spirits would hunt the spirits of buffalo. The *Gilgamesh* epic, an ancient Babylonian legend, refers to a resting place of heroes and hints at a tree of life. In the pyramids of Egypt, the embalmed bodies had maps placed beside them as guides to the future world. The Romans believed that the righteous would picnic in the Elysian Fields, while their horses grazed nearby. Seneca, the Roman philosopher, said, "The day thou fearest as the last is the birthday of eternity." Although these depictions of the afterlife differ, the unifying testimony of the human heart throughout history is belief in life after death. Anthropological evidence suggests that every culture has a God-given, innate sense of the eternal—that this world is not all there is.[38]

What those statistics and those words from celebrities and everyday people alike from cultures around the world all have in common is that they are merely subjective opinions that are not worth betting your eternal destination on. The fact that no human being knows for certain what will happen to our souls upon death cannot be overstated. In light of all that we have discussed throughout each chapter, we know opinions can have serious, eternal consequences. Thus, if Jesus is the Son of God (and we have very reasonable evidence to trust that He is), then if we live by subjective opinions alone and not what He specifically says about our origin, meaning and purpose, morality, and the afterlife, then our very souls are in deep trouble upon death. Alcorn continues with this line of thought:

> For [everyone] who believes [they're] going to Hell, there are 120 who believe they're going to Heaven. This optimism stands in stark

SALVATION

contrast to Christ's words in Matthew 7:13-14: "Enter through the narrow gate. For wide is the gate and broad is the road that leads to destruction, and many enter through it. But small is the gate and narrow is the road that leads to life, and only a few find it." . . . Judging by what's said at most funerals, you'd think nearly *everyone's* going to Heaven, wouldn't you? But Jesus made it clear that most people are *not* going to Heaven. . . . We dare not "wait and see" when it comes to what's on the other side of death. We shouldn't just cross our fingers and hope that our names are written in the Book of Life (Revelation 21:27). We can know, we *should* know, before we die. And because we may die at any time, we need to know *now* – not next month or next year. "Why, you do not even know what will happen tomorrow. What is your life? You are a mist that appears for a little while and then vanishes" (James 4:14). It's of paramount importance to make sure you are going to Heaven, not Hell. The voice that whispers, "There's no hurry; put this book down; you can always think about it later," is not God's voice. . . . The reality of Hell should break our hearts and take us to our knees and to the doors of those without Christ. Today, however, even among many Bible believers, Hell has become "the *H* word," seldom named, rarely talked about.[39]

Psychology has traditionally held a negative view of religion in general. Sigmund Freud, for example, while admitting it had made significant contributions to cultures in various ways, stated religion served as a crutch when we face the harsh realities of life. For instance, when we hear at funerals that our loves ones who have gone before us are the lucky ones because they are in a better place, that is merely something we tell each other in order to make life more palatable. Instead of dealing with problems in a rational manner, said Freud, those who are religiously committed simply regress to childhood and long for the existence of a powerful father who unconsciously is projected into the form of a supernatural god who rescues his supplicants from tribulations of life. According to Freud, culture would advance in maturity by embracing science as the lone, rational approach to solving life's issues. Freud's critique of religion had been highly influential on psychology, as many researchers avoided the study of religion and spirituality because the subject seemed too ethereal, unscientific, or controversial.

Furthermore, as we have discussed in previous chapters, influential atheists refer to Christians as being uneducated, ignorant, stupid, insane, and even wicked. Yet, that is exactly the opposite of what we find when following the evidence wherever it leads. The Christian can be completely confident in their trust in Christ. Once we collect all of the evidence and see that science simply had to catch up with the Bible. As Jesus preached and as the disciples in ancient times lived, trust in Christ is the hope of the world; an exciting adventure, the greatest love story and rescue mission of all time and, most importantly, the truth. Author and speaker Natasha Crain similarly states, "Christianity is not a useful fiction designed to make your life more bearable. . . . It is the truth about reality."[40]

We have ample reason to believe that Christianity is true from the overwhelming historical evidence. On top of that, when we add together the evidence (and we could have included much more had time allowed for it) from all other avenues of investigation, like death by a thousand paper cuts, we see they paint an entirely reasonable picture of the God of the Bible being the true Creator of the universe, Designer of the universe, and the Giver of the moral law. One can no longer attempt to justify disbelief in God overall or not accepting Christ as their Savior due to a head issue. Instead, it would merely be a matter of the heart. This would be to approach life intellectually even worse than an atheist. Where an atheist rules out the existence of God before even looking at the evidence, their preconceived philosophical bias shows a heart issue based on feelings alone instead of a head issue. These are the same people who push women and children aside as they run for the emergency escape hatches and lifeboats, covering their eyes from God while claiming the design and planning of the universe, consciousness, free will, morality, the resurrection (with the hallucination theory), and so on are *all illusions*. If you have made it to this point, then obviously you know the evidence well. Thus, for you to still not trust in God would be to have an even more severe feelings based heart issue that keeps you from accepting reality.

There may come a day when you find yourself walking down the hallway of a hospital, remembering each room your parents were in. And, yet, you know you will never see their face light up because they have not had a visitor all day and they missed you. No more phone calls from them; their voices lost in the wind. There may come a day when you find yourself burying your own child who, at the young age of 20 got killed by a drunk driver. You ponder on how their life was taken from them at no fault of their own, all while you watch the swing they played on sitting eerily still. No one is guaranteed another day. As we cited in our first chapter, with roughly 156,000 people dying each day and 57 million each year, death barely misses us with every passing day.[41] We are still on this side of eternity, and we *must* wake up to reality. A handful of those who "get it" cannot do the immense job alone of leading everyone to Christ – especially those who *you* are closest to that need to hear the Gospel message. You must know God and make Him known. Trust Him in times of happiness, trust Him in times of pain, and trust Him that He will give you the strength to comfort others and lead them to His salvation in ways that only *you* can. Look first to your family – even to those who have been to church every single time the doors are open. Perhaps they have never asked to be saved. Look into the innocent eyes of your young children and grandchildren, nieces and nephews. *You* must be their rock. *They* are your life's purpose.

CROSSING OPINION

BIBLIOGRAPHY

CHAPTER 1

1. Ravi Zacharias, Has Christianity Failed You (Grand Rapids, MI: Zondervan, 2010), pg 50-51
2. https://youtube.com/watch?v=CI8UPHMzZm8
3. http://christianpost.com/news/u-s-church-leaders-youth-ministers-address-christian-youth-fallout-13940/
4. Sean McDowell, Apologetics for a New Generation (Eugene, OR: Harvest House, 2009), pg 18
5. Religulous. Directed by Larry Charles. Performances by Bill Maher. Lionsgate, 2008
6. http://foxnews.com/tech/2015/07/09/worlds-smallest-bible-is-size-grain-sugar.html
7. Inspired by Norman L. Geisler & Frank Turek, I Don't Have Enough Faith to Be an Atheist (Wheaton, IL: Crossway, 2004), pg 40
8. Longmire, Season 5, Episode 10
9. https://twitter.com/benshapiro?lang=en, February 5, 2016
10. https://twitter.com/benshapiro?lang=en, March 23, 2017
11. http://educateforlife.org/greg-koukl-relativism-discussion-starters/
12. Sean McDowell, Ethix (Nashville, TN: B&H, 2006), pg 26
13. Josh McDowell & Sean McDowell, Evidence for the Resurrection (Ventura, CA: Regal, 2009), pg 107
14. Allan Bloom, The Closing of the American Mind (New York, NY: Simon and Schuster, 1987), pg 25-26
15. http://pewforum.org/2008/12/18/many-americans-say-other-faiths-can-lead-to-

eternal-life/).
16. http://images.oprah.com/images/obc_classic/book/2008/anewearth/ane_chapter1_transcript.pdf
17. http://youtube.com/watch?v=noO_dCWtB1E
18. http://texasmonthly.com/story/willie-nelson-0
19. Time Magazine, April 26, 1999
20. Timothy Keller, The Reason for God (Toronto: Penguin, 2008), pg 8-14
21. Ibid, pg 15-16
22. Alex McFarland, The 10 Most Common Objections to Christianity (Ventura, CA: Regal, 2007), pg 148
23. Sura 4:157-158
24. Doctrine and Covenants 9:8-9
25. Quran 53:1-9
26. Jeremiah 17:9
27. Philip Schaff, History of the Christian Church, col. 1 (New York, NY: Charles Scribner's Sons, 1882), pg 175
28. https://www.who.int/news-room/fact-sheets/detail/the-top-10-causes-of-death
29. The 10 Most Common Objections to Christianity, pg 147
30. C.S. Lewis, God in the Dock: Essays on Theology and Ethics (1994), pg 101
31. John 14:6
32. https://youtube.com/watch?v=6md638smQd8
33. https://washingtonpost.com/news/wonk/wp/2017/06/15/seven-percent-of-americans-think-chocolate-milk-comes-from-brown-cows-and-thats-not-even-the-scary-part/?utm_term=.5279a9854d47

CHAPTER 2

1. Leo Tolstoy, A Confession
2. Mark Mittelberg, Confident Faith (Carol Stream, IL: Tyndale, 2013), pg 172-173
3. Lee Strobel, The Case for a Creator (Grand Rapids, MI: Zondervan, 2004), pg 105
4. J.Y.T.Greig, ed., The Letters of David Hume (Oxford: Clarendon Press, 1932), 1:187
5. https://youtube.com/watch?v=hXPdpEJk78E
6. http://content.time.com/time/covers/0,16641,20010625,00.html

BIBLIOGRAPHY

7. https://en.wikiquote.org/wiki/Ice_Age:_Collision_Course
8. http://apologeticspress.org/apcontent.aspx?category=9&article=2106
9. Isaac Asimov, "In the Game of Energy and Thermodynamics You Can't Even Break Even," Smithsonian Institute Journal, June 1970, pg 6
10. Norman L. Geisler & Frank Turek, I Don't Have Enough Faith to Be an Atheist (Wheaton, IL: Crossway, 2004), pg 76-77
11. https://scientificamerican.com/article/it-s-official-the-universe-is-dying-slowly/
12. http://ism.ucalgary.ca/Star_Formation/How_Often.html
13. Robert Jastrow, God and the Astronomers (New York, NY: W.W. Norton, 1978), pg 111
14. http://space.com/17661-theory-general-relativity.html
15. http://haydenplanetarium.org/tyson/read/1996/11/01/outward-bound
16. http://nationalgeographic.com/magazine/2005/05/einstein-relativity-cosmology-space-time-big-bang/
17. http://press.princeton.edu/chapters/s7324.html
18. Paul Davies, "Space-time Singularities in Cosmology and Black Hole Evaporations" in: Fraser J.T., Lawrence N., Park D.A. (eds) The Study of Time III (New York, NY: Springer, 1978), pg 78-79
19. Stephen Hawking and Roger Penrose, The Nature of Space and Time (The Isaac Newton Institute Series of Lectures) (Princeton: Princeton University Press, 1996), pg 20
20. Robert Jastrow, God and the Astronomers (New York, NY: W.W. Norton, 2000) pg 32
21. http://w.astro.berkeley.edu/~mwhite/darkmatter/bbn.html
22. http://astronomy.ohio-state.edu/~ryden/ast162_5/notes19.html
23. http://astronomy.ohio-state.edu/~ryden/ast162_10/notes44.html
24. https://map.gsfc.nasa.gov/universe/bb_tests_ele.html
25. J. Warner Wallace, God's Crime Scene (Colorado Springs, CO: David C. Cook, 2015), pg 34-36
26. I Don't Have Enough Faith to Be an Atheist, pg 82
27. http://planck.cf.ac.uk/science/cmb
28. Michael Lemonick, Echo of the Big Bang (Princeton University Press, 2005), pg 64
29. http://skyserver.sdss.org/dr1/en/astro/universe/universe.asp
30. https://nasa.gov/exploration/whyweexplore/Why_We_24.html

31. Hugh Ross, The Creator and the Cosmos (Colorado Springs, CO: NavPress, 1995), pg 57
32. Alexander Vilenkin, Many Worlds in one: The Search for Other Universes (New York, NY: Hill and Wang, 2006), pg 58-60
33. Daniel Dennett, Breaking the Spell: Religion as a Natural Phenomenon (New York, NY: Viking, 2006), pg 244
34. Frank Turek, Stealing from God: Why Atheists Need God to Make Their Case (Colorado Springs, CO: NavPress, 2015) pg 3-4
35. Alex McFarland, The 10 Most Common Objections to Christianity (Ventura, CA: Regal, 2007) pg 47-48
36. https://youtube.com/watch?v=pO3mryntXwo
37. Stephen Hawking, A Brief History of Time (New York, NY: Bantam, 1988), pg 127
38. John Boslough, Stephen Hawking's Universe (New York, NY: Quill, 1985), pg 109
39. Paul Davies, "The Birth of the Cosmos," in God, Cosmos, Nature and Creativity, ed. Jill Gready (Edinburgh: Scottish Academic Press, 1995), pg 8-9
40. Arthur Eddington, The Expanding Universe (New York, NY: Macmillan, 1933), pg 178
41. http://nytimes.com/1978/06/25/archives/have-astronomers-found-god-theologians-are-delighted-that-the.html
42. "A Scientist Caught Between Two Faiths: Interview with Robert Jastrow," Christianity Today, August 6, 1982
43. Stephen Hawking and Leonard Mlodinow, The Grand Design (New York, NY: Bantam, 2010), pg 180
44. https://ispot.tv/ad/7b4y/craftsman-made-to-make
45. The Case for a Creator, pg 106-107
46. https://theatlantic.com/technology/archive/2012/04/has-physics-made-philosophy-and-religion-obsolete/256203/
47. I Don't Have Enough Faith to Be an Atheist, pg 81-82
48. https://youtube.com/watch?v=CwwUnsqA5gI
49. Stephen Hawking, "Origin of the Universe" lecture, 1988
50. A Brief History of Time, pg 136
51. Robert Jastrow, God and the Astronomers (New York, NY: W.W. Norton & Co, 1978), pg 16

BIBLIOGRAPHY

52. Genesis 1:1
53. Robert Jastrow, Until the Sun Dies (New York, NY: W.W. Norton & Co, 1977), pg 21
54. God and the Astronomers, pg 14
55. Fred Heeren, Show Me God: What the Message from Space Is Telling Us About God (Wheeling, IL: Day Star, 2000), pg 177
56. Echo of the Big Bang, 2005, pg 64
57. George Smoot and Keay Davidson, Wrinkles in Time (New York, NY: Avon, 1993), pg 189
58. The New York Times, March 12, 1978
59. E.g., Job 9:8; Psalm 104:2; Isaiah 40:22, 42:5, 44:24, 45:12, 48:13, 51:13; Jeremiah 10:12, 51:15; Zechariah 12:1
60. The Case for a Creator, pg 127-128

CHAPTER 3

1. William S. Paley, Natural Theology or Evidences of the Existence and Attributes of the Deity, 1802
2. Paul Davies, "Taking Science on Faith," New York Times, November 24, 2007
3. Freeman Dyson, Disturbing the Universe (New York, NY: Harper and Row, 1979), pg 250
4. Sean McDowell, "Praise The Lord," TBN, May 31, 2012
5. Michio Kaku, Parallel Worlds: A Journey through Creation, Higher Dimensions, and the Future of the Cosmos (New York, NY: Anchor Books, 2005), pg 247
6. Lee Strobel, The Case for a Creator (Grand Rapids, MI: Zondervan, 2004), pg 145
7. Paul Davies, Cosmic Jackpot (New York, NY: Houghton Mifflin, 2007), pg 149
8. Stephen Hawking, A Brief History of Time (New York, NY: Bantam, 1988), pg 125
9. Stephen Hawking and Leonard Mlodinow, The Grand Design (New York, NY: Bantam, 2010), pg 160-161
10. Hugh Ross, The Creator and the Cosmos (Colorado Springs, CO: NavPress, 1995), pg 115
11. http://reasonablefaith.org/transcript-fine-tuning-argument
12. Lee Strobel, The Case for Faith (Grand Rapids, MI: Zondervan, 2000), pg 101

13. http://discovery.org/f/11011
14. Roger Penrose, The Emperor's New Mind (New York, NY: Oxford, 1989), pg 344
15. "Your World with Neil Cavuto," Fox News, February 27, 2015
16. http://reasons.org/articles/anthropic-principle-a-precise-plan-for-humanity
17. Lee Strobel, The Case for a Creator (Grand Rapids, MI: Zondervan, 2004), pg 179
18. Ibid, pg 180
19. https://youtube.com/watch?v=IMbEVv3IsGY
20. The Case for a Creator, Ibid.
21. Ibid, pg 181
22. Ibid, pg 182
23. Albert Einstein, Living Philosophies
24. http://nytimes.com/2010/07/22/science/space/22star.html?_r=0
25. Mishurov, Y. N. & Zenina, I. A., "Yes, the Sun is Located Near the Corotation Circle," Astronomy and Astrophysics, 1999, v.341, pg 81-85
26. The Case for a Creator, pg 183-184
27. Ibid, pg 191
28. http://news.nationalgeographic.com/news/2002/03/0307_0307_waterworld.html
29. http://newsweek.com/kic-8462852-alien-megastructure-dimming-astronomers-baffled-616346
30. https://finance.yahoo.com/news/scientists-days-finding-mysterious-star-221657896.html
31. https://space.com/34303-alien-megastructure-star-strange-dimming-mystery.html
32. http://npr.org/sections/13.7/2015/10/27/452276775/maybe-it-s-time-to-stop-snickering-about-aliens
33. http://dailymail.co.uk/sciencetech/article-4872004/Tabby-s-star-NOT-caused-alien-megastructure.html
34. http://news.yahoo.com/astronomers-star-three-super-earths-195105678.html
35. http://popularmechanics.com/space/a18573/closest-habitable-planet-wolf-1061/
36. https://sciencealert.com/astronomers-discover-closest-potentially-habitable-planet-wolf-1061c
37. https://yahoo.com/news/hawking-launches-biggest-ever-search-alien-life-140432362.html
38. https://usatoday.com/story/news/nation-now/2017/08/02/nasa-hiring-planetary-protection-officer-protect-earth-alien-harm/532221001/

BIBLIOGRAPHY

39. http://reasonablefaith.org/transcript-fine-tuning-argument
40. The Case for a Creator, pg 81
41. Richard Dawkins, The God Delusion (Boston, MA: Houghton Mifflin, 2006), pg 169-170
42. The Grand Design, Ibid
43. Paul Davies, The Mind of God (New York, NY: Simon and Schuster, 1992), pg 169
44. The Grand Design, Ibid
45. http://discovermagazine.com/2008/dec/10-sciences-alternative-to-an-intelligent-creator
46. David Shukman (2010), "Professor Stephen Hawking Says No God Created Universe," BBC News, http://www.bbc.co.uk/news/uk-11172158
47. https://newscientist.com/article/mg22129520-900-when-does-multiverse-speculation-cross-into-fantasy/
48. John Polkinghorne, Serious Talk: Science and Religion in Dialogue (London: Trinity Press International, 1995), pg 6
49. https://newscientist.com, Ibid
50. Lee Smolin, "You Think There's a Multiverse? Get Real," New Scientist, 2015
51. http://smithsonianmag.com/science-nature/can-physicists-ever-prove-multiverse-real-180958813/
52. http://discovermagazine.com, Ibid
53. George F.R. Ellis, 2011, "Does the Multiverse Really Exist?" Scientific American, pg 39-41
54. Robin Collins, "The Teleological Argument," The Blackwell Companion to Natural Theology (Malden, MA: Wiley-Blackwell, 2009), pg 263
55. Paul Davies, "Taking Science on Faith," The New York Times, November 24, 2007, http://nytimes.com/2007/11/24/opinion/24davies.html?_r=0
56. "The Creation Question: A Curiosity Conversation," Discovery Channel, 2011
57. http://reasons.org/files/compendium/compendium_part2.pdf
58. http://apologeticspress.org/apcontent.aspx?category=12&article=310
59. The Mind of God, pg 16, 232
60. Robert Augros & George Stanciu, The New Story of Science (Gateway, 1984), pg 70
61. http://discovermagazine.com/2008/dec/10-sciences-alternative-to-an-intelligent-creator

62. http://discovermagazine.com, Ibid
63. The God Delusion, pg 188
64. Owen Gingerich, "Dare a Scientist Believe in Design?" in John Templeton, Evidence of Purpose (New York, NY: Continuum, 1994), pg 24
65. William Dembski, Mere Creation: Science, Faith & Intelligent Design (Downers Grove, IL: InterVarsity, 1998), pg 40
66. Fred Heeren, Show Me God (Wheeling, IL: Searchlight Publications, 1995), pg 200
67. Robert Jastrow, "A Scientist Caught Between Two Faiths," Christianity Today, August 6, 1982
68. Frank Tipler, The Physics of Immorality: Modern Cosmology, God, and the Resurrection of the Dead (New York, NY: Anchor Books, 1994), preface
69. http://www.nytimes.com/2003/04/12/opinion/a-brief-history-of-the-multiverse.html?mcubz=3
70. https://yahoo.com/finance/news/neil-degrasse-tyson-thinks-theres-170000249.html
71. E.g., Isaiah 40:22; Job 26:7

CHAPTER 4

1. John F. Kennedy; Remarks at the Dinner for the America's Cup Crews, September 14, 1962
2. Charles Darwin, On the Origin of Species, (London: Murray, 1859), pg 305
3. Raymond Barber, What the Bible Teaches, 2000, pg 47
4. Letter to J.D. Hooker, February 1, 1871, in Francis Darwin, The Life and Letters of Charles Darwin, 1877
5. On the Origin of Species, pg 413-414
6. http://pewforum.org/religious-landscape-study/belief-in-god/
7. "The One Where Heckles Dies," Friends, Season 2, Episode 3, https://youtube.com/watch?v=cXr2kF0zEgI
8. Richard Dawkins, The Greatest Show on Earth, (New York, NY: Free Press, 2009), pg 8
9. "Iconoclast of the Century: Charles Darwin," Time, December 31, 1999
10. Marvel, "Captain America: The Winter Soldier," 2014

BIBLIOGRAPHY

11. M. Richardson & G. Keuck, "Haeckel's ABC of Evolution and Development," Biological Reviews of the Cambridge Philosophical Society 77, no. 4 (2002): pg 495-528
12. http://pbs.org/wgbh/nova/id/pred-nf.html
13. Lee Strobel, The Case for a Creator (Grand Rapids, MI: Zondervan, 2004), pg 51
14. Elizabeth Pennisi, "Haeckel's Embryos: Fraud Rediscovered," Science, September 5, 1997, Vol. 277, No. 5331: 1435
15. Nigel Hawkes, The Times (London), August 11, 1997, pg 14
16. Richardson & Keuck, Ibid
17. Stephen Jay Gould, "Abscheulich! (Atrocious!)," Natural History, March 2000, pg 42-45
18. Ibid
19. Ibid
20. On the Origin of Species, pg 189
21. Ernst Haeckel, Human Stem History or Phylogeny, 1905, pg 502; Thomas Henry Huxley, 1869, pg 129-145
22. http://evidencepress.com/articles/ultimate-irreducible-complexity/
23. Lee Strobel, The Case for Faith (Grand Rapids, MI: Zondervan, 2000), pg 97-100
24. The Case for a Creator, pg 210
25. Howard Berg, quoted in ed., William A. Dembski and Michael Ruse, Debating Design: From Darwin to DNA, pg 324
26. https://creation.com/the-amazing-motorized-germ
27. Ibid
28. On the Origin of Species, pg 155
29. Francis Darwin, ed., The Life and Letters of Charles Darwin, Vol. II (New York, NY: D. Appleton and Co, 1899), pg 67
30. Michael Behe, Darwin's Black Box: The Biological Challenge to Evolution (New York, NY: Free, 1996), pg 185-186
31. Richard Dawkins, Climbing Mount Improbable (New York, NY: W.W Norton, 1996), pg 77
32. T. S. Kemp, Fossils and Evolution (New York, NY: Oxford University Press, 1999), pg 253
33. Michael Denton, "An Interview with Michael Denton," Access Research Network, Vol. 15, No. 2, 2005

34. On The Origin of Species, pg 280
35. Ibid, pg 95
36. Lorraine Glennon, Our Times: An Illustrated History of the 20th Century, 1995, pg 94
37. http://history.com/news/piltdown-man-hoax-100-years-ago
38. The Case for a Creator, pg 64-65
39. U.S. News & World Report, February 14, 2000
40. The Case for a Creator, pg 62
41. https://scientificamerican.com/article/how-fake-fossils-pervert-paleontology-excerpt/
42. Richard Dawkins, The Blind Watchmaker (New York, NY: W.W. Norton, 1986), pg 229-230
43. James Agresti, Rational Conclusions, (Documentary Press, 2009), pg 289
44. Colin Patterson, April 10, 1979, as quoted in Luther Sunderland, Darwin's Enigma, 1998, pg 101-102
45. William Dembski and Jonathan Wells, The Design of Life (Dallas, TX: Foundation for Thought and Ethics, 2008), pg 50
46. Jonathan Wells, The Politically Incorrect Guide to Darwinism and Intelligent Design (Washington, DC: Regnery, 2006), pg 36
47. Michael Denton, Evolution: A Theory in Crisis (Chevy Chase, MD: Adler & Adler, 1986), pg 250
48. Bill Gates, The Road Ahead (New York, NY: Penguin, 1996), pg 228
49. https://newscientist.com/article/mg22530084-300-glassed-in-dna-makes-the-ultimate-time-capsule/
50. The Blind Watchmaker, pg 116
51. Antony Flew and Roy Abraham Varghese, There is a God: How the World's Most Notorious Atheist Changed His Mind (New York, NY: HarperOne, 2007), pg 128

CHAPTER 5

1. The God Delusion Debate: Richard Dawkins vs. John Lennox, October 3, 2007 (Birmingham, AL: New Day Entertainment, 2007)
2. Lee Strobel, The Case for a Creator (Grand Rapids, MI: Zondervan, 2004), pg 39-40

BIBLIOGRAPHY

3. Lee Strobel, The Case for Faith (Grand Rapids, MI: Zondervan, 2000), pg 97
4. John Horgan, "In the Beginning," Scientific American, February 1991
5. The Case for a Creator, pg 40-41
6. The Case for Faith, pg 97-100
7. Stephen Meyer, Signature in the Cell: DNA and the Evidence for Intelligent Design (New York, NY: HarperCollins, 2009), pg 212
8. Fred Hoyle, The Intelligent Universe (London: Michael Joseph Limited, 1983), pg 17
9. Fred Hoyle, "Hoyle on Evolution," Nature, Vol. 294, No. 5837 (November 12, 1981), pg 105
10. The Case for a Creator, pg 238, 243-244
11. Richard Dawkins, Climbing Mount Improbable (New York, NY: W.W Norton, 1996), pg 77
12. Michael Denton, Evolution: A Theory in Crisis (Chevy Chase, MD: Adler & Adler, 1986), pg 264
13. Dean Kenyon, interview in Unlocking the Mystery of Life, (Illustra Media), May 3, 2003
14. Soren Lovtrup, Darwinism: The Refutation of a Myth (London, 1987) pg 422
15. Colin Patterson, "Evolutionism and Creationism," speech given at the American Museum of Natural History, New York, November 5, 1981
16. The Case for a Creator, pg 257
17. William Dembski and Charles Colson, The Design Revolution: Answering the Toughest Questions About Intelligent Design (Downers Grove, IL: IVP Books, 2004), pg 263
18. Unlocking the Mystery of Life, Ibid
19. Michael Behe, Darwin's Black Box: The Biological Challenge to Evolution (New York, NY: Free, 1996), pg 148
20. Climbing Mount Improbable, Ibid
21. Richard Dawkins, The Blind Watchmaker (New York, NY: W.W. Norton, 1986), pg 229-230
22. Candace Adams, "Leading Nanoscientist Builds Big Faith," Baptist Standard, March 15, 2000
23. Jill Lawless, "Typing Monkeys Don't Write Shakespeare," Associated Press (May 9, 2003)

24. The Case for a Creator, pg 246-249
25. Frank Turek, Stealing from God: Why Atheists Need God to Make Their Case (Colorado Springs, CO: NavPress, 2015), pg 59
26. Richard Dawkins, The Greatest Show on Earth, (New York, NY: Free Press, 2009), pg 216
27. The Blind Watchmaker, pg 29
28. Ibid, pg 1
29. Francis Crick, What Mad Pursuit: A Personal View of Scientific Discovery (New York, NY: Basic Books, 1988), pg 138
30. https://youtube.com/watch?v=ubIpoPjBUds
31. Thomas Nagel, The Last Word (Oxford University Press, 1997), pg 130-131
32. http://arn.org/docs/pjweekly/pj_weekly_010813.htm
33. Richard Lewontin, "Billions and Billions of Demons," The New York Review of Books, January 9, 1997, pg 31
34. Hubert Yockey, Information Theory and Molecular Biology (Cambridge, NY: Cambridge University Press, 1992), pg 284
35. https://townhall.com/columnists/dineshdsouza/2008/11/24/when-science-points-to-god-n1103628
36. Michael Ruse, "Saving Darwinism from the Darwinians," National Post (May 13, 2000), pg B-3
37. Stealing from God: Why Atheists Need God to Make Their Case, 167-168
38. Stephen Hawking, A Brief History of Time (New York, NY: Bantam, 1988), pg 46
39. Stealing from God: Why Atheists Need God to Make Their Case, pg 172-173
40. Lanny Swerdlow, "My Short Interview with Richard Dawkins" (1996)
41. Ernst Mayr, "Darwin's Influence of Modern Thought," Scientific American 28, no 1, 2000, pg 78-83
42. https://youtube.com/watch?v=CzSMC5rWvos
43. Richard Dawkins, lecture from "The Nullifidian," December, 1994
44. Richard Dawkins, "Is Science a Religion?," The Humanist, January/February 1997, pg 26
45. Jeffrey Burton Russell, Exposing Myths About Christianity (Madison, WI: Intervarsity Press, 2012), pg 147
46. Max Planck, Where is Science Going?, tran. James Murphy (Muriwai Books, 1932), pg 168

BIBLIOGRAPHY

47. Charles Darwin, On the Origin of Species, (London: Murray, 1859), pg 2
48. https://evolutionnews.org/2009/02/poll_shatters_stereotypes_with/
49. W.R. Thompson, quoted from introduction to On the Origin of Species (New York, NY: E.P. Dutton, 1956)
50. Antony Flew, There Is a God: How the World's Most Notorious Atheist Changed His Mind (New York, NY: HarperOne, 2008), pg 75
51. Ibid
52. Ibid, pg 88
53. George Gaylord Simpson, The Meaning of Evolution (Cambridge: Harvard University Press, 1967), pg 345
54. Carl Sagan, Cosmos (New York, NY: Ballantine Books, 1985), pg 1-2
55. "Master of the Universe," BBC, 1990
56. Victor Stenger, The New Atheism: Taking a Stand for Science and Reason (Amherst, NY: Prometheus, 2009), pg 76
57. Richard Dawkins, River out of Eden: A Darwinian View of Life (New York, NY: Basic Books, 1996), pg 133
58. Lawrence Krauss, "A Universe from Nothing," Oxford University
59. http://buzzfeed.com/tomchivers/when-i-was-a-child-i-spake-as-a-child#.yqBENoyBKX
60. Autobiography of Mark Twain (Berkeley/Los Angeles, CA: University of California Press, 2010)
61. http://arn.org/docs/orpages/or161/161main.htm
62. Bertrand Russell, Why I Am Not a Christian (New York, NY: Simon and Schuster, 1957), pg 106
63. Ibid, pg 107
64. Jean-Paul Sartre, Nausea, 1938
65. Carl Sagan, speech at Cornell University, October 13, 1994
66. https://economist.com/blogs/graphicdetail/2016/04/daily-chart-20
67. http://nytimes.com/2013/05/03/health/suicide-rate-rises-sharply-in-us.html?_r=1
68. Ibid
69. Genesis 1:1
70. Genesis 1:2-27

71. Ephesians 2:10
72. Acts 3:15
73. Psalm 139:13-14
74. Jeremiah 1:5
75. Psalm 147:4; Matthew 6:26
76. https://nypost.com/2017/12/11/former-facebook-exec-social-media-is-ripping-apart-society/
77. Ecclesiastes 2:10-11
78. https://youtube.com/watch?v=0SVZvWaMWsA
79. Philippians 3:8
80. https://youtube.com/watch?v=QN43j1hXiZk
81. Ecclesiastes 3:11
82. Matthew 22:37-39
83. Matthew 11:28-29
84. Augustine, Confessions
85. Philippians 2:3-4
86. http://livestream.com/princetonalliance/events/1986126
87. John 7:38
88. Romans 1:20
89. https://youtube.com/watch?v=yZLzLVAUJiU&feature=youtu.be
90. Eric Metaxas, Miracles: What They Are, Why They Happen, and How They Can Change Your Life (New York, NY: Penguin, 2014), pg 55-56
91. https://songselect.ccli.com/Songs/4774372/master-designer-of-heaven-and-earth

CHAPTER 6

1. https://barna.com/research/the-end-of-absolutes-americas-new-moral-code/
2. http://equip.org/article/philosophical-problems-with-moral-relativism/
3. Louis Pojman, Ethics: Discovering Right and Wrong (Belmont, CA: Wadsworth, 1999), pg 31-32
4. Polly Nelson, Defending the Devil: My Story As Ted Bundy's Last Lawyer (New York, NY: William Morrow, 1994) pg 319
5. Norman L. Geisler & Frank Turek, I Don't Have Enough Faith to Be an Atheist

(Wheaton, IL: Crossway, 2004), pg 182

6. http://equip.org/article/philosophical-problems-with-moral-relativism/
7. Sean McDowell, Ethix (Nashville, TN: B&H, 2006), pg 30, 37
8. C.S. Lewis, Mere Christianity (New York, NY: Macmillan, 1952), pg 25
9. J.P. Moreland, The God Question: An Invitation to a Life of Meaning (Eugene, OR: Harvest House, 2009), pg 84-85
10. J.P. Moreland, Love Your God with All Your Mind (Colorado Springs, CO: NavPress, 1997), pg 153
11. http://gocomics.com/calvinandhobbes/1989/04/09
12. http://www.barna.com, Ibid
13. Richard Dawkins, A Devil's Chaplain: Reflections on Hope, Lies, Science, and Love (New York, NY: Houghton Mifflin, 2003), pg 34
14. Richard Dawkins, The God Delusion (Boston, MA: Houghton Mifflin, 2006), pg 307
15. http://byfaithonline.com/richard-dawkins-the-atheist-evangelist/
16. Ibid
17. E.g., https://youtube.com/watch?v=wQ-aqnDHqqA
18. Frank Turek, Stealing from God: Why Atheists Need God to Make Their Case (Colorado Springs, CO: NavPress, 2015), pg 93-96
19. John Warwick Montgomery, The Law Above the Law (Minneapolis, MN: Dimension Books/Bethany Fellowship, 1975), pg 24-25
20. http://theatlantic.com/magazine/archive/1998/04/the-biological-basis-of-morality/377087/
21. Charles Darwin, The Descent of Man, pg 91
22. Ibid, pg 88-89
23. http://peta.org/blog/rat-pig-dog-boy/
24. https://thetimes.co.uk/article/when-i-see-cattle-lorries-i-think-of-the-railway-wagons-to-auschwitz-m3t0hntmk
25. James Rachels, Created from Animals: The Moral Implications of Darwinism (New York, NY: Oxford University Press, 1990), pg 186
26. Peter Singer, Practical Ethics (Cambridge: Cambridge University Press, 1979), pg 122-123
27. http://petersinger.info/faq/
28. https://washingtontimes.com/news/2015/jun/16/peter-singer-princeton-

bioethics-professor-faces-c/

29. Michael Tooley, "Abortion and Infanticide," in Rights and Wrongs of Abortion, ed. Marshall Cohen, Thomas Nagel, and Thomas Scanlon (Princeton, NJ: Princeton University Press, 1974), pg 57

30. Jeffrey Reiman, Critical Moral Liberalism (Lanham, MD: Rowman and Littlefield, 1997), pg 121

31. http://libgallery.cshl.edu/items/show/52538

32. T.G. Crookshank, The Mongol in Our Midst (New York, NY: E.F. Dutton, 1924)

33. https://answersingenesis.org/charles-darwin/racism/did-darwin-promote-racism/

34. The Descent of Man, pg 201

35. Francis Darwin, The Life and Letters of Charles Darwin, Volume 1, pg 316

36. Stephen Jay Gould, Ontogeny and Phylogeny (Cambridge, MA: Harvard University Press, 1977), pg 127

37. Adolf Hitler, Mein Kampf (London: Hurst & Blackett, 1939), pg 239-242 =w_5EwYpLD6A

38. Opfer der Vergangenheit, 1937

39. https://youtube.com/watch?list=PLR8eQzfCOiS0OTxoa5BkD21Bxw2O72kHD&v

40. George William Hunter, A Civic Biology: Presented in Problems (1914), pg 196

41. A. E. Samaan, From a Race of Masters to a Master Race: 1948 To 1848 (2013), pg 382

42. David Monaghan, "The Body-Snatchers," The Bulletin, November 12, 1991

43. Nick Kemp, Merciful Release: The History of the British Euthanasia Movement (Manchester University Press, 2002), pg 19

44. Peter Singer, Writings on an Ethical Life (New York, NY: HarperCollins, 2001), pg 77-78, 220-221

45. http://youtube.com/watch?v=j3EVJZEX6Bw

46. "The Tonight Show with Jay Leno," April 29, 2013

47. Richard Taylor, Ethics, Faith and Reason (Prentice Hall, 1984), pg 14

48. J. Warner Wallace, God's Crime Scene (Colorado Springs, CO: David C. Cook, 2015), pg 170

BIBLIOGRAPHY

CHAPTER 7

1. Frank Turek, Stealing from God: Why Atheists Need God to Make Their Case (Colorado Springs, CO: NavPress, 2015), pg 31
2. Ibid, pg 34
3. David Silverman, Fighting God: An Atheist Manifesto for a Religious World (New York, NY: Thomas Dunne Books, 2015), pg 232
4. Lee Strobel, The Case for a Creator (Grand Rapids, MI: Zondervan, 2004), pg 262
5. https://youtube.com/watch?v=SDV2EgVC8KI
6. Maxwell Bennett and Peter Hacker, Neuroscience and Philosophy: Brain, Mind, and Language (New York, NY: Columbia University Press, 2007), pg 143
7. God's Crime Scene, pg 125
8. Eugune Aserinsky and Nathaniel Kleitman, "Regularly Occurring Periods of Eye Motility, and Concomitant Phenomena, During Sleep," Science, Volume 118, (September 4, 1953), pg 273-274
9. https://youtube.com/watch?v=en-3Bz1RMig&list=PLm5UJ3igmxa K0hHMoI-qQfSiGv4k-lgqy&index=3
10. John Searle, The Rediscovery of the Mind (Cambridge, MA: MIT Press, 1994), pg 48-49
11. Michael Ruse, Can a Darwinian be a Christian?: The Relationship between Science and Religion (New York, NY: Cambridge University Press, 2001), pg 73
12. Colin McGinn, Can We Solve the Mind-Body Problem? (Oxford University Press, 1989), pg 349
13. Colin McGinn, The Mysterious Flame: Conscious Minds in a Material World (New York, NY: Basic Books, 1999), pg 13-14
14. The Case for a Creator, pg 278-279
15. Ibid, pg 269-271
16. Ibid
17. Richard Dawkins, River Out of Eden: A Darwinian View of Life (New York, NY: Basic Books, 1995), pg 133
18. https://youtube.com/watch?v=o-ZpV3-mzRc
19. Ibid
20. http://arn.org/docs/orpages/or161/161main.htm

21. Ben Stein & Kevin Miller (2008), "Expelled: No Intelligence Allowed"
22. Francis Crick, The Astonishing Hypothesis: The Scientific Search for the Soul (New York, NY: Touchstone, 1995), pg 3
23. Stephen Hawking and Leonard Mlodinow, The Grand Design (New York, NY: Bantam, 2010), pg 32
24. Sam Harris, Free Will (New York, NY: Free Press, 2012), pg 5
25. John Searle, The Mystery of Consciousness (New York, NY: New York Review of Books, 1997), pg 154
26. J. B. S. Haldane, "When I am Dead," Possible Worlds and Other Essays (London: Chatto & Windus, 1927), pg 209-210
27. Charles Darwin, letter to William Graham, July 3, 1881
28. http://reasonablefaith.org/is-the-foundation-of-morality-natural-or-supernatural-the-craig-harris
29. Michael Ruse, "Evolutionary Theory and Christian Ethics," in The Darwinian Paradigm (London: Routledge, 1989), pg 262, 268-89
30. Michael Ruse and Edward O. Wilson, "The Evolution of Ethics," in Philosophy of Biology, ed. Michael Ruse (New York, NY: Macmillan, 1989), pg 316
31. http://reasonablefaith.org/can-we-be-good-without-god
32. Ravi Zacharias, Jesus Among Other Gods: The Absolute Claims of the Christian Message (Nashville, TN: Thomas Nelson, 2000)
33. Frank Turek, Stealing from God: Why Atheists Need God to Make Their Case (Colorado Springs, CO: NavPress, 2015), pg 92
34. http://abc.net.au/tv/qanda/txt/s3469101.htm
35. Thomas Huxley, "Evolution and Ethics," Evolution and Ethics and other Essays (New York, NY: D. Appleton, 1899), pg 83
36. Robert Morey, Death and the Afterlife (Bloomington, MN: Bethany House, 1984)
37. Stealing from God, pg 212-213
38. Norman L. Geisler & Frank Turek, I Don't Have Enough Faith to Be an Atheist (Wheaton, IL: Crossway, 2004), pg 163
39. Edward Feser, The Last Superstition: A Refutation of the New Atheism (South Bend, IN: St. Augustine's Press, 2010), pg 10
40. Fyodor Dostoyevsky, The Brothers Karamazov, Part 4, Book 11, Chapter 4
41. Immanuel Kant, Critique of Practical Reason (1788)

BIBLIOGRAPHY

42. George F.R. Ellis, as quoted in Marianne Freiberger, "Why does cosmology need philosophy?" (September 23, 2014)
43. Julian Baggini, Atheism: A Very Short Introduction (Oxford University Press, 2003), pg 41-51
44. Richard Dawkins, The God Delusion (London: Bantam Press, 2006), pg 232
45. Russ Shafer-Landau, Whatever Happened to Good and Evil? (Oxford University Press, 2004), pg viii
46. http://reasonablefaith.org/is-the-foundation-of-morality-natural-or-supernatural-the-craig-harris
47. E.g., Quran IX. 105, II. 278, II. 282, XIX 97
48. E.g., Quran II. 99, III. 33
49. http://reasonablefaith.org/concept-of-god-in-islam-and-christianity
50. Bukkyo Dendo Kyokai, The Teaching of Buddha (1966), pg 62
51. Malachi 3:6
52. Hebrews 13:8
53. James 1:17
54. Ezekiel 33:11
55. Deuteronomy 10:17
56. Matthew 5:44
57. 1 John 4:7-10
58. http://americanhumanist.org/news/details/2008-11-humanists-launch-godless-holiday-campaign
59. http://americanhumanist.org/news/details/2009-11-humanists-launch-first-ever-national-godless-holiday
60. The God Delusion, pg 241
61. http://washingtonpost.com/wp-dyn/content/article/2007/07/13/AR2007071301461.html
62. Daniel C. Dennett, Breaking the Spell: Religion as a Natural Phenomenon (New York, NY: Viking, 2006), pg 279
63. http://blogs.wsj.com/speakeasy/2010/12/19/a-holiday-message-from-ricky-gervais-why-im-an-atheist/
64. https://dailywire.com/news/25479/shapiro-discusses-free-will-noted-atheist-sam-daily-wire

65. http://theinterrobang.com/penn-jilllette-rapes-all-the-women-he-wants-to/
66. http://crossexamined.org/turek-shermer-debate-what-best-explains-morality-god-or-science/
67. Romans 2:14-15
68. http://isites.harvard.edu/fs/docs/icb.topic1034793.files/Euthyphro.pdf
69. William Lane Craig, On Guard (Colorado Springs, CO: David C Cook), pg 136
70. Scott Rae, Moral Choices: An Introduction to Ethics (Grand Rapids, MI: Zondervan, 1995), pg 48
71. Ibid
72. Genesis 1:26, 27
73. http://time.com/4403510/george-w-bush-speech-dallas-shooting-memorial-service/
74. http://str.org/articles/evil-as-evidence-for-god
75. Luke 24:39; John 4:24
76. Case for a Creator, pg 275, 281, 286

CHAPTER 8

1. Bart D. Ehrman, Did Jesus Exist? The Historical Argument for Jesus of Nazareth (New York, NY: HarperOne, 2012), pg 5-7
2. https://youtube.com/watch?v=Ant5HS01tBQ
3. Ehrman, Did Jesus Exist? (New York, NY: HarperOne, 2013), pg 5
4. William Lane Craig, On Guard (Colorado Springs, CO: David C. Cook, 2010), pg 184
5. Lee Strobel, The Case for the Real Jesus (Grand Rapids, MI: Zondervan, 2007), pg 113
6. Ibid, pg 112
7. On Guard, pg 184-185
8. Flavius Josephus, Antiquities of the Jews, 18.63-64, tran. Shlomo Pines
9. Josephus, Antiquities of the Jews, 20.9.1.
10. Tacitus, The Annals, 15.44
11. Pliny the Younger, Letter, 10:96
12. Suetonius, Life of Claudius, 25.4

13. Suetonius, Life of Nero, 16
14. Celcus, On the True Doctrine: A Discourse Against the Christians, tran. R Joseph Hoffman (New York: Oxford University Press, 1987), pg 116
15. The Works of Lucian of Samosata, tran. Fowler, H W and F G. Oxford: The Clarendon Press. 1905
16. Gary Habermas, The Historical Jesus, (Joplin, MO: College Press Publishing, 1996), pg 193-194
17. Luke 23:44-46
18. Matthew 27:51
19. Julius Africanus, Chronography, 18:1
20. Paul Maier, Pontius Pilate (Wheaton, IL: Tyndale House, 1968), pg 366
21. Paul Maier, In the Fullness of Time (Grand Rapids, MI: Kregal, 1991), pg 197
22. Gary Habermas and Michael Licona, The Case for the Resurrection of Jesus (Grand Rapids, MI: Kregel, 2004), pg 233
23. Lee Strobel, The Case for Christ (Grand Rapids, MI: Zondervan, 1998), pg 53
24. The Case for the Real Jesus, Ibid
25. Gary R. Habermas, The Risen Jesus & Future Hope (Lanham, MD: Rowman & Littlefield, 2003), pg 9-10
26. The Case for the Real Jesus, pg 113-114
27. The Case for Christ, pg 51
28. Mark 3:21-30, 6:34-46, 7:31-8:10-21, 8:31, 9:2-10, 30-34, 10:13-17, 33-41; Luke 7:36-50, 9:51-55; John 7:5, 8:59, 10:30-33
29. Luke 22:33
30. Mark 14:32-72
31. Matthew 27:55-56; Mark 15:40; John 19:25
32. Luke 24:1-12
33. 1 Corinthians 1:23
34. Deuteronomy 21:22-23
35. Matthew 27:57-60; Mark 15:42-46; Luke 23:50-53; John 19:38-42
36. William Lane Craig, Reasonable Faith: Christian Truth and Apologetics, 3rd edition (Wheaton, IL: Crossway, 2008), pg 364
37. Luke 24:1-11
38. Talmud, Sotah 19a

39. Talmud, Rosh Hashannah 1.8
40. Josephus, Antiquities of the Jews, 4.8.15
41. John 20:3-9
42. Mark 16:9
43. Matthew 28:2-4, 11-15
44. Justin Martyr, Dialogue with Trypho, 108
45. Tertullian, De Spectaculis, 30
46. Reasonable Faith, pg 370
47. Michael Grant, Jesus: An Historian's Review of the Gospels (New York, NY: Macmillan, 1992), pg 176
48. Jacob Kremer, Die Osterevangelien — Geschichten um Geschichte (Stuttgart: Katholisches Bibelwerk, 1977), pg 49-50
49. Luke Timothy Johnson, The Real Jesus (San Francisco, CA: Harper San Francisco, 1996), pg 136
50. Acts 1:3; 1 Corinthians 15:5-8
51. Gerd Lüdemann, What Really Happened to Jesus?, trans. John Bowden (Louisville, KY: Westminster John Knox Press, 1995), pg 80
52. The Case for the Real Jesus, pg 119
53. Ibid
54. Paul Little, Know Why You Believe (Wheaton, IL: Scripture Press, 1967), pg 173
55. N.T. Wright, "The New Unimproved Jesus," Christianity Today (September 13, 1993), pg 26
56. Acts 6:7
57. C.H. Dodd, "The Appearances of the Risen Christ: A Study in the Form Criticism of the Gospels," in More New Testament Studies (Manchester, UK: University of Manchester Press, 1968), pg 128
58. Acts 26:24-28
59. The Case for Christ, pg 54
60. Galatians 1:16-19
61. 1 Corinthians 15:3-7
62. Gerd Lüdemann, The Resurrection of Jesus, trans. John Bowden (Minneapolis, MN: Fortress, 1994), pg 38
63. Richard N. Ostling, "Who Was Jesus?" Time Magazine (August 15, 1988)

64. The Case for the Real Jesus, pg 116-117
65. Acts 7:58-60; 8:1-4; Philippians 3:4-6
66. Acts 26:9-11
67. Acts 9:1-5
68. 2 Corinthians 11:24-28
69. Acts 11:26
70. Eusebius, Church History. 2.25-26
71. http://bbc.co.uk/religion/0/20767427
72. Tertullian, Scorpiace XV
73. Matthew 13:55-56
74. Mark 3:35
75. Eusebius, Ecclesiastical History, 2.23
76. Acts 1:14
77. Galatians 2:9
78. Josephus, Antiquities 20:200

CHAPTER 9

1. Paul Copan, Will the Real Jesus Please Stand Up?: A Debate between William Lane Craig and John Dominic Crossan (Grand Rapids, MI: Baker, 1998), pg 61-62
2. Schweitzer, Quest, pg 56
3. Gary R. Habermas, The Risen Jesus & Future Hope (Lanham, MD: Rowman & Littlefield, 2003), pg 14
4. Raymond E. Brown, "The Resurrection and Biblical Criticism," Commonweal, Vol. 87; No. 8 (November 24, 1967), pg 233
5. William Lane Craig, Reasonable Faith. Christian Truth and Apologetics, 3rd edition (Wheaton, IL: Crossway, 2008), pg 62-63
6. http://reasonablefaith.org/the-resurrection-of-jesus
7. William Lane Craig, On Guard (Colorado Springs, CO: David C. Cook, 2010), pg 251
8. John 10:30-31
9. Eric Metaxas, Miracles, pg 103
10. Josh & Sean McDowell, Evidence for the Resurrection, pg 172

11. Ibid, pg 180-181, 193
12. Wilbur M. Smith, Therefore Stand: Christian Apologetics (Grand Rapids, MI: Baker Book House, 1972), pg 373-374
13. John Lennox, Gunning for God: Why the New Atheists are Missing the Target, pg 207
14. Eric Metaxas, Miracles: What They Are, Why They Happen, and How They Can Change Your Life (New York, NY: Penguin, 2015), pg 104-105
15. Charles Colson, Breakpoint Online Commentaries, April 29, 2002
16. Lee Strobel, The Case for the Real Jesus (Grand Rapids, MI: Zondervan, 2007), pg 146
17. Bill White, A Thing Incredible (Israel: Yanetz Ltd., 1976)
18. Richard Carrier, "The Spiritual Body of Christ," The Empty Tomb, pg 156
19. Lee Strobel, The Case for Christ (Grand Rapids, MI: Zondervan, 1998), pg 238
20. The Case for the Real Jesus, pg 141-143
21. J. Warner Wallace, Cold-Case Christianity: A Homicide Detective Investigates the Claims of the Gospels (Colorado Springs, CO: David C. Cook, 2013), pg 42
22. John 19:34
23. The Case for Christ, pg 213
24. Eusebius, Ecclesiastical History, Book 4, ch 15
25. Bert Thompson and Brad Harrub, "An Examination of the Medical Evidence for the Physical Death of Christ," http://apologeticspress.org/apcontent.aspx?category=13&article=145
26. David Friedrick Strauss, The Life of Jesus for the People, vol. 1, second edition, pg 412
27. Bart Ehrman, How Jesus Became God: The Exaltation of a Jewish Preacher from Galilee (New York, NY: HarperOne, 2014), pg 164
28. http://garyhabermas.com/articles/trinityjournal_latetwentieth/trinityjournal_latetwentieth.htm
29. A. N. Wilson, Jesus: A Life (New York, NY: W.W Norton & Company, 2004), pg 243-244
30. Norman L. Geisler & Frank Turek, I Don't Have Enough Faith to Be an Atheist (Wheaton, IL: Crossway, 2004), pg 313
31. Lee Strobel, "The Case for Faith" lecture at Biola University

BIBLIOGRAPHY

32. https://reasonablefaith.org/videos/interviews-panels/helsinki-finland-interview-with-william-lane-craig/
33. Quran 4:157
34. E.g., John 14:10; 1 Corinthians 13:2; 2 Timothy 3:16-17; 2 Peter 1:20-21

CHAPTER 10

1. Genesis 2:16-17
2. Genesis 3:1-5
3. Genesis 3:6-19
4. https://youtube.com/watch?v=q3HaugarsfU
5. Isaiah 53:5
6. Zechariah 13:6
7. https://youtube.com/watch?v=NIVUdQ6FJfE&feature=relmfu
8. https://everystudent.com/wires/atheist.html
9. Romans 10:9, 13
10. John 6:37
11. Andrew Farley, The Naked Gospel (Grand Rapids, MI: Zondervan, 2009), pg 147
12. E.g., Quran 5:9; 7:6-9; 23:102-103; 42:26
13. Quran 46:9
14. E.g., LDS Bible Dictionary, pg 697; Doctrine and Covenants 58:42-43; 2 Nephi 9:23-24; 25:23; Alma 11:37; 34:30-35; Articles of Faith, pg 92; Doctrines of Salvation vol.1 pg 134; vol.3 pg 91
15. Daniel H. Ludlow, A Companion to Your Study of the New Testament, pg 222
16. Moroni 10:32
17. Mormon Missionary Discussion F, Uniform systems for teaching families, pg 35-36
18. http://pewforum.org/2008/12/18/many-americans-say-other-faiths-can-lead-to-eternal-life/
19. http://pewforum.org/religious-landscape-study/belief-in-god/
20. John 14:6
21. "The Wayfaring Stranger"
22. E.g., Isaiah 65:17; 66:22; 2 Peter 3:13; Revelation 21:1
23. Randy Alcorn, Heaven (Tyndale House Publishers, 2004), pg 17-18

24. Revelation 22:3
25. Heaven, pg 78-80
26. 2 Samuel 12:23
27. Luke 16:19-31
28. Luke 17:1-4
29. 1 Corinthians 15:35-45
30. Philippians 1:23
31. Psalm 84:10
32. Revelation 21:3-4
33. 2 Thessalonians 1:9
34. Luke 16:22-23
35. Craig Groeschel, The Christian Atheist: Believing in God but Living As If He Doesn't Exist, Grand Rapids, MI: Zondervan, 2010), pg 195-199
36. Ibid, pg 211-214
37. DreamWorks, "Madagascar: Escape 2 Africa," (2008)
38. Heaven, Introduction
39. Ibid, pg 23-24
40. https://twitter.com/Natasha_Crain/status/918876736128823296
41. https://www.who.int/news-room/fact-sheets/detail/the-top-10-causes-of-death

Made in the USA
Columbia, SC
08 June 2019